# Restructuring the Soviet Economy

T0358497

*Restructuring the Soviet Economy* addresses the fundamental economic problem facing the Soviet government at the present time. How can an economy which has been centrally planned for 60 years make the testing and painful transition to market-based principles? The Soviet experience in the latter half of the 1980s suggests that it is going to be a much more difficult task than was initially believed in either East or West. This book seeks to uncover the underlying reasons for the paralysis of *perestroika*. It focuses on the crisis points – some new, some perennial – of the economy: the relationship between the enterprise, the regions and the centre, agriculture, investment, inflation, and the budget deficit.

This is a clear and concise treatment of an area which the non-specialist often finds obscure. It is analytical, without being too technical for the non-economist. It will appeal to students of Soviet studies, economics and European affairs.

**David A Dyker** is currently Senior Lecturer in Economics at the School of European Studies, University of Sussex. He has studied the Soviet Union and Eastern Europe for over 20 years, during which he has travelled in the area extensively. He is also a consultant with wide experience of advising government and business, particularly on matters of East-West trade. His previous publications include *The Process of Investment in the Soviet Union* (Cambridge University Press, 1983), *The Future of the Soviet Planning System* (Croom Helm, 1985), *The Soviet Union Under Gorbachev* (editor, Croom Helm, 1987) and *Yugoslavia: Socialism, Development and Debt* (Routledge, 1990).

# Restructuring the Soviet Economy

David A. Dyker

London and New York

First published 1992
by Routledge
11 New Fetter Lane, London EC4P 4EE

Simultaneously published in the USA and Canada
by Routledge
a division of Routledge, Chapman and Hall, Inc.
29 West 35th Street, New York, NY 10001

Reprinted 2001

*Routledge is an imprint of the Taylor & Francis Group*

Typeset by Columns Design & Production Services Ltd, Reading

Printed & bound by Antony Rowe Ltd, Eastbourne

*British Library Cataloguing in Publication Data*
Dyker, David A. (David Alexander) *1944–*
 Restructuring the Soviet Economy
 1. Union of Soviet Socialist Republics. Economic
 conditions
 I. Title
 338.947

ISBN 0–415–05679–9
ISBN 0–415–06761–8 (pbk)

*Library of Congress Cataloging in Publication Data*
Dyker, David A.
 Restructuring the Soviet Economy/David A. Dyker
 Includes bibliographical references and index
 ISBN 0–415–05679–9 – ISBN 0–415–06761–8 (pbk)
 1. Soviet Union—Economic policy—1985–  2. Central planning—
 Soviet Union  3. Perestroika  I. Title
 HC336.26.D95  1991
 338.947′009′049—dc20

# Contents

# Figures and Tables

## FIGURES

## TABLES

# Preface

The genesis of this book lies in a project dating from 1988 to produce a new and updated edition of my *Future of the Soviet Economic Planning System*, first published in 1985. As I started to rewrite, however, I found myself in an uneven contest with the pace of events. It soon become clear that the title of the original book was no longer appropriate. By 1990 the whole status of socialist planning itself had become one of the principle issues on the policy-making agenda of the Soviet authorities. And however bleak the outlook from the standpoint of the first year of a new decade, it was clear that the future had, in a sense, already arrived.

The result of this process of continuous adjustment is the present work. The first three chapters have survived with only minor emendations from the 1985 volume. Chapters 5 and 6 have been substantially rewritten. Chapters 4 and 7 are wholly new. I am grateful to Professor Holland Hunter of Haverford College for many useful comments and criticisms on the original book, and to the Volkswagen Foundation which financed an invaluable term's sabbatical at the Cologne *Bundesinstitut für ostwissenschaftliche und internationale Studien*. I must also record my thanks to my old colleagues at that institute, for the support and stimulation they gave me during the project's initial stages. The final version of the book would have been the poorer had the British Academy and the Soviet Academy of Sciences not facilitated my visit to Moscow in May 1990. Finally, my thanks are due to the editors of *Recherches Economiques de Louvain*, who kindly allowed me to reproduce material from 'The dynamics of the Gorbachev reforms: a crisis of reconstruction', published in vol. 56 (1990), no. 2 of that journal.

David A. Dyker
University of Sussex
1991

# Chapter 1

# The historical origins of the Soviet planning system

## INTRODUCTION

In an age when we still largely identify planning, at least in its more centralized form, with the Soviet Union, it is worth reflecting on the fact that the birth of Soviet planning owed little to any theoretical work on the principles of economic planning. The Marxian classics say little about socialist planning except that it would be necessary (Marx 1968; Engels 1962), and Lenin seems to have been half contemptuous, half unaware of the problem of managing a planned economy (Lenin 1966). Pioneering Soviet efforts to construct a national input–output table (Popov 1926; *Materialy* . . ., 1932) and formulate a multisectoral growth model (Fel'dman 1928) had little impact on practical policy-making. Leonid Kantorovich published a preliminary account of his seminal work on linear programming in 1939 (Kantorovich 1939), but did not develop it fully until after the Second World War. The importance of Kantorovich's work was not recognized in the Soviet Union until the late 1950s (Kantorovich 1960). The parallel American work on linear programming began in the 1930s, but operational methods for applying the technique were not fully developed until 1947 (Dorfman *et al.* 1958, p. 3; Dantzig 1963; pp. 12–13). Economists like Kritsman, who worked in Gosplan (the State Planning Commission) during the 1920s, made substantial progress with the ideas of iteration and linkage as a way of understanding the interrelationships of the economy (Kritsman 1921). As a 20-year-old graduate of the university of Leningrad, Wassily Leontief began his work on the input–output technique in 1926 with a brief article criticizing the 1926 Popov report. But he

*Table 1.1* Industrial production in selected industrial branches, 1913 and 1926

|  | 1913 | 1926 |
|---|---|---|
| Coal (millions of tons) | 29.0 | 27.6 |
| Electricity (millions of kWh) | 1,945 | 3,508 |
| Pig iron (thousands of tons) | 4,216 | 2,441 |
| Steel (thousands of tons) | 4,231 | 3,141 |
| Cotton fabrics (millions of metres) | 2,582 | 2,286 |

*Source*: Nove 1969, p. 94

then left the USSR, and his first systematic presentation of input-output analysis, using US data, appeared in 1936 (Leontief 1936). Again, as with linear programming, full development of this piece of theoretical apparatus had to wait until after the war. If we want to understand where Soviet planning comes from, then, we should not be looking in books, but rather at the circumstances of the year 1930.

That was the year in which the first five-year plan really got under way. It was in December 1929 that the decision was taken to try to fulfil the plan nine months ahead of schedule, the first major operational impetus in Stalin's strategy of 'planning for the impossible'. It was around the same time that heavy industrial targets were upped, while light industrial targets were reduced, heralding the arrival of the 'priority principle' as a key tactical element in the Soviet economic system (Nove 1969, pp. 187–9). January 1930 saw the beginning of a bloodily coercive collectivization campaign which would leave no one in doubt as to what the 'command principle' was to mean under Stalin. It is surely not an exaggeration to say that, material incentives or no, underfulfilment of plans in the 1930s was simply viewed as treason (Nove 1969, pp. 216–18). This obsession with growth and structural change at all costs was, of course, a reflection not only of Stalin's politics, but also of the economic conditions of the time.

The Soviet Union in the 1920s was an industrializing country, but it was industrializing slowly, and from a low base. The First World War, the Revolution and the Civil War took a terrible toll of production potential, and aggregate industrial production in 1926 was not much higher than it had been in 1913. Table 1.1 presents figures for physical production in some key sectors.

Thus Soviet coal output in 1926 was a little below that of Bulgaria in 1982: Soviet steel output in 1926 was slightly above that of its little Black Sea ally in 1982 (Economic Commission for Europe 1983, p. 163). In 1926 26.3 million people out of a total population of 147 million lived in towns, with about 11 million in non-agricultural employment (Nove 1969, pp. 145 and 267). There was widespread rural overpopulation, and while it is impossible to be precise, we must presume that the marginal product of agricultural labour was very low. The savings/investment ratio was around 12.5 per cent of national income in 1928 (Gregory and Stuart 1981, p. 386). Repudiation of the international debts of the Tsarist regime, coupled with the difficult international economic conditions of the post-Wall Street crash period, ensured that any increase in the rate of accumulation would have to be internally financed. Natural conditions were not conducive to high levels of agricultural productivity, with long cold winters, drought problems in the south, and acid soils in the north. Endowment with industrial raw materials was, by contrast, extremely good. Coal was abundant in the Donbass (Ukraine) and Kuzbass (western Siberia), oil in Transcaucasia, and the Urals were rich in ferrous and non-ferrous metals. In some ways, then, the Soviet Union c. 1930 was a typical developing country, with a relatively low level of accumulation and substantial surplus agricultural population. But she could not count on large-scale capital transfer from abroad – for better or worse. More unequivocally, she had a firm, if small, industrial base, and the kind of raw material endowment which ensures that industrialization drives did not lead straight to balance of payments problems.

It stood to reason, then, that Soviet planning had to be planning for development – in the first instance planning to *create* industry rather than planning how to *run* industry: and just as Soviet planning in practice predates most modern theory of planning, so the Soviet approach to development predates most modern development theory. But here there was a Marxian literature, originating largely in the debates of the 1920s in the Soviet Union itself. The principal protagonists in those debates, Nikolai Bukharin and Yevgenii Preobrazhenskii, took up positions which could be more or less identified with, respectively, the 'balanced growth' and 'unbalanced growth' schools in post-war development economics. This is not the place to go into detail on a fascinating episode of intellectual history (see Erlich 1960; Jasny 1972). But Stalin's strategy for growth was essentially a rather crude version of the Trotskyist Preobrazhenskii's theory. Development was identified with industrialization, industrialization would be impossible without capital-intensive techniques, which meant high savings/investment ratios. In the absence of any chance of foreign loans this meant that some kind of 'primitive socialist accumulation' (Preobrazhenskii's phrase) or 'pumping-over' (Stalin's phrase) at the expense of the numerous, if impoverished, peasantry would be a necessary condition of any sharp increase in the rate of accumulation. Development would be essentially autarkic in relation to production, if not in relation to technology. That presented no problems as far as raw material supplies were concerned, but it did mean that processing capacity would have to be a priority. It also meant that the Soviet Union would have to build up its engineering industry at top speed, simply to provide the machines to raise the investment ratio. It is not difficult in this context to understand why Stalin laid such stress on heavy industry. High rates of growth of national income were viewed partly as an end in themselves, partly – certainly by Preobrazhenskii – as a means of ensuring a rapid increase in employment (there were 1.6 million registered unemployed in 1929 (Nove 1969, p. 115)).

We have to be a little careful about identifying the idea of Stalinist development strategy with the outcome. Collectivization was implemented with such clumsy brutality that a great deal of capital stock, including livestock, was destroyed. Though net investment in agriculture was low throughout the Stalin period, substantial capital inputs had to be made throughout the 1930s to compensate for the losses incurred during collectivization – tractors to replace horses, for example. Contemporary research suggests that there was, in fact, a net 'pumping-over' *into* agriculture in the 1930s (Ellman 1979, pp. 92–6). And if creation of employment was a goal, then results over the first five-year plans were almost embarrassingly successful. Total non-agricultural employment was planned to reach 15,764,000 by 1932–3, but in fact reached 22,804,000, with employment in large-scale industry and construction rising to almost twice the planned level (Nove 1969, p. 195).

Development economists have in fact pin-pointed duality in technology, with main-line activities being developed on a highly capital-intensive basis and auxiliary operations continuing on a

Table 1.2 Soviet national product, factor inputs and productivity, average annual rates of growth, 1928–40

| Net national product | 1937 rouble factor cost | 4.2 |
| | Composite price base[a] | 9.3 |
| Employment | | 3.7 |
| Reproducible fixed capital | 1937 roubles | 9.8 |
| | Composite price base | 11.0 |
| Selected inputs (labour, capital, agricultural land) | 1937 weights | 3.8–4.2 |
| NNP per worker | Output at 1937 rouble factor cost | 0.5 |
| | Output on composite price base | 5.4 |
| NNP per unit of fixed capital | Output at 1937 rouble factor cost, capital in 1937 roubles | −5.1 |
| | Output and capital on composite price base | −1.6 |
| NNP per unit of selected inputs | Outputs at 1937 rouble factor cost, inputs using 1937 weights | 0.1–0.5 |
| | Output on composite price base, inputs using 1937 weights | 4.9–5.3 |

Source: Bergson 1978, p. 122

Note: [a] With rates of growth 1928–37 calculated in 1928 prices, and rates of growth 1937–40 calculated in 1940 prices.

highly labour-intensive basis, as a key feature of Soviet development patterns (Wilber 1969, Ch. 5). Now there is nothing in the Preobrazhenskii–Stalin line of thought to give this *ex ante* legitimacy – rather it was Bukharin who had talked about the value of intermediate technology. In any case, as we shall see later, the peculiar form that dual technology takes in the Soviet Union is a largely unintended effect of certain characteristic weaknesses in the planning system. Nevertheless, on balance early Soviet industrialization was a fairly labour-intensive process, with labour productivity growing at much more modest rates than national income. Table 1.2 summarizes output and input trends, as recalculated in Net National Product (NNP) terms by Abram Bergson.

We immediately encounter the classic index number problem: outputs can only be aggregated on the basis of a chosen set of prices, and different price weights may produce quite different aggregate output estimates. We should not be surprised that rates of growth of national income calculated predominantly in early-year prices are much higher than rates calculated in late-year prices, since prices of the new products which give the impetus to economic growth tend to be high on first introduction, then fall sharply as mass production is developed. The contrast between the two NNP figures in Table 1.2 does, indeed, serve to highlight the dramatic extent of structural change in the Soviet economy over this crucial decade or so. But whereas national income grew impressively at 4–9 per cent, labour productivity grew rather ordinarily at 1–5 per cent.

Even more striking is the sharply negative rate of growth of capital productivity over the given period. We would expect a substantial element of short-term diminishing returns when the volume of investment rises as rapidly as 14.5 per cent per annum (Gregory and Stuart 1981, p. 337). But in the context of almost unlimited long-term investment opportunities capital was never anything else but a very scarce resource in the Soviet Union of the 1930s. With the wholesale introduction of new technologies from the west, furthermore, the production possibility frontier was being moved outwards all the time. Thus the capital productivity figures for the period 1928–40 are surprisingly unimpressive. To make sense of this we have to move from the strategic to the tactical level, from the conceptual to the implementational.

## CENTRALIZATION AND THE COMMAND PRINCIPLE

It is not difficult to see why Stalin favoured a quasi-military, command approach in stategic decision-taking. He was obsessed with speed, and even Winston Churchill discovered that when you want something very different done very quickly you have to give people orders (see Devons 1950). At the level of specific tasks for specific sectors and enterprises, too, there is a strong theoretical case for using direct instructions as a basis for plan implementation. The pioneers of the post-war period developed theorems permitting the derivation of optimal sets of prices from optimal sets of outputs: thus a planning board would be able to operate a system of indirect centralization, calculating optimal prices and simply telling its enterprise managers to maximize profits. Now of course the Soviet planners of the 1930s did not have these theorems at their disposal, neither did they have the computers without which major planning operations of this kind are not possible.

But the theorems do in any case suffer from very serious limitations – in particular they cannot cope with externalities and increasing returns. If a given level of aggregate output is to be specified there is no alternative to specifying corresponding disaggregated levels of output. Contemporary theorists have come up with sophisticated proposals for combining price and output planning (Heal 1973), but it is obvious why the Soviet planners of the 1930s took a simpler approach. Faced with politically determined aggregate targets – for key sectoral production series rather than national income – they proceeded on the basis of essentially arithmetical division and sub-division of tasks among administrative intermediaries and enterprises. This kept their own life as simple as possible, and it provided easily understood targets for unsophisticated managers and workers – not just easily understood, but easily assimilable, since they related the particular to the general in a very obvious way.

Even so, the sheer volume of planning operations imposed on the central planners was such as to make it impossible to do all the strictly necessary calculations properly. Although the hierarchy of Soviet planning developed into a fairly neat, three-tiered system, running Gosplan → sectoral ministry → enterprise it is important to note that this was in no way a multi-level planning system in the sense used by Kornai (Kornai 1969). Rather than just disaggregating down to the intermediate level and leaving the ministries to do the rest, Gosplan was responsible for production planning right down to the level of individual commodities. The State Planning Commission had no executive power, however, and this is where the ministries came in. It was their job to give Gosplan's targets an organizational dimension, by translating them into specific targets for specific enterprises, and to ensure that those enterprises pulled their weight. But the ministries were entrusted with the actual planning of only a few hundred commodity groups of mainly intrasectoral significance.

This did not stop the ministries from developing into very powerful institutions – as we shall see in Chapter 6 their role in the investment field has always been crucial. Rather it is merely to say that the nature of the division of labour between Gosplan and the ministries meant a great deal of overlap between the two instances

*Figure 1.1* The organizational structure of the Soviet economy, *c.* 1930–57

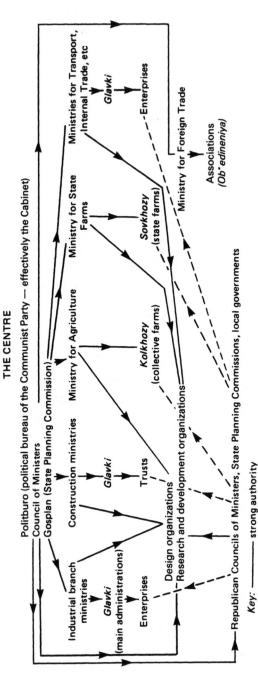

THE CENTRE

Politburo (political bureau of the Communist Party — effectively the Cabinet)

Council of Ministers

Gosplan (State Planning Commission)

Industrial branch ministries

Construction ministries

Ministry for Agriculture

Ministry for State Farms

Ministries for Transport, Internal Trade, etc

*Glavki* (main administrations)

*Glavki*

*Glavki*

Enterprises

Trusts

*Kolkhozy* (collective farms)

*Sovkhozy* (state farms)

Enterprises

Design organizations

Research and development organizations

Ministry for Foreign Trade

Associations (*Ob″edineniya*)

Republican Councils of Ministers, State Planning Commissions, local governments

Key:
——— strong authority
– – – weak authority
▲ ▲ ▲ denotes direction of authority

in terms of the planning and assignment of commodity targets, and that meant that the central planners had to try to cope with some thousands of product groups. Given the limited computational technology of the time it was therefore quite impossible for Gosplan staff to work out the full implications of any adjustments to plans that might have to be made. Their Material Balances method of plan construction illustrated in Table 1.3 has the simplicity and convenience of double-entry bookkeeping, and its attractions to computerless planners are obvious. But because it does not lay out the information in matrix form, it provides no direct basis for calculating secondary effects of changes in particular plan magnitudes.

The planning process as it evolved in the 1930s would start with a set of very rough 'control figures' (*kontrol'nye tsifry*) which the centre would send down through the hierarchy of ministry and enterprise, and on the basis of which producing units would make their preliminary requests for supplies. What happens when projected supply and demand for product X do not quite match? In principle adjustments should be made not only to planned levels of output of the inputs into product X, but also to planned levels of inputs into those inputs, and so on for a certain number of iterations which will be determined by the structure and complexity of the economy. But whereas all this can be done on the basis of a single input–output table, it may involve looking at dozens of Material Balances, the interrelations between which are not clearly shown. Understandably, then:

> Because the calculation of changes in the Material Balances is very labour-intensive, and because in practice there is not enough time for the completion of such work, sometimes only those balances which are linked by first-order relationships are adjusted. As regards relationships of the second order, never mind those of the third and fourth order, adjustments in the balances are made only in cases where the magnitudes involved are large.
>
> (Efimov 1957, p. 107)

Certainly the characteristically Stalinist habit of starting the planning process from key intermediate goods rather than final goods reduces the number of iterations required for a given level of consistency.

*Table 1.3* Material Balance for product X (in hundreds of thousands of tons)

| Resources | Distribution |
| --- | --- |
| 1 Production (subdivided by republics)<br>2 Imports<br>3 Other sources<br>4 Stocks at suppliers at beginning of plan period (subdivided by republic) | 1 Production needs (subdivided by republics and ministries)<br>2 Free market allocation[a]<br>3 Exports<br>4 Other needs<br>5 Stocks at suppliers at end of year<br>6 Reserves |

*Source*: Ellman 1970, p. 87.
*Note*: [a] Free market allocation refers to supplies which go outside the sphere of state-sector production, i.e. all goods for final consumption, and also producer goods for the collective farm sector.

Nevertheless in practice Soviet plans were often not even approximately consistent; in the purely technical sense Soviet planning has always been over-centralized. Now the Marxian classics are certainly predominantly centralist in tendency: yet we must surely seek essentially functional explanations for the extraordinary persistence of this feature of Soviet planning. These seem to fall into two categories.

First, over-centralization may have a rationale in terms of the resource endowment situation of the early period of planning; it certainly does have one in terms of the operation of the command principle. Shortage of trained managers is a characteristic of the resource endowment situation in all developing economies, and Stalin had made things worse with his purges of 'bourgeois specialists'. A high degree of centralization may have permitted the authorities to concentrate what cadres they had to maximum effect. Certainly it allowed them to use men with no managerial training as factory directors. On the other hand, it tied up middle-level administrators in bureaucratic wrangling, leaving them less time to be effective captains of industry. Less equivocally, one cannot in practice operate the command principle throughout an industrial economy unless one is prepared to work at a very high level of centralization. Specificity is the essence of target planning, for once we get beyond the agrarian, semi-subsistence level the scope for distortion of ill-defined output targets is almost unlimited, as we shall see later on. But if sufficiently clear instructions are to be issued for every major product group and for each producing unit, and in the absence of multi-level planning, then the centre cannot but be saddled with a colossal burden of work. With multi-level planning much of this burden could be devolved to intermediate planning bodies, but relationships between centre and intermediate level would then have to be organized at least partly on a parametric basis (see Chapter 3). So if pure command principle were wanted – and as we have seen there were substantial reasons for wanting just that – a degree of over-centralization would have to be tolerated.

But, second, the system was in any case a good deal more flexible in practice than our initial sketch suggests. Whatever the algebraic limitations of the Material Balances method, it has the great virtue that it does not fetishize reported input–output coefficients. In an economy going through as rapid a process of structural transformation as the Soviet one during the 1930s it would be quite unreasonable to assume fixed 1–0 coefficients. With a number of industries, e.g. the vehicle industry, being built up virtually from scratch, and with major new capacities being commissioned everywhere, economies of scale were naturally of substantial importance. Equally important, the novice industrial work-force introduced a volatile dimension into productivity trends which must have made them often impossible to plot: 'much damage was done by sheer clumsiness: expensive imported machines were smashed by inexperienced labourers or unqualified substitute-engineers' (Nove 1969, p. 197).

Given all this it is easier to understand why planners were so blasé about leaving 'holes' in the plan. It is also easier to understand why they were prepared to turn consistency problems into a vehicle of taut planning. Where gaps in plans appeared, ministries and enterprises would normally be told simply to produce more with given planned inputs, or the same with fewer inputs. Downwards adjustment was avoided if at all possible. Thus pressure for maximum output was applied in a situation where the concept of full capacity had little meaning. Ministries would be left to juggle with their array of production capacities, and enterprise targets were frequently chopped and changed throughout the year.

If bottlenecks proved unamenable to this treatment, the ultimate fail-safe was the priority principle. We saw how, right from the start, Stalin was prepared to play around with production targets in the interests of the heavy-industrial core of the economy (see p. 20). Throughout the 1930s and 1940s the priority principle was used consistently as a basis for ensuring that input flows would ultimately correspond to those output requirements. Thus, if plan fulfilment in priority sectors was threatened, resources would simply be physically shifted across to them from the 'soft' sectors – usually agriculture and light industry. Plans for the latter were often substantially underfulfilled during the 1930s (Hunter 1964). In other words, the planners were quite prepared, *in extremis*, effectively to decentralize much of the system, as non-priority sectors were implicitly left to fend for themselves. In agriculture Stalin even countenanced the creation of a small, subsidiary private sector – to a great extent in order to ensure that peasants did not starve to death under the rigours of the priority principle. Thus there can be no priority principle without the principle of command. And the obvious wastefulness of the priority principle, as resources are directed and redirected without regard for the logic of continuous production processes, is itself a reflection of the nature of taut planning as a tactic of resource *mobilization* rather than of resource *allocation*.

## THE THEORY AND PRACTICE OF RESOURCE MOBILIZATION

As we move from the general to the particular in our analysis of classical Soviet growth tactics we have to pose three major questions. First, how exactly do we expect taut planning to extend production possibilities? Second, what are the mechanics whereby the abundant resources of labour and industrial raw materials are mobilized? Third, where does the 'scarce' factor of capital fit into all this? Post-war development theory can give us substantial help in relation to the first question.

In his *The Strategy of Economic Development* (1958) Albert Hirschman proceeded from a strategic concept based on un-balanced growth to develop the notion of linkage. He used this to explain what an unbalanced growth path means at the level of the sector and the firm. 'Leading' projects would create backward linkage, by creating technologically determined demands for inputs – thus, for example, the setting up of a vehicle plant would create a derived demand for metals, plastics, automatic control mechanisms, etc. They might also create forward linkage, in the vehicle plant case, by making possible the development of all sorts of transport services. Now Hirschman's theory was developed to interpret market economies, not command economies, and it is clear that the concept of forward linkage is of limited relevance to Soviet-type economies. For an enterprise manager concerned primarily with fulfilling an output target, and bound to his 'planned' suppliers of inputs, the commissioning of new and more efficient capacities to produce these inputs creates little of the pressure it may create in a profit-oriented economy, though it may certainly bring some relief. The notion of backward linkage, by contrast, seems to provide a neat theoretical underpinning for the tactic of taut planning as a way of maximizing output in the short term, given spare capacity. And while in a developing market economy there is always the danger that backward linkage effects will be dissipated through imports, leading to balance of payments crises and stop–go growth patterns, the heavily autarkic Soviet approach ensured that they would be kept within the system. Of course in a Soviet context we are not just talking about pressure exerted by planners on producers. Taut planning operates as much as anything through the application of pressure by one set of planners on another – 'goading the goaders' in Alec Nove's memorable phrase (Nove 1968, p. 308).

How exactly does this tactical element tie in with the overall strategy for growth as adopted in the Soviet Union? Using input–output tables covering the United States, Italian and Japanese economies, Chenery and Watanabe calculated coefficients of the ratio of purchased inputs to the value of total production for a given sector ($u_j$), and the ratio of intermediate to total demand for a given sector ($w_i$) (Chenery and Watanabe 1958). If we interpret the former as a coefficient of backward linkage, and the latter as a coefficient of forward linkage, then we have a basis for assessing the linkage potential of particular sectors of the economy. By adding the two together we can obtain a coefficient of total linkage. Sure enough, we find that the industries with the highest total linkage coefficients include most of Stalin's favourites – iron and steel, non-ferrous metals, oil and oil products, coal products, gas, and metals and coal mining. As Wilber points out, machinery would have done much better in the Chenery and Watanabe tables if finished equipment had been counted as intermediate rather than final production. Likewise electricity would have shown a much higher total linkage coefficient if Chenery and Watanabe had used Soviet statistics, because the ratio of industrial utilization to total utilization of electricity has historically been much higher in the Soviet Union than in the west (Wilber 1969, pp. 89–90).

Thus, overall coefficients of total linkage strongly suggest that Stalin got his sectoral mix right in terms of maximizing potential linkage effects. If, however, we look only at backward linkage effects, the argument is less clear. Iron and steel is almost as impressive on backward as on total linkage, and oil and coal products more or less hold their position. But machinery, metal mining, oil and gas, and coal mining all drop out of 'Division I' on backward linkage. Unless, then, we are prepared to attach more importance to forward linkage than seems a priori reasonable for a command economy, the identification between high linkage coefficients and Stalin's priorities is not complete. But it works for metallurgy, and for parts of the fuel/energy complex. If, of course, we look at structure more generally, in terms of the main sectors of the economy, it is clear that industry as a whole will always exhibit much higher linkage coefficients than agriculture, trade and services, etc. Thus we can perceive here a substantial, but not total, correspondence between strategic and tactical elements in the Soviet approach to economic development.

The linkage factor helps us to place in context the uneven emphasis of the gross output (*valovaya produktsiya*) target in the traditional Soviet planning system. Cost plans there always have been, but they have been by definition of secondary importance. Under the 'classical' system overfulfilling enterprises were allowed to 'bag', if they could, supplementary resources. Thus there was always a degree of *de facto* decentralization on the supply side, even for priority sectors, and it was through this that the impetus to backward linkage was channelled. Semi-legal supply agents called 'pushers' (*tolkachi*) would wheel and deal for scarce inputs often on a barter basis, and local Communist Party cadres too would get involved in this kind of thing when priorities were threatened in their 'parish'. The fact that the planned wages fund for a given year tended to be based on the actual wage expenditure of the previous year made it easy for enterprises to recruit and hold on to labour 'just in case'. Thus the typical production cycle over a one-month operational plan period would start off with a quiet ten days, as everyone recovered from the previous cycle, ten days of 'getting into it', and a final ten days of 'storming' (*shturmovshchina*), as the deadline approached.

It was in those last ten days that underemployed labour would be marshalled, perhaps new workers recruited, and pushers scour the country for key supplies. Of course even if the shadow-price of labour was zero, these new workers had to be housed, and the Soviet Union devoted 18.3 per cent of its total investment effort to housing in 1950 (Dyker 1983, p. 191). But living space per person in the Soviet Union has historically been on the Japanese rather than west European/North American dimension (Wilber 1969, p. 114), and the quality of housing construction has often been poor. There can be no doubt that the residential investment costs of the formation of the new proletariat were kept down to something near a minimum, with the pioneers on the great Siberian projects like the Bratsk hydro-electric station often living in tents (Dyker 1983, Ch. 6).

The issue with respect to material costs is rather more complex. Certainly the system failed to penalize, and perhaps even encouraged, wasteful use of material resources. Certainly Soviet Russia's generous industrial resource endowment meant that this wastefulness did not, on the whole directly incur net foreign currency costs, though with a different development strategy they could, of course, have exported the raw materials. Even with the given development strategy pushers and pushers' operations in any case cost money, or rather resources, and a look at the way that they operated, reveals a very high-cost form of commodity brokerage indeed. As late as the 1960s we find reports of crucial supplies being flown in for an enterprise by specially chartered aircraft ('S veterkom' 1968). And surely wasteful use of resources must have run the Soviet economy into increasing short-run marginal costs, even if not absolute production constraints, as extractive and primary-processing capacity was pressurized to produce over the score? It is, in fact, very difficult to give a confident answer to this question in the absence of comprehensive data on the cost characteristics of Soviet plants in the Stalin period. But research done on the Urals–Kuzbass coal-metallurgy complex, for example, paints a picture of a project with massive initial capital costs (it accounted for 47 per cent of total investment in ferrous metallurgy in 1931) and demanding transport implications, but fairly constant operating costs over a large range of output as the project gradually attained something like full capacity (Holzman 1957; Clark 1956, pp. 216–21). In any case, of course, so many new plants were being opened during the first few five-year

*Table 1.4* Annual growth rates of Soviet net material product
(produced), 1929–38[a]

| 1929 | 16.0 | 1934 | 15.2 |
|------|------|------|------|
| 1930 | 21.0 | 1935 | 19.2 |
| 1931 | 16.8 | 1936 | 29.3 |
| 1932 | 11.3 | 1937 | 12.0 |
| 1933 | 6.5  | 1938 | 8.9  |

*Source:* Clarke and Matko 1983, p. 7.
*Note:* [a] According to official Soviet statistics.

plans that costs were being continually lowered through (borrowed) technological progress.

The way that tautness got through to these, and other, basic industrial capacities was (a) that old, obsolescent capacities would not be shut down as new capacities were commissioned, and (b) that new projects might be forced into production long before full completion, with the period from on-streaming to planned full-capacity operation often very long by international standards. At the same time big projects often languished without enough customers for years after commissioning. The Bratsk hydro-electric station, for example, worked at only 20–30 per cent capacity for the first year or so after completion. The opening of a transmission line to a neighbouring town then raised the figure to 50–60 per cent (Dyker 1983, p. 131). This serves to underline the weakness of forward linkage in a traditional Soviet context, but it does mean that backward linkage effects emanating from manufacturing were that much less likely to be held up by stubborn bottlenecks.

In general, then, fragmentary microeconomic data suggest that taut planning in the early period of Soviet planning did not tend to run the economy into soaring short-run marginal costs in the extractive and primary-processing industries, and this picture is confirmed by the fairly evenly sustained year-by-year growth figures for the first decade presented in Table 1.4 (note that these are official Soviet statistics, which average out to a rather higher growth rate than Bergson calculates on either price base). There was certainly a hiccup at the end of the first, and the beginning of the second, five-year plan. Though ferrous metallurgy output growth was impressive from 1928 to 1932, it fell well short of the 'impossible' plan target, and there was significantly a 30 per cent shortfall in iron ore production. But oil and coal production held up well, and the other major problem areas of this period were outside the sphere of industry proper. By 1932 transport was emerging as a major bottleneck, with targets for railway line construction grossly underfulfilled (Nove 1969, pp. 193–4), and this must have pushed up 'true' c.i.f. costs of deliveries of bulky materials. Problems like this were never to go away altogether, and by 1938 transport bottlenecks had forced the leadership to modify the whole concept of the Urals–Kuzbass Combine. This may well have been a factor in the economic slow-down of the late 1930s, though the impact of the Great Purges (see Conquest 1968) was probably a more crucial one.

But if characteristic Soviet developmental features ensured that there would be no serious problem of increasing marginal costs in the short run, they did so at the cost of ensuring that average costs for each new complex would be consistently high, particularly average capital costs. This helps us to put Bergson's capital productivity figures into perspective, and enables us to pin-point a key weakness of the Stalinist growth strategy. Unskilled labour and to an extent raw materials are properly treated as abundant factors, and consistently made the subject of mobilizatory tactics. Capital should have been treated as a scarce factor, but a number of features got in the way of this.

First, there was a good deal of sheer gigantomania, conditioned partly, perhaps, by an undiscerning application of American experience, and partly by Marxist preconceptions about the role of the rate of interest under socialism. We should certainly not press this latter argument too far. Soviet planners in sectors like energy and transport, faced with alternative technology decisions involving greatly differing degrees of capital-intensity, quickly developed an approach to project appraisal which still forms the basis of officially approved investment effectiveness criteria (see Chapter 6 for details). But these criteria were not permitted to affect strategic decisions on intersectoral allocation of investment funds or lists of 'leading' projects. It has been estimated that by 1940 c.i.f. costs of Soviet cement were 35–40 per cent greater than they would have been under an optimal locational pattern because plants had been built too big, in the absence of substantial economies of scale. As a result, unit transport expenditures on cement were 70 per cent higher than they should have been in that year (Abouchar 1967).

Second, ministries and enterprises, faced with exacting, sometimes unpredictably exacting, output targets, evinced a strong tendency to overbid for investment resources. The fact that up to

1965 the great bulk of investment funds to state organizations was disbursed in the form of non-returnable budgetary grants – in a word that capital was a free good to the ministry or enterprise – obviously facilitated this. The best way to ensure an ample flow of resources in period $t + 1$ in a bureaucratic set-up is to get as many projects as possible started in period $t$, even to the extent of starting things that are not actually in the plan. And given the perennial supply uncertainty which is inevitable in the context of taut planning and 'success indicators' which put all the emphasis on production rather than satisfaction of clients' needs it was in any case in the interests of ministry or enterprise to have as many projects as possible on the go, so that it would always have something it could be getting on with and finishing. This was one of the main reasons for the chronic tendency to *raspylenie sredstv* – 'excessive spread of investment resources' – too many projects going on at any one time, very high volumes of unfinished construction, i.e. 'frozen' capital, and average lead-times, from inception to full-scale production, of two or three times what is normal in the west (Dyker 1983, pp. 36–8).

Third, the peculiarly Soviet pattern of duality in technology was inherently wasteful of capital, whatever it did for the utilization of the labour force. Ministries and enterprises, looking for ways of safeguarding themselves against the effects of supply uncertainty, would seek to divert investment resources towards 'do-it-yourself' operations, thus increasing their degree of organizational autarky. Enterprises could do this perfectly legally on a very small scale through use of the director's or enterprise fund. Ministries could do it legally on a fairly large scale because for so-called 'below-limit' investment they merely received block votes from the centre, leaving them a large measure of freedom in relation to choice of actual projects. The 'limit' appears to have been around 1 million roubles during the Stalin period. In any case, however, ministries have always been prepared to fiddle estimates so that projects properly falling into the 'above-limit' category should in fact go through the books as below-limit (see Chapter 6).

As a result, locational patterns became seriously distorted in many cases. In engineering most nuts and bolts and castings production became concentrated in enterprise 'dwarf-workshops', ill-equipped, certainly, in most cases, but utilizing what equipment they had poorly. Ministries constrained to operate a nation-wide network of plants tended to use small plants in peripheral regions as 'dwarf-workshops writ large' (Dyker 1983, pp. 150–7). This often meant excess capacity, neglect of regional developmental considerations, and highly transport-intensive supply patterns, with small plants in Tashkent or Vladivostock sending components to a main-activity factory in Moscow or Leningrad. Some sectors virtually lost their organizational identity under pressure of the rapacity of the more powerful ministries. In 1957 only 386 out of a total of 15,000 sawmills in the Soviet Union were under the control of the Forestry Ministry (Fridenberg 1957, p. 50).

In sum, then, capital tended to be used wastefully because of its key role as an instrument of mobilization. There is absolutely no evidence whatsover of any systematic planning of overall investment ratios (I/Y) or national and sectoral capital–output ratios (Y/I) until a very late date in Soviet economic history. Rather, investment planning proceeded as an essentially autonomous activity in terms of sectoral and project priorities. This, coupled with the operational obsession with short-term, rather than medium-term, output results, bred an insensitivity to the problem of lead-times amongst planners at central and ministerial level. It was only in 1979 that annual breakdowns of construction work were for the first time included in the so-called 'title list' (*titul'nyi spisok*) – the key summary project planning document which has to be approved by the centre for above-limit projects (Ivanov 1979). This blind spot in turn encouraged a blasé attitude to cost considerations at the level of the design organization (*proektnaya organizatsiya*) entrusted with the elaboration of detailed documentation and drawings.

> Design workers know that in the majority of cases the completion of a new factory will take three, five, or even ten years, and that consequently control over estimated production costs is really not possible. As far as estimated capital cost is concerned, it will in any case be reconsidered in the course of construction.
>
> (Ferberg 1966, p. 41)

Stalin got away with wasteful use of capital: (a) because resources were so abundant, and because the mobilizatory campaign was largely successful; and (b) because he was prepared to push up rates of accumulation and push down levels of consumption beyond what is normally considered acceptable. Between 1928 and 1935 the ratio of gross fixed investment to GNP grew from 12.5 to

32 per cent (Gregory and Stuart 1981, p. 386). In 1932, a couple of years after the start of the collectivization drive, the Soviet countryside was in the grip of a famine that cost the lives of millions of peasants.

> The immediate cause of [the famine] was not poor harvests but the requisitioning of grain from moderate harvests in such quantities that not enough was left for the peasants themselves. The main reasons for this drastic policy appear to have been, first, the attempt to maintain exports of agricultural produce and hence imports of machinery . . .
>
> (Hanson 1968, p. 36)

## THE COMMAND PRINCIPLE AND THE WORK-FORCE

We associate the name of Stalin with terror and forced labour, and there can be no doubt that there was a significant degree of direct militarization of labour in the early Stalin period. By the late 1930s there were several million people in Soviet labour camps. Legislation was introduced in the late 1930s and early 1940s which made provision for the direction of 'free' labour (especially of apprentice labour), and placed serious obstacles in the way of any worker wishing to change his job. Peasants on collective farms were subjected to 'organized recruitment' (Orgnabor) for industrial work, but in practice Orgnabor had little difficulty in fulfilling its quotas, as young country people in particular jumped at the opportunity to get away from the hated collective farms. The negative control imposed by passport restrictions, whereby a peasant could not leave his farm without express permission, was in practice the more onerous. The restrictive measures affecting urban labour fell into disuse after the war, being finally repealed in 1956, and though automatic issuance of passports to peasants only came in the late 1970s, organized recruitment on the old pattern did not survive the war.

Thus, even under high Stalinism the bulk of the working population was constrained by essentially negative controls, with the problem of excessive labour turnover (*tekuchest'*) very much in mind, rather than active direction as such. To this day the police *propiska* (residence permit) regulations are used to stop too many people drifting into the big towns, especially Moscow, in speculative search for work. Sometimes the command principle would boil over from the production sphere into the labour sphere. As late as 1968 there was a report of all the boys at a particular school being 'directed' into the building trade by the local political establishment ('A esli . . .' 1968). This was improper, and was reported with extreme censure. We must presume, however, that hierarchies themselves under pressure from superiors to report plan fulfilment may well have indulged in this kind of thing with some regularity under Stalin. In addition, of course, Communist Party members and new university graduates were quite legally the subject of positive direction.

But if labour was not largely directed, how was it allocated? Not surprisingly, through the market dimensions of wages and bonuses. There is nothing in classical Marxian theory to say that distribution should not be according to work rather than need throughout the intermediate period of socialism leading up to the establishment of full communism (Marx 1968), and Stalin did not, of course, claim that even socialism had been built until 1936. Between 1928 and 1934 the decile ratio (i.e. the ratio of the total earnings of the top 10 per cent of earners to the total earnings of the bottom 10 per cent of earners) for all workers other than collective farmers grew from 3.8 to 4.2. By 1946 it had risen to 6.0 (Wiles 1981, p. 25). The variable element was very substantial for management workers, with their bonuses in the top priority iron and steel industry coming to 51.4 per cent of their basic salary in 1947 (Berliner 1966, p. 116), but it was substantial also for line workers, through the medium of bonuses and various forms of payment-by-results (PBR) schemes. We should not exaggerate the importance of financial inducements in a situation where supplies of many basic consumer goods and services were in gross deficit at fixed prices. On the other hand, privilege – for example access to various kinds of special shops – has always tended to go along with, and reinforce, differentials in wage packets in the Soviet Union (Matthews 1978).

But however effective material incentives may have been in relation to effort (of this more in the next chapter), we must raise a substantial question-mark over their effectiveness in terms of allocation of labour. When unemployment was officially 'abolished' in the Soviet Union, around 1932 and 1933, so were labour exchanges. For the next 35 years or so job information would be purveyed largely through the medium of radio announcements, posters, etc., and recruitment done largely at the factory gate. In the post-war period Orgnabor turned increasingly towards the mobilization of labour for work in the pioneer eastern regions, but on the whole workers thinking of changing jobs had little choice but to go 'on the road' to look for something new, and this helps to explain the problem of excessive job turnover. Planners were often as ill-informed as workers about conditions on the labour market. Soviet researchers working in the 1960s set themselves to discover why, despite the efforts of Orgnabor and the Komsomol (the Young Communist League, which frequently organized 'volunteers' for big pioneer projects), as many people came back from Siberia as went out from 1939 to 1959. Certainly Orgnabor's postwar work had left much to be desired from the point of view of efficiency (Andriyanov 1971), but the more fundamental explanation is quite simply that the special wage coefficients established for Siberia were in real terms illusory. A 1966 calculation showed that the cost of living in eastern Siberia was 20 per cent above that in the central region, while wages were only 18 per cent higher (Gladyshev 1966, pp. 18–19). We must presume that the Soviet planners of the 1940s and 1950s were just not aware of this fact.

In general, then, the authorities appear to have lacked the detailed knowledge required to fashion a comprehensive pattern of wage planning in the pre-reform period of Soviet development. They do not seem to have had at their disposal even the more limited information necessary to make compulsory graduate placement an effective tool of direct labour planning. In practice, this work was devolved to a multiplicity of departments, with predictable results, and was a good deal compromised by the influence of high-placed parents. In any case, many graduates directed to inhospitable areas simply did not turn up (Dyker 1981a, p. 40). On the other hand, educational planning, backed up by substantial investment, has always been a major tool of Soviet development policy. The authorities were very prepared to apply pressure on schoolchildren and students to go into the specialities which would best match their abilities to the needs of the national economy. This, coupled with the on-the-job training schemes characteristic of the Stalin period, ensured that the basic complexion of the labour force conformed with planning priorities. When it came to the allocation of individuals to particular jobs and localities, the system operated very crudely indeed. But this must be seen against the background of a mobilizatory development strategy. Labour productivity was not a key variable in the Stalin period – indeed, on-the-job training made overstaffing in any case unavoidable – and the authorities were more interested in sheer absorption of people into the urban labour force than in details of allocation. Educational policies ensured that the broad pattern of allocation could not go very far wrong.

## CONCLUSION

In putting together a picture of Soviet developmental strategy we may seem to have erred on the side of apology. We must certainly disclaim any intention of implying that the chosen strategy was the best one, even with the given resource endowment. Rather we have sought to demonstrate that the strategy was internally more or less consistent. Of course, the strategy was never laid down on paper in as many words, and the history of its implementation bears the scars of a pragmatism sometimes, perhaps, misled by a crude Marxism. After all the talk about primitive socialist accumulation and pumping-over, it never happened because Stalin made such a bloody mess of collectivization. The politics of class war, it seems, is not conducive to the effective implementation of capital transfers. Not all the excesses on the capital investment front can be put down to the mobilizatory strategy. Gigantomania may not be a Soviet Marxist monopoly, but the labour theory of value is certainly an impediment to the correct appraisal of capital scarcity. In addition, the eccentricities of Marxian macroeconomics, and the Marxian tendency to see capitalist accumulation as something with an independent life of its own, must provide part of the reason for planners' insensitivity to the I/Y and Y/I coefficients. Similarly with labour planning, one cannot help feeling that labour exchanges were abolished basically because they smacked of capitalism, leaving Soviet planners an inadequate basis on which to do a rather tricky job – to plan one major dimension in price terms while most of the others are planned in output terms. Finally, the planning system which grew out of the strategy soon began to exhibit a number of key weaknesses. Here we are firmly back in the realm of the strictly functional, and of the main theme of the present work. In the next chapter we move to a more operational treatment of the Soviet planning system, as a basis for placing those key weaknesses in historical and developmental perspective.

# Chapter 2

# Soviet planning in practice

We saw in the last chapter that the Material Balances system gave Soviet planners a framework within which to use their common sense, rather than a computational technique as such. We also saw how the tactics of taut planning coloured the interpretation of common sense. We now have to look at some of the planning rules of thumb that emerged from all this.

## THE 'RATCHET' PRINCIPLE

There is an inherent informational problem in any command economy. Lower-level executive bodies know that any information they let go about their own production possibilities will affect the level of plan targets in the future. If a manager wants an easy plan the watchwords are audacity about supply needs, and modesty about output potential. It is for this reason that the traditional Soviet process whereby the control figures went down the line to enterprises and back up again to Gosplan tended to turn into a process of negotiation. Enterprises 'poured in the water' and central planners 'cut off the fat'. Ministries did both, depending on which direction they were looking. But because the central planners were known to cut off the fat, enterprise managers in turn felt that they were obliged to pour in the water. All the actors were thus effectively trapped in a behaviour pattern which not even 'socialist consciousness' could break.

What, then, are the principles on which fat was cut off? The Russians call it 'planning from the achieved level' (*planirovanie ot dostignutogo urovnya*). Given that ministries' and enterprises' statements about what they could do could not be trusted, extrapolation of past input and output trends was used as a surrogate for direct information on production possibilities (see Birman 1978). Applied more specifically to growth targets, we call this the 'ratchet' principle, as each new plan provision is calculated on the basis of a mark-up on the achieved level of the previous plan period. I believe that Martin Weitzman is wrong in specifying the ratchet principle in terms of the actual and planned performance in the previous plan period (Weitzman 1980). I would suggest that plan targets have no *ex post* significance. Under the ratchet principle it is strictly the achieved level of previous periods that matters.

But why, the reader may ask, couldn't the planners evolve some kind of way of directly estimating production possibilities? Certainly in the pre-computer age it was difficult to cross-check information coming from different sources for consistency. But the primary factor here was the sheer level of centralization of the system. It is very significant that Granick, in his econometric researches on the ministerial level in the Soviet planning system, found no evidence of the ratchet principle in centre–ministry relationships (Granick 1980). It was manifestly easy enough for Gosplan to make direct estimates of aggregate trends in production capacity of oil, gas, electricity, etc. The problem arose when one got down to the level of individual oil-wells and power stations. It is above all because Soviet planning was not multi-level planning, because Gosplan insisted on planning by sector but also by product, that the system was burdened with a quantitative informational problem to match the qualitative one introduced by the command principle in the first place. It was the combination of the two that made the ratchet principle essential.

But the ratchet principle was important in other ways. The 'always up, never down' aspect is an important aspect of crude growth maximizing tactics, and is obviously related to the tactic of taut planning. In addition, the ratchet helped with consistency problems. If plans, or rather out-turns, were reasonably consistent last year, and if the centre applied a more or less standard mark-up all round, then this year's plans would also be reasonably consistent.

However, while the ratchet principle represents an attempt to adjust to managerial behaviour patterns it does tend to induce modifications in those patterns. Just as perception of the command principle induces capacity concealment, so perception of the ratchet principle induces output limitation. The best way to ensure that the target for period $t + 1$ is not too demanding is to make sure that not too much is produced in period $t$. And of course if a fairly easy target is obtained for period $t + 1$, it is vital that it should not be overfulfilled by too much, for fear of what might happen in period $t + 2$. Thus use of the ratchet principle encouraged managers to place primary emphasis on even, but modest, levels of plan fulfilment.

## THE MICAWBER PRINCIPLE

This is closely related to, but analytically distinct from, the ratchet principle, and brings us into the realm of specific incentive arrangements. Readers well versed in Dickens will remember Mr Micawber's salutary dictum:

> Annual income twenty pounds, annual expenditure nineteen nineteen six, result happiness . . . annual expenditure twenty pounds ought and six, result misery.

Throughout the Stalin period managerial incentive systems were strikingly asymmetrical. In principle, fulfilment would bring a substantial initial bonus, while each percentage point of overfulfilment would bring incremental bonuses. Underfulfilment by just 0.1 per cent would mean no bonuses at all, probably a reprimand, and possibly even demotion if the pattern were repeated. In practice, ministries, which administered the incentive funds, often varied the amount of money going to individual managers arbitrarily, and the only certain principle was that a non-fulfilling manager would get nothing at all (Katsenelinboigen 1978, p. 144).

The Micawber principle is clearly basically an aspect of the crude growth maximization approach. The underlying idea is that underfulfilment, even by a fraction, should be perceived as something essentially shameful. To that extent it merely consolidates one important aspect of the ratchet principle. If we lay great stress on the incentive to overfulfilment, of which Katsenelinboigen bids us beware, then we may look beyond the crude growth maximization idea to perceive a more precise tie-in between Micawber on the one hand and the strategy of unbalanced growth and the tactic of taut planning on the other. If, by contrast, we see the essence of the Micawber effect in terms of placing a high premium on simply avoiding underfulfilment at any cost, then the complementarity of ratchet and Micawber is the more apparent. We should add that the application of the Micawber principle, and the perception of its application by managers, made the ratchet more necessary by exacerbating the tendency induced by the command principle to capacity concealment.

## RATCHET AND MICAWBER AND MANAGERIAL BEHAVIOUR

Taken together, then, these two basic principles, or rather rules of thumb, of Soviet planning procedure helped with informational difficulties, eased the problem of internal plan consistency, and fortified the crude growth maximization approach. At the same time they encouraged output limitation. But how can planning principles which do that possibly contribute anything to growth rates? Have we, in fact, discovered another 'wrong-headed' element in the Soviet approach to planning for development? Perhaps so, but before jumping to conclusions we will do well to look at some of the western literature on workers' reactions to PBR schemes. Even in the United States it is normal for workers on piece-rates to operate a 'bogey'. This is an unofficial quota, beyond which most workers will not produce for fear of giving the management an excuse to 'raise the norms' (Roy 1972). In other words, western managements perceive that under PBR conditions workers have an incentive to conceal capacity, and try to solve the problem by observing output trends very closely; the workers realize that and tailor their output trends accordingly. This is precisely a microcosm of the situation we are analysing in relation to Soviet planners *vis-à-vis* subordinate managers. But the really interesting thing is that although this phenomenon is universal throughout the western industrial world, a British National Board for Prices and Incomes report could conclude that 'there was wide agreement in the general evidence we received that the most usual reason for installing PBR had been to raise output, and that it had been effective in doing so' (National Board for Prices and Incomes 1968, p. 20). Payment by results sets up conflicting pressures in a management system, but both Soviet and western experience indicate that on balance it is good for short-term output trends. This, however, is by no means the end of the story.

## RATCHET, MICAWBER, AND THE LONG TERM

We introduced in Chapter 1 the phenomenon of 'storming' – uneven work tempos – essentially in the context of supply uncertainty and the ways in which enterprise managements react to supply uncertainty. We should note now that under the operation of the ratchet and Micawber principles managers will have an incentive to *shturmovshchina* irrespective of any supply uncertainty. There may be perfectly normal technical reasons why monthly output indices should not be completely even, and why they may be unpredictably uneven for overworked and harassed Gosplan and ministerial officials. It will always be in the interests of a manager in a Soviet-type system to try to iron out any such variations, at least as far as plan fulfilment reporting is concerned. This means that he may indulge in a degree of what is called in British factories 'cross-booking', where output produced (or rather hopefully produced) in period $t + 1$ is reported as being produced in period $t$ (see Lupton 1972). But the scope for this is limited, while the insensitivity of the traditional Soviet planning system to cost indicators meant the scope for storming was always substantial. Thus the concern to maintain even levels of plan fulfilment from one month to the next tended to exacerbate the tendency to sharply uneven tempos of production from one week to the next. A survey conducted over the period October 1965 to March 1966 found that 21–29 per cent of TV sets were produced in the first ten days of the month, 30–33 per cent in the second ten days and 39–48 per cent in the last ten days (Skorodunov 1966, p. 14). But annual plans were also very important from the point of view of bonuses and promotion, and the storming syndrome was correspondingly very evident in the quarterly pattern of plan fulfilment as well, particularly in sectors with longer production cycles. In residential construction, for example, over the twenty-year period 1953–73, 8–11 per cent of completions came in the first quarter, 19–21 per cent in the second quarter, 20–22 per cent in the third quarter, and 46–49 per cent in the fourth (Tsygankov 1976).

Thus we can perceive how very deep-seated were the employment patterns characterized by overmanning and low productivity which the pressure for *shturmovshchina* engendered in the Soviet planning system. Supply uncertainty is partly a result of growth orientation and so is ratchet, while Macawber is largely related to the crude growth maximization approach. More fundamentally, supply uncertainty and ratchet are related to over-centralization, and therefore so is storming and all that it entails. This is a theme to which we will return repeatedly.

The other major side-effect of the operation of the ratchet and

Micawber principles brings us to another crucial dimension of the Soviet, as of any other industrial, economy – research and development and innovation. Western literature has illuminated systematic difficulties in the relationships between Soviet 'scientific-research' organizations and the shop-floor (Hutchings 1976; Amann *et al* 1977). It is not difficult to trace these difficulties back partly to the problem of tailoring a quantity-oriented planning system to institutions the output of which cannot possibly be measured quantitatively. What we are more concerned with here is the general problem of assimilation of new technology at enterprise level, whether that new technology originated from a Soviet R&D establishment or technology transfer from the outside world.

Clearly a command planning system must have some advantages over market systems in relation to the introduction of technical change. As we noted in the last chapter, the technological levels of most sectors of Soviet heavy industry were revolutionized with the building of a series of key new plants in the 1930s. But they were *new* plants. Where the Soviet system did less well was with the introduction of new techniques into established plants, and here we are once again back with the ratchet and Micawber effects. Of course, a planning system oriented towards crude quantity is going to take a dim view of cost-saving innovations. In 1965 a textile factory which had successfully developed some synthetic fibres failed to fulfil its gross output plan, expressed in value terms, because prices for synthetics were set at a lower level than those of conventional materials, presumably because they were cheaper to produce (Demchenko 1965). More generally, however, any innova-tion, even if it were good for gross output, was likely to be bad news in terms of the optimal path (for the manager) of even, modest levels of plan fulfilment. Any stoppage for retooling threatened plan fulfilment in the given plan period, and a manager who was in a position to make up lost ground in the following period and earn overfulfilment bonuses would likely end up with an awful target in the period after that.

We are suggesting, then, that the undoubted technological dynamism (in implementational terms) of the early Stalin period was largely a function of the unusually high proportion of wholly new enterprises amongst the total number of investment projects. Once the Soviet economy had settled down to a more normal relationship between the two kinds of investment, the power of the command principle could no longer match the power of shop-floor defensive reaction. For this the ratchet and Micawber principles were wholly to blame. Once again, we pin-point those two principles as key obstacles to the development of high-productivity manufacturing patterns in the Soviet economy.

These technological considerations bring us into what is perhaps the major area of interest from the point of view of the operational evolution of the Soviet planning system: to what extent have the strengths of the Soviet planning system turned to weaknesses, to what extent have the weaknesses passed from venal to cardinal in the course of economic development and as a function of the rapid growth patterns which the system was precisely designed to foster? The answers to these questions represent a crucial aspect of the background to the emergence of the economic reform movement.

## THE CLASSICAL STALINIST PLANNING SYSTEM IN HISTORICAL PERSPECTIVE

Let us start with the most difficult of this set of issues, that of tautness. There is a theoretical argument to the effect that 'the longer the chain of supply relationship, the more weighty is this element [namely that tautness may increase effort, but it also introduces uncertainty, which reduces effort] in favouring lower but surer targets' (Keren 1972). This seems to fit with the suggestions of common-sense empiricism, and it represents an a priori argument that as an economy grows and becomes more complex, so the virtues of balance may increasingly outweigh the enticements of imbalance. In the Soviet case, however, perhaps the key variable here is the extent to which tautness has been backed up by the priority principle.

As we saw in Chapter 1, the tactical application of that principle in favour of a limited number of heavy-industrial sectors was a key feature of the Stalin period. As soon as Stalin died a process of progressive weakening of the priority principle began. To a degree this represented an 'objective' necessity, which Stalin, had he survived, would have had to face up to. The policy of unbalanced growth at the strategic, sectoral level had by the early 1950s resulted in a situation of gross disequilibrium between industry and agriculture, and Table 2.1 illustrates the long-term production

*Table 2.1* Annual rates of growth of industrial and agricultural gross output, 1928–53[a]

| Industry | | | | Agriculture | | | |
|---|---|---|---|---|---|---|---|
| 1928 | 18.9 | 1941 | −2.0 | 1928 | 2.5 | 1941 | −38.0 |
| 1929 | 19.7 | 1942 | −21.4 | 1929 | −2.4 | 1942 | −38.7 |
| 1930 | 22.2 | 1943 | 16.9 | 1930 | −3.3 | 1943 | −2.6 |
| 1931 | 20.7 | 1944 | 15.6 | 1931 | −2.6 | 1944 | 45.9 |
| 1932 | 14.6 | 1945 | −15.3 | 1932 | −6.1 | 1945 | 11.1 |
| 1933 | 5.2 | 1946 | −16.3 | 1933 | −5.6 | 1946 | 13.3 |
| 1934 | 19.2 | 1947 | 20.8 | 1934 | 5.0 | 1947 | 27.9 |
| 1935 | 22.7 | 1948 | 26.9 | 1935 | 12.3 | 1948 | 11.5 |
| 1936 | 28.7 | 1949 | 19.5 | 1936 | −8.4 | 1949 | 2.1 |
| 1937 | 11.2 | 1950 | 22.7 | 1937 | 22.9 | 1950 | 0.0 |
| 1938 | 11.7 | 1951 | 16.8 | 1938 | −10.5 | 1951 | −6.1 |
| 1939 | 16.1 | 1952 | 11.4 | 1939 | 0.8 | 1952 | 8.6 |
| 1940 | 11.7 | 1953 | 12.0 | 1940 | 16.5 | 1953 | 3.0 |

*Index numbers:*
1913 = 100, 1928 = 132, 1940 = 852      1913 = 100, 1928 = 124, 1940 = 141
1940 = 100, 1953 = 252      1940 = 100, 1953 = 104
*Source:* Clarke and Matko 1983, pp. 10–15.
*Note:* [a] According to official Soviet statistics.

trends which had brought this situation about. Powell's recalculations in terms of Final Industrial Product, which nets out the substantial amount of double-counting in the Soviet Gross Industrial Output series, suggests a slightly lower figure for industrial growth over the Stalin period (Clarke and Matko 1983, p. 204). On the other hand, despite the mobilization of the rural population for the industrialization effort – the urban population grew by 30 million from 1926 to 1939 (Gregory and Stuart 1981, p. 243) – the total farm population does not appear to have dropped much in absolute terms from 1928 to 1953, so that the record on agricultural productivity was just as poor as on output (Gregory and Stuart 1981, p. 253; Clarke and Matko 1983, p. 35). Western research indicates much more effective 'pumping-over' of resources from rural to urban sectors in the period of post-war reconstruction than there had been during the original 'Great Leap Forward' (Karcz 1968). To this extent the continuation of the agricultural price policies of the 1930s had a kind of rationale. But with an ever-increasing urban population the stagnatory trend in production could only go on for so long. In real terms the Soviet grain harvest never regained its 1940 level in Stalin's lifetime

(Nove 1969, p. 303), and Soviet leaders were talking in the early 1950s of 'the grain problem' as if they were back in 1927–8 (even if they were saying that it had been solved by 1952!).

It is not surprising, then, that the post-Stalin 'collective leadership' (Khrushchev was already in charge of agriculture, though he did not consolidate his political ascendancy until 1956–7) made immediate announcement of a series of measures designed to improve the agricultural situation. By 1954 average nominal grain prices were over 700 per cent better than they had been in 1952, and the corresponding figure for meat was nearly 600 per cent (Nove 1969, p. 328). Better prices would not only help to finance better incomes for peasants, they would also permit the *kolkhozy*, which in principle have to finance all their own investment, to push up fixed capital formation in agriculture. That in turn meant that farm machinery and building materials ouput had to be increased, while land improvement schemes would require sharp increases in fertilizer output. Nor were these developments a flash in the pan. Total annual agriculture investment doubled between 1953 and 1955, and has continued to grow remarkably steadily up to the mid-1980s (Clarke and Matko 1983, pp. 17–18). The trend at the strategic level obviously weakened the priority principle as a tactical weapon, since it reduced – greatly if we bear in mind indirect effects – the number of 'soft' sectors available to take the strain when the going got tough.

But there were other, more subjectively political, changes in the period 1953–4 which further weakened the priority principle. Town dwellers were promised not just more and better food – they were also promised a substantial increase in the supply of manufactured consumer goods. (Farmers would obviously not want to spend all *their* increased income on agricultural products.) Plans for investments in consumer manufactures were raised sharply as a back-up to this and prices were slashed in order to create the requisite purchasing power. The primacy of the 'Law of the Faster Growth of the Production of the Means of Production' was even temporarily overturned. These specific measures were not properly thought out – prices were cut over hastily, producing queues, while the new output targets were never met (Nove 1969, p. 325) – and were abandoned after the political demise of Malenkov in 1955. But Khrushchev never went back to the grim, belt-tightening days of Stalin, and American recalculations suggest that per capita consumption in the Soviet Union grew 4.5 per cent per annum in the period 1950–69, as compared to 1.1 per cent for 1928–37 (Gregory and Stuart 1981, p. 360). And though power cuts to student hostels of several days' duration were still common when I was a student in the Soviet Union in the late 1960s, industrial supplies to private consumers would never have the same 'flexibility' again.

Did this weakening of the priority principle in an increasingly complex economy exacerbate supply uncertainty, or force a reduction in the degree of tautness? The answer is probably both, although the evidence is conflicting and inconclusive. If we accept Khrushchev's assessment that organizational-autarkic patterns were becoming markedly worse in the mid-1950s (see Chapter 3), then we can deduce that the underlying supply problem must also have been getting worse. As we shall see later, improvement in supply conditions through changes focusing on the enterprise was a key thrust of the 1965 planning reform. This, of course, strictly proves that the problem was bad, rather than necessarily getting worse. In any case, as we argue below, there were other good reasons why the supply problem might have been getting worse. At the same time, at least part of the reason for the abandonment of the sixth five-year plan in 1957 was that it was 'over-ambitious and unworkable' (Nove 1961, p. 67). Granick, in his study of centre-intermediate planning body relationships, found evidence of a reduction in tautness after 1965 (Granick 1980), and a *Pravda* policy article from the late 1970s talks about 'planned reserves creat[ing] scope for economic manoeuvring within the framework of five-year and annual plans, without breaking or changing them' (Abalkin 1977). On the other hand an input–output exercise carried out on the 1970 plan for Latvia revealed that it was 'impossible' (Gillula and Bond 1977, p. 296). Planning reforms in the Soviet Union have largely been about *implementation*, while tautness/slackness is very much an aspect of plan *construction*. It has, therefore, been one of the aspects of the Soviet planning problem least aired among Soviet economists. But it keeps turning up and we shall be returning to it.

Second, there is the simpler and less controversial issue of success indicators. The gross-output indicator has two main weaknesses. It is insensitive to costs, and it tends to encourage neglect of quality and distortion of specification, particularly in the direction of 'heaviness'. Irrigation work in the North Caucasus in the middle of 1960s, for example, was vitiated by a number of characteristic faults: drainage pipes were laid only 10–15 cm below the surface instead of the normal 70 cm, and the general standard of construction was so low that proper control over the system was not possible – backflows occurred, and sometimes too much water was supplied, so that land had subsequently to be drained (Kalmykov and Filipenko 1966). It is, of course, perfectly clear that pipes are more quickly laid shallow than deep, which suits a target for metres of pipes laid. Apropos of 'heaviness', the hideousness of much Soviet architecture in the Stalin period, with its tasteless embellishments, has been blamed partly on the use of a variant of gross output as principal success indicator in the design sector (Podshivalenko 1965).

We have already argued at length that cost-efficiency considerations were not of paramount importance in the early days of Soviet industrialization. We can add that the scope for quality/specification distortion in basic intermediate sectors like steel, coal, oil and electricity, producing simple, homogeneous commodities, must by definition be fairly limited. We cannot say the same thing about engineering, perhaps the most complex and heterogeneous of all main industrial production lines. Neglect of the systematic production of components and spare parts, under the pressure of the gross-output regime, has indeed been one of the major sources of supply problems in Soviet industry, and has, as we saw in Chapter 1, caused serious distortions in the locational pattern of the engineering industry itself. Nevertheless, on balance it is surely fair to say that Stalin's priority sectors were not the kind likely to be too badly affected by the quality/specification weakness of the gross-output success indicator.

The crucial changes which affected the Soviet Union in the immediate post-war period conditioned an evolution of the balance of advantages of the traditional key success indicator, just as they presaged a transformation of the priority principle. More emphasis on consumption meant more emphasis on the little, on the quality-intensive, on the downright fussy. But just as the economy was becoming bigger and more complex, so the producer goods it required were becoming more sophisticated and more varied. In particular, electronics and chemicals emerged as new key sectors for which gross output was a quite unsuitable success indicator. Most important of all, however, the cost-insensitivity of the old indicator was becoming an increasing liability, as the Soviet economy began to run up against resource constraints. Reference forward to Table 2.4 will confirm that the Soviet labour force grew effectively by only 0.6 per cent per annum during 1956–60 according to Greenslade's recalculations. As the scope for bringing in more 'new' workers from the rural and female populations narrowed, as the rate of natural increase fell, and with the huge loss of life (at least 20 million people) during the war, it was inevitable that the labour supply situation would become tighter. The situation in that crucial first quinquennium of economic reform was exacerbated by a two-hour reduction in the working week in 1956.

As far as raw and energy materials are concerned, the crunch came rather later. Certainly problems with coal supply intensified and Caucasian oil supplies began to dry up, but Khrushchev was able to turn to the readily extractable oil resources of the Urals–Volga region, which by 1960 was accounting for 71 per cent of total Soviet oil output (Saushkin *et al.* 1967. p. 161). By the early 1960s, however, the rate of growth of Urals–Volga oil output was slowing down, and the Soviet oil industry was being forced to move eastwards.

Commercial exploitation of gas in western Siberia started in 1963, and of oil in 1964. Difficult natural conditions, isolated location and lack of existing infrastructure combined to push costs up sharply east of the Urals. Labour productivity on Siberian building sites is only half the Soviet average, projects take two to three times longer to complete than in the central regions of the Soviet Union, and actual construction costs of projects using standard designs exceed planned costs by 30–40 per cent. Permafrost conditions push up basic construction costs by at least 20 per cent, reduce the life-span of installations, and demand maintenance expenditures reaching 50 per cent and more of initial capital costs. Local supplies of building materials are usually inadequate, and have to be supplemented, at high cost in terms of transport, by 'imported' materials. On average, for the oil-bearing regions of western Siberia, 6,000–7,000 roubles' worth of new investment in the non-material sphere (i.e. services, education, housing) was required for each new arrival in the 1970s. In the Middle Ob' area the figure was 20,000 roubles, and in the extreme north of western Siberia around 40,000 roubles. The comparable figure for the central regions of the Soviet Union was 3,000–3,500 roubles (Dyker 1983, pp. 161–2).

Thus as one moves east and north in Siberia, capital costs tend

*Table 2.2* Output–capital ratio (*fondootdacha*) in the extraction of
Soviet gas (in cu.m. per rouble)

|  | 1970 | 1971 | 1972 | 1973 |
|---|---|---|---|---|
| USSR | 163.5 | 144.4 | 118.8 | 97.4 |
| Komi ASSR | 143.8 | 110.0 | 95.9 | 66.9 |
| Kuibyshev and Orenburg provinces | 44.8 | 67.2 | 57.5 | 30.0 |
| Krasnodar province | 136.8 | 115.0 | 74.8 | 54.5 |
| Stavropol' province | 228.3 | 180.6 | 150.1 | 115.3 |
| Tyumen' province | 117.5 | 111.1 | 81.7 | 63.2 |
| Khar'kov province | 260.6 | 220.1 | 180.7 | 150.3 |
| L'vov province | 126.5 | 118.2 | 99.4 | 146.7 |
| Ivano-Frankovsk province | 116.4 | 102.1 | 103.1 | 85.1 |
| Uzbek SSR | 373.2 | 359.9 | 296.3 | 196.6 |
| Turkmen SSR | 391.9 | 325.8 | 276.1 | 201.3 |

*Source:* Khaskin *et al.* 1975, p. 40.

to rise. But very rapid escalation of capital costs with the initiation of new hydrocarbon capacity was by no means a monopoly of Siberia, as the figures on the gas industry in Table 2.2 illustrate. Evidence has not come to hand on whether the Soviet ore-extraction industry has faced similar trends in the post-war period, although stagnating ferrous ore production was certainly one reason for difficulties in iron and steel production in the early 1980s (Dyker 1984). In any case the evolution of the labour and hydrocarbons positions alone has radically changed the balance of mobilizatory and allocative interests, and therefore the balance of good and bad in the gross-output success indicator.

Third, we have to return to the question of piece-work and incentives. We noted that western research finds payment by results the best way to get maximum short-term ouput, even though output limitation through the bogey is universal. Western research also tells us that when workers feel that a particular job is just not worth the trouble at the going rate, they will tend to 'goldbrick' or 'go slow', as a protest. Clearly the rates for many jobs in the Soviet Union under Stalin were very poor, and political pressure was often exerted to make them even poorer. One way to combat the bogey is through 'organized rate-busting', whereby certain individuals are 'bribed' (whether by promise of money or political favours) to break the bogeys systematically. This is essentially what the Stakhanovite movement was. (Stakhanov was a record-breaking coal-miner in the mid-1930s. His records were, however, very much 'set-up jobs' (see Schwarz 1953, pp. 193–7)). Now the normal reaction to this kind of thing in western factories would be gold-bricking. I have seen no evidence of gold-bricking in the Soviet Union during the Stalin period, and would suggest that one of the important economic functions of Stalin's political terror may have been to discourage just that amongst the less politically motivated workers, thus ensuring that the sustained rate-busting campaign was not neutralized. To the extent that Stakhanovites were rewarded in money terms this does help us to understand why Stalin needed an inequitable distribution of income.

I leave it to the political scientists to determine whether elements of political terror survived into post-Stalin Russia. If they did, they certainly did not affect ordinary workers. A 'photograph' of the working day published in *Pravda* in 1968 depicted a three-man brigade of machine operators at a Perm' factory as effectively working barely three hours in the shift (Shatunovskii 1968). 'Socialist competitions' and 'counterpart plans' (*vstrechnye plany*) served as a political vehicle designed to weaken the bogey (and also ease consistency problems) through raising the general level of 'involvement', but their effect was less than decisive. A late 1970s study of disciplinary problems in the construction industry in Penza province highlighted familiar problems like heavy drinking, 'social passivity' and 'negative attitudes to work' among the proximate causes of absenteeism, loafing, etc. More interesting was the finding that disciplinary problems were more serious amongst the more senior, more highly paid workers. A picture emerged of experienced workers almost being able to work when they liked (Reznik 1980). This is in total contrast to even the mildest interpretation of the Stalin period, and it is something on which, as we shall see later, the ex-secret police chief Andropov had very strong views.

Fourth, we must assess the impact of continuing reliance on the ratchet and Micawber principles in the context of rapid quantitative growth and qualitative evolution in the Soviet economy. From the 1960s onwards a trend sets in towards the modification of the classic Micawber principle. In that year Gosplan published a list of products for which overfulfilment was forbidden (Nove 1961, pp. 180–1). After 1965 overfulfilment was more systematically deemphasized through the introduction of reduced norms in cases of overfulfilment for deductions into incentive funds. Indeed, regulations implemented after 1965 introduced a fair degree of symmetry into rules for forming incentive funds, with modified coefficients being applied in cases of underfulfilment.

None of this, however, affected the way in which actual payments from funds were made. Here the principle that bonuses should not be paid at all in cases of underfilfilment of key targets generally remained in force. But the tendency to de-emphasize overfulfilment clearly got through to procedures for bonus payments, if only through the establishment of overall ceilings on total managerial bonus payments, a principle ratified *de jure* in the late Brezhnev period (Adam 1980). Confirmation of the movement away from open-ended encouragement of overfulfilment came in the form of a rather bizarre case, reported in 1976, in which Gosplan fined an enterprise 10 per cent of the cost of the iron used to make over-plan steel, although the iron itself was over-plan production and all orders for iron had been met (Galkin 1976). Of course iron and steel have in general terms been very much deficit commodities in the Soviet Union over the past decade or so. One wonders what the 'steel-eaters' of Stalin's time would have made of all this.

We should not exaggerate the importance of the transition from Micawber to 'modified Micawber' principle. As we saw earlier, the ministries under Stalin never allowed themselves to be tied down by the small print of bonus regulations when it came to rewarding their lieutenants. But the fact that post-Stalin Soviet governments took the trouble to issue regulations on overfulfilment suggests that the issue was of some importance in terms of indicating government preoccupations. Khrushchev was certainly just as growth-oriented as Stalin, but his initial modifications of the Micawber principle, like his abandonment of the sixth five-year plan, seem like the measures of a man who realizes that the most obvious route to high growth will not be the quickest for ever – of a man faced with the totally un-Stalinist problem of excessive retail stocks of goods that no one wanted to buy (cf. earlier discussion of the success indicator problem). For the first time, perhaps, the issue of 'quality of growth' came on to the Kremlin's agenda.

But, of course, the more modified is Micawber, the less there is an element of incentive for overfulfilment, and the more safely we can proceed on the assumption that the two basic operational rules of Soviet planning – the ratchet and Micawber principles – induce enterprises to place the highest priority on the avoidance of underfulfilment, on the maintenance of even, modest levels of fulfilment, with all that that implies for attitudes towards work tempos, manning levels and technical change. Before going on to study how changing conditions affected the importance of these behavioural patterns, we must pause to assess how such changing conditions affected the value of Micawber and ratchet to the central planners.

As far as Micawber is concerned, we have already implicitly answered the question. The modification of Micawber clearly spelled some movement away from crude growth-maximizing tactics, and corresponds to the evidence we adduced of a stuttering retreat from tautness. Had that movement been complete, Micawber could have disappeared quite painlessly. With the ratchet principle the question is more complex and interesting. To the extent that it had been an instrument of taut planning, and to the extent that planning became less taut under Brezhnev, ratchet must have become less important. But to the extent that it helped with consistency problems its role must have developed over the period of 'developed socialism', as the economy became more complex and the priority principle weakened. We can, indeed, take this argument one step further and suggest that increased reliance on the ratchet to approximate a solution to the consistency problem may have weakened the priority principle beyond even what the post-Stalin leadership wanted, because by definition use of the ratchet for this purpose would tend to exclude the possibility of structural readjustment. We shall return to the question of rigor mortis in the structure of the Soviet economy later on. Of course crude growth maximization tactics and consistency were never more than subsidiary aspects of the ratchet principle. As far as ratchet's key role vis-à-vis the informational problem is concerned, we can discern two opposing forces at work. On the one hand, the development of computer technology and information science in general made it easier to cross-check different bodies of information for consistency, and to build up an 'objective' picture of production possibilities. On the other hand, the growing size and complexity of the Soviet economy obviously increased the dimensions of the information problem. All in all, then, we should not be surprised at the extraordinary resilience of the ratchet principle in the period after 1965 in the face of repeated statements from the central political authorities to the effect that it should be excised from the planners' arsenal.

We showed earlier that managerial reaction to the known use of the ratchet and Micawber principles tended to result in overmanning and resistance to technical change at the shop-floor level. We implied that the former problem must have become much more of a headache as labour shortage started to impinge. We suggested that the latter problem must have become more serious as the share of wholly new projects in total investment fell. We can add that the post-war trend towards continuous and integrated process and product innovation (see Pavitt 1980) must have further exacerbated it. Significantly, contemporary Soviet research on technical change tends to identify innovation with the rate of introduction of new products. But is there any evidence that these problems actually became more serious in themselves, i.e. that storming patterns became more accentuated, that enterprise managers became less and less willing to countenance work stoppages for retooling? Here we come up against a problem of methodology. Complaints about these tendencies certainly became more common and more vociferous in the 1950s, but in the absence of, for example, systematic time-series on temporal work patterns in given sectors this really proves nothing. On a strictly a priori basis we would expect that worsening supply uncertainty would tend to make managers even more 'cagey', while any drop in the level of tautness would have the opposite effect. We simply come back, in fact, to Keren's generalized conclusions about optimal tautness. Thus it is the context rather than the essence of these problems which evolves in the post-Stalin period.

## THE SLOW-DOWN

It is not difficult, then, to build up a comprehensive picture of a planning system unable to keep up with the pace of evolution of its own creation, the industrialized Soviet economy. Here again we can pin-point a general weakness of the command economy: it holds no scope for any kind of Schumpeterian or Galbraithian evolution of economic institutions – for better or worse – in the face of changing economic conditions. Soviet planning and management arrangements can only be changed by decree, and decrees, of course, normally follow events. But our subsequent discussion of attempts at reform will, perforce, focus on decrees, large and small, and the manner of their implementation.

Before going on to that, we must document the deceleration in Soviet economic growth which has been implied in much of the forgoing 'qualitative' discussion. As Table 2.3 shows, the CIA is systematically sceptical about the absolute growth rates claimed by the Central Statistical Office (the definitional differences between NMP and GNP are not a substantial factor here), but the two sources do not disagree seriously on trends in growth rates. The CIA figures do tend to flatten out the pattern for the period 1951–65, and for evidence of a slow-down in the immediate post-Stalin period we really have to go to the official Soviet figures. On the other hand, both series portray a recovery of growth rates in the five years after the 1965 planning reform (though again very marginal according to the CIA), and a sharp down-turn in the 1970s. By 1984 even the official Soviet plan fulfilment report is claiming less than 3 per cent.

We can more readily assess the origins of these trends if we look at the figures for factor inputs and productivity over the same period presented in Table 2.4. (Note that these are calculated in term of a set of GNP figures which differ slightly from those in Table 2.3. In order to ensure strict comparability, we cite the five-year averages of the latter set of figures in the table.) Interestingly, labour productivity did not do at all badly in the 1950s, with a 5 per cent growth rate in the period 1956–60 being largely instrumental in keeping the growth rate of GNP above 5 per cent. It was the capital productivity trends for that quinquennium that really looked disturbing, with an already sharply negative rate of growth falling by a further percentage point. There can be no doubt that Khrushchev was, in general terms, aware of these trends, and this helps us to understand why he was so concerned about the capital-wasting penchants of the ministries (see Chapter 3).

In the early 1960s, however, labour productivity growth rates fell sharply, while capital productivity trends fared no better than in the previous five-year period. But it was a sharp improvement in that latter series which formed the basis of improved GNP performance in the period 1966–70, with the labour productivity growth rate remaining at its pre-1965 level. In the early 1970s both series show sharp falls, and the rate of growth of total productivity goes negative for the first time. That startling conclusion is rather dependent on the particular way the calculations were done, but

*Table 2.3* The slow-down in Soviet economic growth

| *(Average) annual percentage change in NMP (official Soviet figures, calculated in constant prices)* | | | | *(Average) annual percentage change in GNP (CIA estimates, calculated in constant prices)* | | | |
|---|---|---|---|---|---|---|---|
| 1951 | 12.2 | 1966 | 8.1 | 1951 | 3.1 | 1966 | 5.1 |
| 1952 | 10.9 | 1967 | 8.4 | 1952 | 5.9 | 1967 | 4.6 |
| 1953 | 9.8 | 1968 | 8.6 | 1953 | 5.2 | 1968 | 6.0 |
| 1954 | 12.1 | 1969 | 4.7 | 1954 | 4.7 | 1969 | 2.9 |
| 1955 | 12.0 | 1970 | 8.9 | 1955 | 8.6 | 1970 | 7.7 |
| 1951–5 | 11.4 | 1966–70 | 7.7 | 1951–5 | 5.5 | 1966–70 | 5.2 |
| 1956 | 11.4 | 1971 | 6.0 | 1956 | 8.4 | 1971 | 3.9 |
| 1957 | 6.7 | 1972 | 3.8 | 1957 | 3.8 | 1972 | 1.9 |
| 1958 | 12.6 | 1973 | 9.1 | 1958 | 7.6 | 1973 | 7.3 |
| 1959 | 7.4 | 1974 | 5.0 | 1959 | 5.8 | 1974 | 3.9 |
| 1960 | 7.7 | 1975 | 4.8 | 1960 | 4.0 | 1975 | 1.7 |
| 1956–60 | 9.2 | 1971–5 | 5.7 | 1956–60 | 5.9 | 1971–5 | 3.7 |
| 1961 | 6.9 | 1976 | 5.3 | 1961 | 5.6 | 1976 | 4.8 |
| 1962 | 5.6 | 1977 | 5.0 | 1962 | 3.8 | 1977 | 3.2 |
| 1963 | 4.1 | 1978 | 4.8 | 1963 | −1.1 | 1978 | 3.4 |
| 1964 | 9.4 | 1979 | 2.6 | 1964 | 11.0 | 1979 | 0.8 |
| 1965 | 6.8 | 1980 | 3.2 | 1965 | 6.3 | 1980 | 1.4 |
| 1961–5 | 6.6 | 1976–80 | 4.2 | 1961–5 | 5.1 | 1976–80 | 2.7 |
| | | 1981 | 3.1 | | | 1981 | 1.1 |
| | | 1982 | 4.2 | | | 1982 | 2.8 |
| | | 1983 | 4.0 | | | 1983 | 3.2 |
| | | 1984 | 2.7 | | | 1984 | 1.4 |
| | | 1985 | 3.7 | | | 1985 | 0.8 |
| | | 1981–5 | 3.5 | | | 1981–5 | 1.9 |

*Sources:* Clarke and Matko 1983, p. 7; Economic Commission for Europe 1983, p. 104; Joint Economic Committee, US Congress 1982, pp. 55–8; CIA 1989, p. 40; *Narkhoz* 1985, p. 410.

total productivity trends would look pretty unfavourable by the early 1970s on any methodology. Thus capital productivity is the 'early turner', with Kosygin's 1965 planning reform apparently reversing the trend temporarily. It is a pity that the breakdown in Table 2.4 does not distinguish primary resources as a factor of production, but if it did we would probably find that a good deal of the sharp deterioration in total factor productivity trends during

*Table 2.4*  Average annual percentage rates of growth of GNP, factor inputs and factor productivity, 1951–75

|                      | 1951–5 | 1956–60 | 1961–5 | 1966–70 | 1971–5 |
|----------------------|--------|---------|--------|---------|--------|
| **GNP**              | 6.0    | 5.8     | 5.0    | 5.5     | 3.8    |
| Inputs               |        |         |        |         |        |
| Total[a]             | 4.5    | 3.9     | 4.1    | 3.9     | 4.1    |
| Labour (man hours)   | 1.9    | 0.6     | 1.6    | 2.0     | 1.9    |
| Capital              | 9.0    | 9.8     | 8.7    | 7.5     | 7.9    |
| Land                 | 4.0    | 1.3     | 0.6    | −0.3    | 0.9    |
| Factor productivity  |        |         |        |         |        |
| Total                | 1.4    | 1.8     | 0.9    | 1.5     | −0.2   |
| Labour (man hours)   | 4.6    | 5.1     | 3.4    | 3.4     | 1.8    |
| Capital              | −2.7   | −3.6    | −3.3   | −1.9    | −3.8   |
| Land                 | 1.9    | 4.4     | 4.4    | 5.8     | 2.9    |

*Source:* Greenslade 1976, p. 279.
*Note:* [a] Inputs have been combined using a Cobb-Douglas (linear homogeneous) production function with weights of 60.2, 36.7 and 3.1 per cent for labour, capital and land respectively.

1971–5 was ultimately imputable to diminishing returns in that area. If we want to pin-point proximate causes of the continued decline in growth rates in the late 1970s and early 1980s we may have to look no further than the figures for the rate of growth of employment, which averaged 1.4 per cent during 1976–80 and 0.95 per cent during 1981–3 (Economic Commission for Europe 1984, Table 3.1.2). It has been estimated that diminishing returns in primary extraction retarded Soviet GNP growth rates by 0.6 per cent per annum during 1976–82 (Hanson 1984).

Of course great care has to be taken in attaching ultimate 'blame' for these adverse trends in growth rates and efficiency. We would expect growth rates to fall off with the attainment of economic maturity, if only because the base on which they are calculated is getting bigger and bigger (see Gerschenkron 1966, for a fuller discussion). We would expect some tendency for capital productivity to fall off as the capital–labour ratio rises; the figures in Table 2.4 show that in the 1950–75 period the Soviet capital stock grew at nearly 10 per cent per annum, while the labour force grew at just 1–2 per cent per annum. And can the upward trend in Siberian energy costs really be blamed on anything else but mother nature?

In fact we can reformulate all of these points to bring in the dimension of the planning system. Why has the Soviet economy

faltered on quantity without picking up substantially on quality?
Given that capital–labour ratios were bound to go on rising as
labour ran short, why has technical progress not done more to keep
down the capital–output ratio? And why amidst all this capital-
deepening, and in the aftermath of an industrialization drive which
shows up weakest of all on productivity, did the rate of growth of
labour productivity manage to *decline* by around three percentage
points over 25 years? The issue of just how inexorable energy cost
trends are is something we will have to come back to in Chapter 6.
But there must be a presumption that a system which reports zero
or negative growth in total productivity is in some sense badly
managed. Planning reform in the Khrushchev period may well
have had a depressing effect on growth rates because of its
piecemeal, disorganized and disorganizing character. As we shall
see in the next chapter, the argument that Kosygin's 1965 reform
provided a short-term fillip to growth rates can be substantiated
fairly directly. But the history of planning reform 1970–82 was the
history of what it failed to achieve, of the trends which it failed to
reverse. We can only agree with the assessment of the secretariat of
the Economic Commission for Europe, namely that:

> Among the most frequently quoted qualitative factors contribut-
> ing to an increase of labour productivity are the introduction of
> new technology, increased use of production capacities, changes
> in the structure of manpower skills, decrease in the number of
> lost working hours and days, reduced unit inputs of energy and
> raw material costs in general, rationalisation in management and
> allocation of resources, and improvement in the organisation of
> production processes. There are plenty of references in policy
> statements, plan and plan-fulfilment documents, and in the
> professional literature . . . to this dimension of labour produc-
> tivity growth, and also to the notable results obtained in this
> regard in many enterprises or branches. Nevertheless, the
> contribution of these factors to changes in labour productivity
> and efficiency in the economy . . . is usually presented in purely
> qualitative terms. It appears that up to now their contribution
> has been potential rather than actual.
>
> (Economic Commission for Europe 1978, p. 77, n. 8)

It will be the task of the next chapter to analyse the reasons for this
failure of actualization.

# Chapter 3

# The reforms of the 1960s and 1970s and why they failed

## THE 'PRE-REFORMS'

Having given Khrushchev credit for perceiving the unfavourable trend in capital productivity in the late 1950s, and for making the link between that and the organizational problems of the ministerial planning hierarchy, we have to give him rather less credit for his attempted solution. To counter departmentalism and its attendant evils of 'long cross-hauls' (see p. 19), neglect of potential external economies of scale in regional complexes, etc., Khrushchev thought to create a network of regional economic councils (*sovnarkhozy*), thus breaking up the traditional concentration of economic administrative power in Moscow. He was able at the same time to get rid of his political rivals, the so-called 'anti-Party Group', whose power base was located in the ministerial structure. But nothing was done to modify the degree of centralization of the system, the success-indicator regime, etc., so that nothing happened to alleviate the supply problem which had lain behind the autarkical tendencies of the ministries. It came as no surprise, then, when the evils of departmentalism were simply replaced by the canker of localism.

If anything, indeed, the *sovnarkhozy* turned out to be even more mischievously autarkic than the ministries had been. Because of the political dimension of the reform, with Khrushchev anxious to reward his own supporters amongst the regionally organized Communist Party hierarchy as well as to squash his rivals, the *sovnarkhozy* were made coterminous with the existing network of politico-administrative republics, provinces, etc. This increased the power and prestige of the local Party apparatus men, but it had three economically deleterious effects. First, it meant that the *sovnarkhozy* were too small – there were originally over a hundred of them. Second, it meant that their boundaries had in most cases no economic rationale. Taken together, those two characteristics meant that the 'natural' degree of autarky of the *sovnarkhozy* was in most cases very low, so that the autarkical tendencies were that much more damaging, while the scope for 'rational complex development' was severely limited. In addition, the fact that many Soviet administrative subdivisions are ethnically based allowed an element of sheer local nationalism to enter in and exacerbate localistic tendencies. This was particularly marked in Central Asia, where each of the four union republics was given its own *sovnarkhoz* (Dyker 1983, especially Ch. 6).

Khrushchev may also have hoped that the regionalization of the intermediate planning hierarchy might lessen the degree of *raspylenie sredstv* (excessive spread of investment resources). If so, he was to be disappointed – that problem too seemed to get worse under the *sovnarkhozy*, partly because of difficulties with the regionalization of the building industry, and partly because the intensely autarkical tendencies of the *sovnarkhozy* ultimately made the supply situation even worse, certainly as far as investment supplies were concerned. Khrushchev's first attempt at reform was, then, a total failure, and by 1962 the *sovnarkhozy* had been largely emasculated, though they were not officially abolished until Kosygin reinstated the ministerial system as part of his 1965 planning reform.

It is odd that Khrushchev continued through the early 1960s to play 'bureaucratic musical chairs' with the creation of all sorts of new central and regional planning bodies which simply further confused an already unwieldy structure. At the same time he has to take some credit for starting the process of reappraisal of the basic element in plan implementation, the success-indicator regime, a process which was to continue throughout the late 1960s and early 1970s. In 1959 he tried the most obvious approach to the problem of making the system more cost-conscious – he introduced cost reduction as an explicit key indicator, having equal status with gross output. Of course, this did not work. Enterprises quickly discovered that with a captive market the easiest way to cut costs is to skimp on materials and quality. But the lesson was learned that any basically physical planning indicator is bound to induce concentration on some dimensions of the production/realization cycle to the neglect of others. With limited and clear-cut priorities and abundant resources this could almost be an advantage, but as the strategic emphasis moved more in the direction of balanced growth and the resource availability situation tightened, so the need to evolve some kind of synthetic indicator, which would reflect all key aspects of that cycle, intensified. This is the background to the emergence of the notion that the success indicator the Soviet economy needed was profit.

Yevsei Liberman published his classic article 'The plan, profits and bonuses' in *Pravda* in 1962 (Liberman 1962). The article was important as a political signal that the profit-based reform idea was on the official agenda, rather than in terms of its specific content which was diplomatically vague. But we can perceive three main threads in the thinking of the reforming economists of the early 1960s in relation to profit. First, but not necessarily most important, there was the notion of profit as an indicator of the optimal static allocation of resources. Second, there was the more dynamic, more X-efficiency oriented idea that use of profit as a success indicator would push producing units in the direction of more rapid technical change and higher quality standards. Thus both the cost and quality/specification weaknesses of the gross output indicator would be avoided. Third, there was a purely organizational argument in favour of profit, inasmuch as it could be used not only as a success indicator, but also as a direct source of incentive payments which of course gross output never could. Implicit in all this was the idea that planning in general would become more parametric, i.e. based more on coefficients which are 'constant in the case under consideration but which may vary from case to case' (Bullock and Stallybrass 1977, p. 455), whether they be prices, bonus coefficients, plough-back ratios or whatever; in a word, Liberman's approach was ultimately based on the notion of stable norms.

In 1963 a pilot scheme was set up in the Bol'shevichka and Mayak textile enterprises involving use of profit as a success indicator, and with some degree of freedom of price formation and possibly also some contract flexibility conceded to enterprises. The pilot scheme was subsequently extended to other enterprises, but its usefulness was limited by the fact that reformed enterprises still had to operate in a largely unreformed environment. In any case, the experiment was quickly overtaken by political events, with Khrushchev falling from power in September 1964, to be replaced by a 'collective leadership' led by Leonid Brezhnev as Party boss and Andrei Kosygin as prime minister, i.e. effectively super-minister for industry. But however much of a break this may have signified in terms of political style, as the new leadership took pains to dissociate itself from Khrushchev's 'hare-brained schemes', there was a very substantial degree of continuity on the planning reform dimension. When Kosygin announced his comprehensive planning decree in September 1965, it did, indeed, appear as if the Bol'shevichka/Mayak experiment was simply to be extended throughout the Soviet industry.

## THE 1965 PLANNING REFORM

The main elements in the reform were as follows:

First, the total number of planned indicators for the enterprise was to be cut from around 30 to 7 – sales, rate of profit on capital, level of profit, wages fund, basic assortment, payments to and from the state budget, and centralized investment. The first three of these were designated as key indicators, determining bonuses, etc. The norm would be a combination of sales and rate of profit, with sales being replaced by level of profit for some enterprises. Other permutations were subsequently introduced, but not such as to represent any serious modification of the system. Profit was thus well and truly established as a keystone of the planning system, but with a modified output indicator (in the form of sales) sharing pride of place. A priori, this seemed a theoretically sound and pragmatically sensible combination.

Second, the incentive system was revamped. There would now be three funds: the material incentive fund, which would pay bonuses to managerial and shop-floor workers alike; the socio-cultural and housing fund; and the production development fund to finance decentralized investment. (See pp. 49–50 for a discussion of this last fund.) The socio-cultural and housing fund was an important innovation, because of the key incentive effect of housing provision in an environment characterized by shortage of accommodation. The material incentive fund gave the enterprise a formally constituted bonus fund of its own for the first time – previously, as we saw earlier, managerial bonuses had come from ministerial funds, while line workers had been paid out of the wages fund. The wages fund would continue to be one source of shop-floor incentives, but the emphasis would shift to the new fund. The general weight of bonus payments in relation to total remuneration was increased. The scope for earning bonuses increased for everyone, but proportionately more for managerial workers, though overall average differentials between managerial and line workers decreased somewhat between 1965 and 1973 (Yanowitch 1977, p. 30). The whole system was to be based on stable norms.

Third, a reform of the price system was set in motion, to be completed by 1968. The old price system, with its great and often arbitrary variations in margins over costs and high incidence of 'planned loss-makers', was quite unsuitable for a success-indicator system in which profit played a large part. There was some movement towards scarcity pricing in the area of factor pricing, with the introduction of a standard capital charge on all industrial fixed capital on which loan interest was not being paid. The charge was, however, set at the very low level of 6 per cent. Some limited forms of rental payment were introduced in the extractive industries (Fedorenko 1968), but these fell far short of a generalized system of payment for the use of unique natural advantages. As far as wholesale and retail prices are concerned, the aim of the reform was simply to establish some kind of uniformity in profit rates between different sectors and enterprises. It was, in fact, very much a cost-plus price reform, based on a kind of modified ratchet principle. It succeeded in ironing out some of the anomalies of the old system but left light industry with systematically higher profit rates than heavy industry, and permitted the survival of a good deal of planned loss-making – inevitably, since no generalized land rent structure had been introduced. In a word, it did nothing to introduce scarcity pricing at the wholesale and retail levels.

Fourth, the system of finance for centralized investment was to be moved away from its traditionally almost exclusive reliance on the non-returnable budgetary grant. Retained profits and bank credit were programmed to develop as major alternative forms of finance for fixed capital investment. Despite the establishment of almost ludicrously low rates of interest, originally as little as 0.5 per cent, bank credit did not take off in its new role, perhaps because the new price structure gave many enterprises such high gross profit margins that plough-backs were just too easy. By 1972 only 33.8 per cent of total centralized investment in Soviet industry was being financed from the budget, with as much as 60 per cent being funded from retentions. Bank credit accounted for just 6.2 per cent of the total in that year (Pessel' 1977, p. 51).

Fifth, there was to be a limited marketization/decentralization of the system in relation to some minor subsectors of the economy. With the creation of the production and development fund, the importance of decentralized investment increased sharply, and by 1972 it was accounting for nearly 20 per cent of total state investment (Solomin 1977, p. 62). While the introduction of the possibility of financing centralized investment from profits represented in essence no more than an accounting change, the planning of decentralized investment projects was to be strictly the preserve of the enterprise management, subject to planned limits for aggregate decentralized investment. Would-be decentralized investors were permitted to place special orders for investment supplies with other enterprises on the basis of a new enterprise statute which established the right of primary producing units:

> to accept orders from other enterprises and organizations for above-plan production on the basis of materials supplied by the client, or using own materials and waste products – on condition that this is not to the detriment of the fulfilment of the state plan and obligations according to agreements.
>
> (Bodashevskii 1968)

There would be a new flexibility in supply arrangements for a number of basic commodity categories. A provision whereby certain oil products, construction materials, and chemicals could be obtained at *snabsbyty* (supply depots) without the classical *naryad* (allocation certificate) was introduced in certain areas in 1966 ('Sistema material'no-tekhnicheskogo snabzheniya' 1969). The 'supply on the basis of orders' (*snabzhenie po zakazam*) system in the construction sector – presumably a development of non-allocational supply for the building industry (Chernyavskii 1976) – was experimentally introduced in 1970. A decree passed in 1969 provided for the transfer of whole enterprises on to non-allocational supply in certain cases. But dispensing with the *naryad* was an essentially limited step, probably removing a form-filling irritation rather than revolutionizing the supply system. Non-allocational supply involved no freedom of price formation, and may have involved little effective freedom of contract, as it is not clear to what extent enterprises may have been permitted to 'shop around' among *snabsbyty* in different areas.

A more radical departure was the creation of a network of wholesale shops to ply small-scale wholesale (*melkooptovyi*) trade. Wholesale shops operated largely without any kind of constraint in terms of how much of what they might supply to whom. As of 1969 just 30 per cent of the turnover of these shops was subject to 'limits', whereby ministries retained quantitative control over allocations of key commodities to particular shops, though enterprises still did not require formal *naryady*. By the mid-1970s the proportion of the total turnover of the shops subject to limits may have risen to around two-thirds (Rabinovich 1976, pp. 169, 219). Small-scale wholesale shops were primarily concerned with selling goods in small batches. There seems to have been virtually complete freedom of contract here, subject to plan targets for total turnover, but wholesale shops do not appear to have been allowed to fix their own prices. The 1965 reform also created the category of 'wholesale fairs' (*yarmarki*) as one-off occasions to bring prospective suppliers and buyers of 'bits and pieces' together, and these must have been permitted a degree of freedom of price formation to function at all. Commission shops, which basically existed to permit private individuals to sell off unwanted goods, but which were systematically used for procurement purposes by the R&D establishment, were subject only to the constraint that goods could not be sold at a price higher than that of the same commodity in a state shop (Katsenelinboigen 1978, p. 174).

The distinctions between these various categories of more flexible supply arrangements were in practice less than clear, so that it is difficult to be sure about the coverage of published figures on the volume of transactions they involved. In 1965 the total turnover of wholesale-trading organizations (which may or may not have included non-allocational supply) was just 70 million roubles, and by 1968 it had grown to 583 million roubles, with an expected figure of 885 million roubles by 1969 – about 0.3 per cent of Soviet national income in that year ('Sistema material'no-tekhnicheskogo snabzheniya' 1969). In 1968 small-scale wholesale trade proper accounted for just 0.5 per cent of total supply turnover (Gofman and Petrakov 1968), but by 1974 wholesale trade as a whole represented 3–5 per cent of total trade (Drogichinskii 1974, p. 31).

Another major element of limited marketization introduced into the system in 1965 related to subsidiary industrial activity in the countryside, a key subsector in the context of the seasonality of much agricultural work and the poverty of urban-industrial supplies to the countryside. It was the 1967 decree on agriculture that spelt out the new regime in this connection, and though the exact extent of autonomization of subsidiary industrial activity was left a little unclear, a legal source from 1973 stated that

> *Kolkhozy, sovkhozy* and other agricultural enterprises, and inter-*kolkhoz* organizations, sell the output of subsidiary enterprises and workshops on the basis of agreements concluded with the state trading network, industrial enterprises, consumer cooperatives, and other economic organizations. *Prices and technical production specifications are agreed on by the parties concerned* [emphasis added]. There is an established procedure for supplying subsidiary enterprises with the necessary materials, equipment and credit.
>
> (Lur'e 1973, p. 23)

This suggests that the only specific constraint imposed on these kinds of economic activity should be through the retention of some degree of central control over the supply (to the subsidiary enterprise) and credit sales. In the 1970s Gosbank did, in fact, extend six-year loans to *sovkhoz* and inter-*kolkhoz* organizations, though not to *kolkhozy* as such, for the construction of subsidiary enterprises (Pronin 1969, p. 47). On the other hand, mushroom gathering seems to have been subject to strict quotas and procurement prices (Barsukov 1971, p. 7), and the general rule that subsidiary industrial activity should never be to the detriment of basic agricultural activities meant that the central authorities retained substantial powers of occasional interference.

Subsidiary industrial activity in the countryside, covering canning and processing, building materials production, construction itself, timber and textiles, was worth 4.7 billion* roubles in 1966 (Gusev 1970, p. 6), and 8.5 billion roubles in 1970 (Gusev 1971, p. 7) – almost three per cent of Soviet national income in that year. In some regions it accounted for 50 per cent of *kolkhoz* income from sales in 1970 (Utochkin and Kuznetsov 1970, p. 95).

Sixth, the reform decree also predicated a new emphasis on 'direct links' between enterprises, without explaining, even in general terms, what this was to mean. The radical interpretation of direct links, which was espoused by the 'marketing' faction of the Soviet economics profession at the time, saw it as a complement to the development of more flexible supply arrangements, an aspect of a comprehensive transition to 'state wholesale trading' as the basis of the planning system. In this reading, direct links would certainly

---

* The US billion (1,000 million) has been used throughout.

involve some generalized freedom of contract, and perhaps also some freedom in the price-fixing domain. In the conservative interpretation of direct links, by contrast, enterprises with established supply links would simply come together to work out, and commit themselves to, details of specification and assortment: no extra freedom in relation to the basic contract or the prices at which deliveries were invoiced would necessarily be implied.

Seventh, although the ministerial system was re-established, the centre sought to limit the redepartmentalization of the supply system (no doubt with the possible resurgence of autarkical patterns in mind) by creating a national network of supply depots under the aegis of a new body called Gossnab – State Supply Committee. (A committee of the same name had existed before 1953.) Gossnab would do the bulk of the detailed Material Balance work at the plan compilation stage, leaving Gosplan to concentrate on the 'commanding heights' – that still meant Gosplan handling about 2,000 commodity groups, and Gossnab about 18,000. But through its national network Gossnab would also supervise the actual consignment of planned deliveries.

The eighth element in the package related to innovation. As we said earlier, the new profit success-indicator was clearly expected to strengthen the incentive to innovation at the shop-floor level. But in 1969 a follow-up decree established special prices and bonus schemes to stimulate the introduction of new products.

Finally, another follow-up decree of 1969 recommended the extension of an experiment which had been going on for two years at the Shchekino Chemical Combine (Tula province). The essence of this experiment was simple enough – managers were given the right to make workers redundant, though they were supposed to help them find new work, and use part of the funds thus released to increase incentive payments to the rest of the work-force. This gave concrete expression to some vague statements from 1965 about increasing managerial rights in the personnel area. Traditionally, Soviet directors had had very limited powers of dismissal, and though this did not stop individual directors taking the law into their own hands on occasion, it did create a level of job security virtually unknown for blue-collar workers in the west. This helps us to understand how the kind of easy-going work practices we mentioned in the last chapter could survive, and it did, of course, all fit in quite nicely with the extensive employment patterns characterizing Stalinist development strategy. But by the same token a Soviet government inreasingly forced to look to the labour productivity variable for prospects of future growth was bound to wonder whether they could go on affording a tenured work-force. In 1971, 121 enterprises were on the Shchekino system, and by 1975 the chemicals industry had been largely transferred on to the experiment, though Shchekino-system enterprises still employed only 3 per cent of the total labour force in that year (Dyker 1981a, p. 58).

Preoccupation with the problem of efficient allocation and utilization of the work-force also showed up in the development, from 1966, of a network of employment offices (*sluzhba truda*) under the aegis of republican committees for labour resource utilization. This represented the first systematic approach to the problem of labour placement (*trudoustroistvo*) since the abolition of the old labour exchanges in the early 1930s, and by 1970 *sluzhba truda* were processing more than a million workers annually in the Russian Soviet Federated Socialist Republic (RSFSR) (accounting for about half the population of the USSR) alone. Labour placement remained basically a republican matter through the Brezhnev period, although the republican committees for labour resource utilization were subordinated to a reorganized All-Union State Committee for Labour and Social Problems (Goskomtrud) in 1977 (Dyker 1981a, p. 43).

## THE 1965 PLANNING REFORM IN RETROSPECT

In a constantly changing world the assessment of economic policy measures is notoriously difficult, but we can start off here by looking back at Table 2.4 and reminding ourselves that the fillip to Soviet economic growth in the late 1960s was primarily associated with an improvement in the capital productivity situation – at least to the extent that the continued downward trend in that variable proceeded substantially more slowly than it had been doing. Micro-economic analysis confirms that the introduction of the capital charge (at too low a level or not), and the institution of rate of profit on capital as a key success indicator, did induce enterprise managers to unload large volumes of excess equipment – of course under the old system 'hoarding' was costless, and could pay big dividends because it gave pushers something they could swap when trying to solve supply problems (Schroeder 1968).

But the failure of the reform to do anything to the rate of growth of labour productivity, in an era before rising primary material costs had really started to bite, suggests a failure to engineer the desired 'change of gear', a failure to make an effective transition from extensive to intensive development. Certainly we have to be careful about judging the effect of the reform in crudely quantitative terms. Good weather and good harvests in a number of years in the later 1960s provided a fillip to aggregate growth rates which had nothing to do with planning reforms, inside or outside agriculture. In any case the quality problem had been a major issue in the discussion leading up to the reform, and travellers' reports from the Soviet Union in the immediate post-reform period suggest that there was some general improvement in quality, while trends in exports of the more sophisticated types of goods showed Soviet industry in a fairly good light. But complaints in the Soviet press about quality problems of the traditional type, to the extent of track suits with different lengths of arms or legs, were as frequent after 1965 as before – no doubt partly because the authorities were increasingly concerned about the problem (Dyker 1976, pp. 62–3). And of course precisely because of the increasing complexity and technical sophistication of the economy, these problems tended more and more to hamper industry itself. The supply situation in relation to spare parts remained critical, despite the wholesale shops, and the incidence of pushing, if anything, actually increased:

'Pushers' . . . continue to perfect their 'weapons'. And it seems to me that their activity has intensified in recent times. Managers took to the new arrangements on supplies with alacrity. . . . And suddenly, after all this, it turns out that there are more 'pushers' than ever, for all your 'economic levers'. . . . A contradiction? Certainly, and it makes you think.

(Ryzhov 1972, p. 3)

We shall return to the interpretation of that contradiction on p. 63.

No less suggestive in terms of the underlying supply problem is the fact that, despite the creation of the Gossnab system, departmentalist autarkical tendencies reasserted themselves in the years after 1965 with extraordinary vigour. In the period 1965–9 the number of building and building-maintenance organizations in the city of Odessa grew four times, with all the new ones being under different departments (Koppel' and Brig 1969). Other sources from around that time emphasized continuing supply uncertainty as a major reason for the survival of *shturmovshchina* into the new system (Dyker 1976, pp. 63–4). Marginal improvements there may, then, have been, but all the characteristic efficiency problems of the traditional system seem to have carried over into the new. To find out why, we have to look more closely at the provisions of the Kosygin reform.

Perhaps the most striking feature of the 1965 provisions was that they involved virtually no overall decentralization of the system. The reduction in the total number of planning indicators sent down to the enterprise represented only a formal decentralization – in practice it had, of course, always been beyond the capabilities of the planning hierarchy to ensure consistency between 20 or 30 indicators, and that is precisely one of the reasons why in practice gross output tended to have an almost unique priority. Cutting down the total number of planning indicators removed an irritation from the life of the Soviet manager, but in terms of the key indicators which determined bonuses, promotion, etc. the situation actually became more complex. The central authorities continued to try to plan production assortment at enterprise level in considerable detail, and if we look at the number of commodity groups planned centrally we find that it fell from c. 20,000 in the late 1960s to around 15,500 in 1977 ('Problemy razrabotki . . .' 1977, p. 115). In computational terms this is not a significant change. Despite the increasing availability of computers, the technology of Soviet plan construction had consequently changed strikingly little by the mid-1970s:

> Each year Gosplan USSR works out some hundreds of material balances by product types, and a great deal of experience has been accumulated in this field. Inter-product and intersectoral balances, which can provide a greater degree of consistency between the production and allocation of goods in interlinked sectors, are less widely used. In the organs of Gossnab USSR balancing has still not been widely developed as a basis for the production of material-technical supply plans.
>
> (Rabinovich 1976, p. 214)

The various components of partial decentralization discussed on pp. 49–52 were of course not substantial enough to affect the overall level of centralization, whatever their potential 'qualitative' significance. And the tradition of administrative control over prices was reconsecrated in the price reform of 1966–7 to such a degree that even wholesale shops and the like were probably given very little freedom in this domain. Under the original provisions, the formation and disbursement of bonus funds were to be on the basis of rules which left a good deal of freedom to the enterprise. But by 1971 changes were being introduced which reasserted the right of ministries to modify bonus rules.

The transition to profit as a key success indicator implied a degree of transition to a more parametric system, to a system just as centralized, perhaps, but less directly centralized. In fact, the Soviet planners did, under the reform, insist on setting targets for profit. It is difficult to see any good reason for this – rather, it smacks of the obstinacy of the old habits of command. But with sales targets being imposed as well, for perfectly good reasons we must add, the command principle was clearly much less modified at that general level than it might have been. It was modified very significantly in the peripheral areas of radical marketization, but once again we have to say that even in potential terms this was very small beer. Procedures were introduced into R&D planning whereby special price differentials and coefficients tied bonuses directly to the return on innovations (Cooper 1979). As we shall see in Chapter 6, similar approaches were tried out experimentally in construction. Thus movement away from the command principle tended to affect specific sectors or subsectors, rather than the planning system as a whole. As far as enterprises are concerned, the classic principle that they be instructed how much of what to produce or realize, from whom to obtain their inputs, and to whom to send their outputs, remained largely untouched.

How did all this affect the actual operation of the new success indicators? Let us take sales first. It is not clear, in a situation where customer enterprise cannot argue about prices or change suppliers, that a switch from output to sales as key output-based indicator will make a great deal of difference. One can easily find cases from the post-reform period where badly substandard consumer goods were simply sent back to the producer (see Dyker 1976, p. 63), and under the new success indicator this did mean automatic loss of bonuses. But of course even under the old system managers who pushed their luck too far on the quality side tended to run into political sanctions – hence the indignant articles in *Pravda* from which we learn so much. More important is what happens when deliveries from one industrial enterprise to another are substandard, or inaccurately specified, without being totally useless. The trouble with sending the whole lot back is that this will almost certainly mean that the manager will fail to fulfil the monthly or quarterly plan, thus breaking golden rule number one of the Soviet executive bent on survival. And if, under the pressure of the given enterprise's own plans, a substandard consignment were wholly or partly used, the right to sue the supplier is forfeited under Soviet commercial law (Vlasov 1984). Even if specification is so far out that the supplies cannot be used, they can, of course, always be hoarded with a view to disposing of them through the pusher network on which the manager was in any case the more dependent, the more often mis-specified deliveries are received. While the 1965 planning reform introduced a significant sanction' on the hoarding of capital goods, it did not materially alter the situation with respect to supplies in general.

In a market economy clients initially respond to quality and specification problems by demanding price discounts, or making threatening noises about changing supplier in the future. The problem in the Soviet case, with the introduction of a sales success indicator not backed up by substantial decentralization or relaxation of the command principle, is that the ultimate sanction was the only one available; no basis whatsoever was created for the development of any regularized process of continuous adjustment in the matching of supplies and demands.

We can say exactly the same things about the introduction of profit as a success indicator. With fixed prices and captive customers a supplier can improve the profit position by skimping, or using shoddy materials, just as he can the position with a straight cost-reduction indicator. With hundreds of thousands of prices to be fixed by the State Committee for Prices, it is unavoidable that there will be inconsistencies in the profitability of individual items. Bonus-maximizing managers will be able to increase profits by distorting assortment towards product lines carrying higher profit margins, and once again the client enterprise will be prevented by the rigidity of the price and contract system from making any kind of flexible response. Under the 1965 provisions the authorities sought to retain direct control over assortment – they were not looking to the profit success indicator to do the job for them. But because general over-centralization prevented them from exercising that control effectively, a vacuum was created which the profit success indicator was prevented from filling by continued restrictions in the price and contract area. If, of course, an expected consignment simply does not turn up at all, there is absolutely nothing an enterprise in a Soviet-type system can do, whatever the success-indicator regime, except resort to political string-pulling and the pusher network. There were other problems with the profit-based indicators. The combination of cost-plus pricing, failure to institute a proper profit-maximizing rule, and failure to permit any sharp increase in the degree to which resource flows were permitted to respond to price/profit signals, meant that profit was largely unable to function in its allocative role. To the extent that it was, it may have tended to misallocation rather than allocation. Rate of profit did reinforce the capital-dishoarding effect of the capital charge. But it was a peculiarly unsuitable indicator to introduce at a time when enterprises were being brought more into the investment decision-making process. Clearly an enterprise which has, for any reason, an above-average gross rate of profit on existing capital stock will be discouragd by this indicator from undertaking any new investment which would pull that average down, irrespective of its net present value. The failure of the price reform to iron out historical anomalies in sectoral profit rates made this problem that much more serious (Liberman 1968, pp. 54–5; Bunich 1967, p. 47).

To sum up, then, profit in the given context earns just about zero marks in relation to resource allocation. It was prevented by the continued rigidity of the price and contract set-up from making anything like its potential contribution in terms of general X-efficiency problems. It did, however, work perfectly well as a basis for financing enterprise funds.

The second major specific difficulty with the 1965 reform related to the position of intermediate planning bodies. As we noted in Chapter 1, the traditional planning system was remarkably simple in terms of how the line of command operated. The centre dished out aggregate output targets to the ministries and main administrations, and they broke them down into specific targets for producing units. Ministerial workers were not on bonus schemes as such, but in more general terms their prospects depended on performance in relation to plan just as much as those of enterprise managements. Plan fulfilment, in a word, meant exactly the same thing for everyone, from Gosplan planners down to shop-floor workers. The 1965 reform changed all that. Ministries, etc. would remain, or rather be re-established, as essentially administrative bodies, receiving aggregate instructions from Gosplan in terms of gross output. This stood to reason, because sales contracts were imposed on enterprises, not ministries. It did, however, create a problem of 'translating' output targets into sales targets, and it is hardly surprising that in the early days of the reform the ministries were frequently accused of setting unofficial gross output targets for their enterprises.

But the problem went deeper than that. Now that enterprises 'paid' in various ways for their capital stock as they had never done before, what happens if a ministry or *glavk* decides to transfer equipment from one enterprise to another? Should this be forbidden, or should compensation be paid when it does occur? More generally, the fact that intermediate planning bodies were not on *khozraschet* (business accounting) like their subordinate enterprises meant (a) that they did not have formally constituted profit-and-loss accounts and incentive funds; and (b) that they were not juridical persons, so that enterprises had no basis for litigation against them if they acted in a way detrimental to the local interests of the enterprise. Under the new system, with enterprises constrained to place much more emphasis on financial flows, this emerged as a serious problem.

The approach of the Brezhnev/Kosygin government to that problem was to try to push the *khozraschet* principle further up the planning hierarchy. By the late 1960s one ministry – the Ministry for Instrument Making – was already on a regime involving 'elements of *khozraschet*', though this does not appear to have meant much more than 100 per cent self-financing of centralized investment in the sector. Experiments with ministerial *khozraschet* continued into the mid-1970s, but more substantial progress was made at the level between ministry and enterprise. During the early reform period a number of *glavki* were put on *khozraschet*, but that approach was superseded with the decree on the association (*ob"edinenie*), published in 1973. This created a highly complex system at the sub-intermediate level, in which the norm was for so-called *production* associations to group together fairly small numbers of associated enterprises, with the latter sometimes (but not always) losing their juridical independence, and *industrial* associations taking over the role of the old *glavki*. Production associations were always on full *khozraschet*, and there appear to have been substantial elements of *khozraschet* at industrial association level. But the *ob"edinenie* reform at best shifted the incidence of the problem of dovetailing administration and the post-reform interpretation of *khozraschet* to a higher instance (Dyker 1983, p. 34). Indeed clashes between ministry and association were surely inevitable as long as the former was forced to work with a system still plagued by supply uncertainty and still containing substantial elements of tautness. In such an environment they could hardly be expected to ensure plan fulfilment without recourse to their traditional ploys of chopping and changing plan targets for subordinates, shifting around resources, etc.

The association reform was not only about the balance of administration and *khozraschet*. Recognizing that the general measures of 1965 had not resulted in any dramatic improvement in the supply situation, and that in this context it was going to be very difficult to control organizational-autarkical tendencies, the authorities sought through the establishment of production associations to create rationalized combinations of main-activity and ancillary enterprises which would at least cut the cost, in terms of transport and excess capacity, of organizational autarky. They do not appear to have been particularly successful in this (Golub' 1974), no doubt partly because it was left to the ministries to do the rationalizing. Finally, the Soviet leadership saw in the 1973 decree a basis for improving the innovation performance of the Soviet economy. This statement in itself implies that the approach to the innovation problem embodied in the decrees of 1965 and 1969 had not worked. Let us investigate that proposition.

Just as profit with fixed prices and contracts may not in practice stimulate high quality and the study of clients' needs, so it may not necessarily create effective incentives to innovation. With sales targets to be fulfilled, furthermore, and the ratchet principle still very much alive (see discussion on pp. 62–3), enterprise managers may be sceptical about innovation even when it is likely to improve profit performance. In any case, none of this has any effect on the flow of R&D from research institutes to producing units in the first place. The 1969 decree did little apropos the latter problem, except to instruct the institutes to mend their ways. In relation to the former, its reliance on special prices and bonuses for innovations ran into two types of difficulty. First, the special price system was over-complex and badly designed, so that enterprises might often be stimulated to do the wrong thing (Lavelle 1974). Second, there is the problem of simulation. The easy way to earn special innovation bonuses is through 'innovation' rather than innovation. The more sophisticated an economy becomes, the more emphasis it places on consumer goods, the greater the scope for such simulation becomes. By giving associations their own R&D

facilities (some special mixed 'scientific-production associations' were also created) the authorities obviously hoped to speed up the process of communication from research team to production unit. They seem also to have believed that the association would be in a position to take a longer view on the merits of innovation. In practice, continued 'petty tutelage' over the new sub-intermediate bodies ensured that their view on this could not be very different from that of an enterprise (see Zakharov and Petrov 1974).

Perhaps the most significant failure of the Kosygin reform was in relation to limited liberalization in specific subsectors. Let us start by looking at decentralized investment. The first thing that happened there was that would-be investors, replete with production-development funds, ran into serious difficulties in getting hold of the physical resources to make their decentralized investment plans reality (Gorushkin 1969). In a Soviet-type economy, giving institutions funds to finance essentially unplanned activities may run into the problem that other institutions have not been assigned plans to produce the corresponding supplies – hence the importance of the change in the enterprise statute cited earlier. Enterprises, it was hoped, would feel encouraged to produce lines not included in the plan, or to produce extra output on planned production lines, thus improving performance in relation to the profit indicator, though not, presumably, in relation to basic sales and assortment plans.

That this did not happen seems to be largely related to the vigorous survival of the ratchet and modified Micawber principles into the post-reform period (Dyker 1981b, pp. 127–8). Enterprises had little choice but to remain above all concerned that sales/output plans be fulfilled, and at best indifferent to the production of large-scale over-plan surpluses (Zangurashvili 1976). They must have remained positively reluctant to report any such surpluses, so that unofficial direct disposal would in any case have been considered preferable to official. The operation of the ratchet and Micawber factors may have been strengthened in this regard by more general systemic tendencies. To the extent that the planning balance remained taut, there may not have been, with the best will in the world, much potential surplus around (see Varavka 1975), while surpluses that were reported were often quickly gobbled up by intermediate planning authorities (Protsenko and Soloveichik 1976, p. 24). Ministries, still obsessed with minimizing a supply problem that had been eased to only a minor degree, proceeded with their traditional autarkic policies to the extent of making it extremely difficult for enterprises to take on extra commitments to 'outsiders'. Cases were even reported of ministries issuing formal regulations obliging subordinate enterprises to give priority to intrasectoral supply, even in cases where allocation certificates had not been issued by Gossnab (Khashutogov 1976).

The second thing that happened with decentralized investment, round about 1969/70, was that it began to sort out its supply problems with a vengeance, to the extent that in 1971 the plan for total decentralization was overfulfilled by 26 per cent, while the plan for centralized investment was underfulfilled by 4 per cent. In 1971 there was no fewer than 880 projects under construction that were outside the plan, but using materials and men earmarked for planned projects ('Vypolnenie plana . . .' 1972, p. 3). It seems clear that enterprise managers, originally baulked by the weakness of formal supply arrangements for decentralized investment, were by the early 1970s turning to the unofficial pusher network to filch supplies away from centralized investment. This helps us to understand the paradox noted earlier of an apparent increase in the activity of pushers after the reform.

The development of subsidiary industrial production in the countryside followed a very similar pattern, and for the same ultimate reason. 'The supply to *kolkhozy* of equipment for processing and subsidiary production is not a function of state organisations' (Pozdnyakov 1968, p. 101). Trading organizations could, on the basis of what amounted to barter agreements, transfer goods from the 'market fund' to collective and state farms for use as 'raw and ancillary materials' (Pronin 1969, p. 48). Payment for these deliveries might be made in the form of counterpart consignments of the finished goods. Industrial enterprises were encouraged to sell of surplus machinery, inventory, raw materials and offcuts to agricultural organizations. But many reports indicate only fractional satisfaction of subsidiary industrial supply needs from official allocations. In some cases, e.g. that of timber, it may have been possible to meet the bulk of needs from own supplies and direct supplies from local enterprises (Sokolov 1969). But even with state farms, which might presumably tend to get better treatment than *kolkhozy*, the acuteness of the problem is underlined by the testimony of a *sovkhoz* director:

Early in the morning I rush off to the *oblast'* centre, 80 kilometres

away, abandoning a mass of production affairs. Having spent the
day running around construction and supply organizations I
return late. The foreman is waiting for me. What about the
bricks, the things for the carpenters? He doesn't even bother to
ask about roofing felt and glass.

(Vasil'ev 1968, p. 10)

Despite this, agro-industrial operations flourished, partly because
they fulfilled very great needs, partly because the freedom of
movement conceded them made possible unofficial supply operations on a grand scale. It is reported that 37 per cent of all cases of
misappropriation in Odessa *oblast'* in 1971 occurred in the
subsector, with a corresponding figure for 1972 of 24 per cent. At
one point more than 200 illegal subsidiary enterprises were
operating in the province, many of them created by 'sharpers'
(Yasinskii 1973, p. 19). A legal specialist reported that among the
most common forms of unlawful act committed on *kolkhozy* were

deals between collective farms and private go-betweens involving
the sale of *kolkhoz* production or the acquisition of materials.
Violations of the second type are particularly common, which is
largely explicable in terms of deficiencies in the organization of
material-technical supply to *kolkhozy*.

(Tarnavskii 1973, p. 26)

The kinds of problems that decentralized investment and subsidiary industrial activity ran into, and the way these problems
were solved, highlighted the failure of the various kinds of free
trade introduced to take off in a big way, which in turn reflected
the failure of the reformed planning system to create effective
incentives for the production of special orders. Of course, because
sales is a gross indicator the new system failed in any case to
obviate the traditional disincentive to produce even *planned* quotas
of bits and pieces. Most fundamentally, the failure to decentralize
meaningfully meant that the planners could not give up the
ratchet, which meant that managers could not give up their anti-
ratchet ploys. Table 3.1 gives a revealing picture of the operations
of an apparently fairly successful wholesale shop in Odessa. The
most significant thing to emerge from the table is that the bulk of
purchases were coming from the supply network itself, including
other free trading organizations. (This means, by the way, that
official figures on shop turnover must have exaggerated their real

*Table 3.1*  Percentage breakdown of decentralized purchases of
material resources by the universal shop under the
Odeselektromashsnabsbyt administration

| Decentralized purchases | Total | Purchases within the zone of the administration | Purchases within the zone of the administration |
|---|---|---|---|
| From industrial enterprises | 24.6 | 37.9 | 17.9 |
| From *snabsbyt* organizations under Gossnab USSR | 53.1 | 4.0 | 77.2 |
| of which from small-scale wholesale shops | (16.9) | (0.4) | (25.0) |
| From trade and *snabsbyt* organizations under ministries and departments | 22.3 | 58.1 | 4.9 |
| Total | 100.0 | 100.0 | 100.0 |

*Source:* Rabinovich 1976, p. 171.

importance because of elements of double-counting.) The proportion of total purchases coming directly from industrial enterprise
was fairly low overall, and was even lower in relation to non-local
enterprises. Some proportion of purchases from the trading
network must have represented indirect purchases of enterprise
surpluses, but the bulk of these must surely have reflected
'shunting-around' of planned, but incorrectly despatched, consignments. This confirms the failure of free trading organizations to
emerge as powerful instruments for the redistribution of surplus
production coming directly from enterprises under the 1965 reform.

We should certainly not exaggerate the quantitative importance
of these elements of autonomization introduced by Kosygin –
around 1970 they probably added up to just about 10 per cent of
Soviet national income. But they graphically illustrate the key
principle that a degree of general decentralization is a necessary
condition of more radical autonomization in particular subsectors,
that the 'stable norms' slogan is meaningless in an over-centralized
economy. Just as interesting is the way in which the Soviet
authorities reacted when things began to get a little out of hand.
Perceiving the ever more vigorous development of the 'second
economy' within the industrial supplies field, perceiving the threat
to central priorities posed through the undermining of centralized
investment plans by decentralized, the leadership decided on a
sharp clamp-down. In 1973 the overfulfilment of decentralized

government plans was banned (Isaev 1973, p. 32). By 1975 decentralized investment had fallen to 15 per cent of total state investment (Gribov 1976, p. 88), while by that year production development funds were already being commonly used to finance centralized investment (Dementsev 1975). By 1976 it had become 'a pure formality that investments implemented on the basis of the production development fund . . . are called decentralized' (Pessel' 1977, p. 56). The early 1970s saw a powerful government impetus towards the creation of inter-*kolkhoz* and mixed *sovkhoz–kolkhoz* associations, involving agricultural activity and subsidiary industrial operations. As far as the latter are concerned, there was a considerable degree of variation in the specific planning arrangements involved (see Dyker 1981b, pp. 140–1), but it is clear that the general tenor of the new arrangements was to deprive the subsidiary industrial sector of its autonomy.

> The progressive transformation of associations into basic *khozraschet* links leads to a reduction in the number of production units, brings them closer to the central state organs of administration, and makes it possible to improve the centralised management of their activity.
>
> (*Ekonomicheskie Problemy* . . . 1976, p. 278)

As far as free trade is concerned, of course, development was never so vigorous as to raise the issue of reassertion of control.

## GOING THROUGH THE MOTIONS: THE BREZHNEV ASCENDANCY

Though never officially superseded till the advent of *perestroika*, in a sense the Kosygin reform died at some point in the early 1970s. To understand why, we have to look more closely at the political economy of the reform process. Up until 1968 the more uncompromising marketizers among the reformists were still hoping for a decisive move in the direction of market socialism through a radical interpretation of direct links. This would obviously have directly facilitated the development of wholesale trade, but it would also have done so indirectly by permitting substantial decentralization and therefore leaving the ratchet principle largely redundant. Political developments in 1967 and 1968 put an end to this hope.

The economic and political reforms in Czechoslovakia, culminating in the Prague Spring and the Soviet invasion in August 1968, alerted the Soviet establishment to the general political dangers of allowing too much economic reform. (In Hungary Kadar's power and prestige permitted the introduction of a new economic model that was as low-profile on the political side as it was radical on the economic.) More specifically, the professional Party apparatus – the city and provincial Party secretaries, etc. – read a lesson which was, indeed, already there to be read from the Yugoslav experience. In a creaky, over-centralized system, the Party apparatus man has a key trouble-shooting role to play – a role which because of the dominance of supply problems in everyday production life tends to reduce to that of a kind of super-pusher. Without actually being on formal success-indicator regimes, local Party secretaries are judged by the economic success of their parishes in much the same way as managers and ministerial administrators. To ensure that success, *apparatchiki* must make systematic use of political influence and cajolery to keep supply lines open. This makes for a hectic life, but it also gives a powerful political group a strong vested interest in the very weaknesses of the traditional planning system. The more successful is economic reform, the more the *apparatchik* finds himself out of a job, as became evident in Czechoslovakia as early as 1967 (Urbanek 1968). Just as Brezhnev, with his impeccable apparatus background, was establishing his political ascendancy, so it became clear that, whatever this round of Soviet economic reform was to mean, it was not to mean the dismantling of physical allocation of industrial supplies.

But as we have seen in relation to decentralized investment, agro-industrial activity, etc., it was inevitable, once that decision had been taken, that the elements of autonomization which survived the 1968 reaction should come into direct conflict with the *dirigiste* planning still prevalent in the rest of the economy. It is perfectly understandable that the leadership and apparatus could not tolerate the threat to state priorities posed by decentralized investment in the early 1970s or the mushrooming of the 'grey' economy in the countryside. Given their political preconceptions and perception of self-interest, it is hardly surprising that they interpreted the paradoxes of those developments as proof that market socialism does not work, rather than as proof that market socialism cannot work unless you give it a chance. As we saw earlier, one can make exactly the same point about use of profit as a success indicator. We should not be surprised if the establishment interpretation was that the failure of profit in that role in the late 1960s and 1970s was evidence of its inherent weaknesses, rather than of the inappropriateness of the medium in which it was asked to operate.

The fourfold increase in world oil and gold prices at the end of 1973, representing the culmination of a process of realignment of primary material prices which had, for instance, already seen timber prices rise by several hundred per cent, introduced a new dimension into the situation. With much-enhanced hard currency purchasing power, Brezhnev seems to have thought that increased imports of western technology would be an adequate substitute for sustained economic reform (Kaser 1975, pp. 204–5). Soviet imports of machinery and equipment from the west increased by 96 per cent between 1974 and 1975 (Economic Commission for Europe 1977a, p. 103). Thus political preferences, the organizational implications of the same, and the *deux ex machina* of the oil crisis conspired to bring an end to the first major impetus to planning reform in the Soviet Union. The 1970s witnessed a progressive de-emphasis of profit as a success indicator, and a tendency to return to the use of simple, as opposed to synthetic, indicators. At the same time the role of profits as a source of enterprise finance was if anything somewhat enhanced, and this reflected an ongoing concern to make the planning system, still essentially a centralized command system, more sensitive to costs and to rates of value-added. Indeed the mid-1970s saw the development of a new success indicator which focused on net output in a way that no standard Soviet indicator had ever done.

The obvious virtue of a value-added success indicator is that it avoids the tendency to induce excessive buying-in of materials, excessive bulk, neglect of components, etc. built in to any gross indicator, be it gross output or sales. The drawback to crude net output indicators is that they tend to induce precisely the opposite distortion – excessive in-plant processing, as the Soviet planners found from experiments carried on at the time of Khrushchev (see Nove 1961, p. 159). The clever thing about the new indicator of the 1970s – normed net ouput (*normativnaya chistaya produktsiya*), hereafter NNO – is that it obviated this problem. NNO is calculated on the basis of sector- or product-based norms for the relationship of net output, defined as wage costs plus profit, to total sales. Thus in principle, and as long as the ratchet is not around, an enterprise which effects a given level of sales with a less-than-normal level of wage expenditure will improve its profit, and hence its fund-forming position, while still fulfilling its NNO target. The enterprise does, in fact, have an incentive to minimize unit processing costs, subject to the fulfilment of the NNO target (Rogin 1979).

NNO was developed with the problem of measuring labour productivity particularly in mind, so that its relationship to the general strategic issues facing the Brezhnev government need hardly be spelt out. It involves a number of fairly familiar implementational problems: as long as prices and contracts are fixed, enterprise can simulate good NNO performance just as they can good profit performance; as long as NNO is calculated on the basis of sales, which in the given context is not very different from gross output, then any distortions in the reporting or indeed the execution of that planned task will be reflected in the reported level of NNO (Hanson 1983). More fundamentally, any advantages that the new indicator might have are surely more than cancelled out by the enormous number of calculations it imposes on already overworked planners. The more highly aggregated the NNO coefficients, the more scope there is for enterprises to spot and concentrate on product lines which are 'more advantageous' in terms of giving a higher level of normed net output than actual wage costs plus normal profit. NNO really has to be operated on the basis of highly disaggregated coefficients, or else combined with highly detailed assortment plans. Either way, it is bad news for the people who actually have to work the details out.

But whatever the operational drawbacks of NNO, its development did represent some increase in the level of sophistication of Soviet planning. As we shall see in Chapter 6, a similar experimental trend in the investment and construction sphere extended to the disappearance of the traditional command principle as such. But on the general balance of centralization the trend was at best equivocal, at worst in the 'wrong' direction, and this confirms the pattern we noted at the basic Material Balances level.

The essence of Brezhnev's economic policy orientation is perhaps most clearly evoked by the history of the Shchekino experiment in the 1970s. By 1980 2,003 enterprises and production associations were working on the full system, with a further 7,251 using 'specific elements of the method' (Fil'ev 1983, p. 59). It is difficult to know precisely what this meant in employment terms, but it is unlikely that as of 1980 much more than around 10 per cent of the Soviet industrial labour force was working under the full system. Reports on the effectiveness of Shchekino were uniformly positive. In the Shchekino combine itself (now renamed the Azot association) 1,814 men – 23 per cent of the work-force – were made redundant during 1967–80, with labour productivity increasing 4.1 times over the same period. In industry as a whole, 968,000 persons, representing 6 per cent of the total work-force, were made redundant during 1976–80, and the money saved in 1980 alone, (in terms of wages fund economies) amounted to 287 million roubles (Fil'ev 1983, pp. 58–9). The method is also credited with a sharp reduction in the rate of labour turnover (Mirgaleev 1977, pp. 104–5). Why did the Brezhnev leadership not extend it further? There seem to be two main groups of reasons – technico-planning obstacles to universalization, and fears that it might ultimately work too well.

The first problem the Soviet authorities encountered as they tried to push the system outside the chemicals industry was that the technology and history of many key sectors, e.g. engineering, simply did not suit Shchekino as originally developed. In straightforward production line industries with limited product ranges, like the energy sectors, chemicals and petro-chemicals, subtantial scope was found for the conflation of jobs – nearly half the redundancies at Azot from 1967 to 1980 came into this category. But a Leningrad survey showed that the scope for that kind of economizing of labour in engineering plants is quite limited (Fil'ev 1983, p. 61). What keeps labour productivity down in machine-building is the prevalance of large, non-specialized factories, carrying full complements of auxiliary processes and services operating on an under-capitalized, labour-intensive basis. This of course, is a very specifically Soviet form of overmanning, induced by the powerful tendency to organizational autarky we discussed earlier. To break the pattern would require: (a) a solution to the basic supply problem; (b) a major restructuring of production profiles. These requirements take us far beyond the limits of the Shchekino method – indeed they take us right back to the general planning issues posed in 1965.

Second, superior bodies were often less than sympathetic to the experiment. Ministries failed to make appropriate adjustments to wages funds in connection with major investment programmes, leaving some enterprises without the funds to pay Shchekino supplements. Gosplan and the Ministry of Finance changed the rules so that any Shchekino economies in wages funds not used to pay supplements had to be transferred back to the state budget. Throughout the 1970s workers found themselves deprived of Shchekino wage supplements as new wage tariffs were drawn up (Fil'ev 1983, pp. 67–8) – note how once again the ratchet rears its ugly head. Given the pressure on managers to retain some surplus labour for all the reasons we discussed earlier, and given the sometimes dubious and ephemeral nature of the material incentives, it is not clear that there was a consistently powerful motivation for managers or workers to follow the method.

Perhaps most important of all, the Brezhnev government baulked at the danger that large-scale redundancy might turn into large-scale unemployment. It is very significant that the Shchekino system was widely introduced only in highly dynamic sectors like chemicals, where it was possible to reabsorb most of the redundant labour within the same enterprise or association. Nearly half of the total number of workers made redundant in industry from 1976 to 1980 were found new jobs at their existing place of work (Fil'ev 1983, p. 59). The development of labour placement services during the 1970s obviously strengthened the basis for reabsorption of redundant workers, but, as many western countries have discovered in the last ten years, labour from traditional heavy industries can be extraordinarily difficult to redeploy. For the typical Soviet worker, with a low real wage and little effective participation in decision-taking, the kind of job security which only white-collar workers enjoy in the west has been a major focus for identification with the system. To the extent that Brezhnev's political base was as much among the traditional working class as among the Party apparatus, it is not difficult to see why he was reluctant to be over-hasty in the extension of the Shchekino system.

As we saw in Chapter 2, the post-reform wager on the foreign technology card did not work. Soviet growth rates fell steadily from the mid-1970s onwards, and nothing happened to modify the adverse productivity trends already strongly in evidence in the early 1970s. Part of the reason for this lies in the fact that neither the reform nor the reaction substantially touched two of the weakest areas of the Soviet economy – agriculture and investment/construction. We will be discussing the special problems of those sectors in Chapters 5 and 6. In addition, as energy material extraction costs in the Soviet Union rocketed, the rental element in Soviet oil and gas export revenues diminished, while commitments to supply energy to east European allies became economically increasingly onerous. In January 1975 a system was introduced whereby intra-CMEA international trade prices were calculated on the basis of a five-year moving average of world prices, adjusted annually (Economic Commission for Europe 1977b, pp. 124–5). This ensured an improvement in terms of trade for the Soviet Union as energy prices were pulled up towards the world level, but it also meant that as long as the trend in world energy prices continued upwards intra-CMEA delivery prices could never quite catch up.

More generally, however, Brezhnev surely erred in believing that planning reform and increased import of technology could be anything but complementary. Western specialists disagree on the impact of technology transfer on Soviet economic performance (Gregory and Stuart 1981, p. 403), but it is beyond dispute that its impact has been substantially below its potential, simply because of inefficiency at the assimilation stage. A study of a group of chemicals turnkey projects exported from the UK to the Soviet Union came up with an average total lead-time, 'from first enquiry to completion (handing over)' of 6 years and 10 months, as compared to a corresponding figure, for projects done in western Europe, of 2.25 to 3.5 years. Thus the Russians are almost as slow at completing imported as domestic investment projects, even where all the construction and installation work is done, or supervised, by western firms. Some of the 'excess' in the chemicals sample related to negotiating time, but even the contract completion stage took on average 2.5 to 3 years longer than it would have in western Europe (Hanson and Hill 1979, p. 594).

Quite apart from this, and quite apart from the very specific problems with success indicators, etc. which the moratorium on reform inevitably entailed, the 1970s witnessed the onset of a degree of sectoral rigidity which made effective policy initiatives increasingly difficult. It is ironic that the experiment with decentralized investment was wound up essentially in defence of the sacred priority principle, because that principle seemed increasingly ineffectual as the Brezhnev era progressed. We touched on what may be part of the reason for this in Chapter 2 – increased reliance on the ratchet principle to provide an approximation to plan consistency necessarily produced a tendency to structural conservatism. More fundamentally, however, the process of escalation of priorities which had begun on the death of Stalin had come to its logical conclusion. Thus the Economic Commission for Europe, in relation to eastern Europe as a whole, hypothesized that:

one possible explanation for the slow pace of change in investment structures, apart from resistance to change within the existing structure, may lie in the multitude of criteria for investment priorities. Export promotion, orientation towards domestic resources and the consumer market, savings in labour, fuel and raw material inputs, increased intensiveness in research and advanced technology, are only the most frequently quoted. The application of so many priority criteria in the allocation of investment resources may slow down changes in the pattern of investment allocation, and produce mixed tendencies in relation to planned developments.

(Economic Commission for Europe 1978, p. 76)

The issue of economic reform, then, would not go away, and 1979 promised to be the worst year yet for growth rates. It came as no surprise when a new planning decree was published in July 1979.

## THE 1979 'MINI-REFORM'

The main features of the decree (see Figure 3.1) were as follows (V TsK KPSS . . .' 1979; 'Ob uluchshenii . . .' 1979):

1 Success indicators: in sharp contrast to the optimism about the role of profit in 1965, the 1979 approach saw no surpassing virtue in any single indicator. Sales would continue to serve as the basis for assessment of fulfilment of contracts (with the implication that there would be no incentive for overfulfilment) ('Planovye pokazateli . . .' 1979). Profit would still figure as an indicator, but in some cases, presumably those of planned loss-making enterprises, would be replaced by cost-reduction. The precise role of NNO as an output indicator was left vague, but it was specified that NNO should, as a general rule, be used as the basis for calculating labour productivity, now established as a key success indicator. Ministries would continue to have plans for gross output, as would some associations and enterprises. Increased stress on details of assortment (cf. earlier remarks about NNO on pp. 68–9), and increased optimism about the possibility of measuring quality directly, gained expression in the notion of 'output in natural terms' (*proizvodstvo produktsii v natural'nom vyrazhenii*) as a key operational indicator ('Planovye pokazateli . . 1979). Bonus funds would be formed

out of profits with the fund-forming norms calculated on a profit base. These norms would relate to labour productivity, deliveries and assortment/quality (Hanson 1983, pp. 5–6).

2 Transition to the production association system was to be completed by 1981–2.

3 Integrated and comprehensive incentive fund arrangements were to be introduced from 1981 at ministerial, industrial association, and production association levels.

4 The conservative interpretation of direct links was to be universalized by 1980.

5 Stable norms (i.e. no ratchet principle) and symmetrical bonus systems (i.e. no Micawber principle) were to be (once again) introduced. Unused remainders of funds should be carried over to subsequent years.

6 Ministries should stop chopping and changing plans. In particular, they should not normally adjust plans downwards. But they should have the power to allow associations and enterprises to reduce levels of production, and modify associated planning indicators, if this permitted introduction or increase in production of high technology goods or new high-quality consumption goods. They should in addition be permitted to establish a reserve of up to 5 per cent of total investment votes.

7 Counter-plans, once adopted, would now count as part of the state plan for plan-fulfilment assessment purposes. Special bonuses were to be created for 'rate-busting'.

8 Renewed emphasis was placed on the development of wholesale fairs.

9 Decentralized investments financed from the production development fund should be decided on independently by the association or enterprise, but then incorporated into the ministerial plan. The number of sources of finance for decentralized investment was, however, programmed for reduction, and above-plan profit was specifically excluded from that number ('Poryadok . . .' 1979).

10 The brigade system of work-team organization developed in construction (see discussion in Chapter 6) was to be extended economy-wide.

11 The Shchekino system was programmed for generalization, with special supplements of up to 50 per cent of basic wage payable from wages fund economies. Management was to be allowed

greater freedom in disposing of these economies. Upper limits on enterprise work-forces were to be established.

12 The number of commodity groups planned at the central level was to increase.

13 By 1980, ministries were to prepare 'passports' for each association and enterprise on which would be stated all basic technical information about the organization, especially in relation to capital stock.

14 There was to be a shift in emphasis away from short-term towards medium-term and long-term planning. The five-year plan should form the crux of the planning system, and twenty-year programmes for scientific and technical progress, broken down into five-year periods, should be worked out and corrected every five years. Gosplan should in addition elaborate a ten-year outline of strategic lines of development on the same revolving five-year basis.

15 Rental elements should be taken more into consideration by planners. A systematic water charge to enterprises was to be introduced.

This is a difficult piece of planning legislation to assess. There seems to have been a kind of paralysis in Soviet policy implementation in the last few years of the Brezhnev era; no doubt the increasing rigidity of the structure of the economy may have been partly responsible for this, but there was also a purely political element relating to the expectation of a change in leadership. In any case, that change came within a little more than three years, with the death of Brezhnev in November 1982. Rather than attempt a systematic follow-up on the provisions of the mini-reform, then, we may find it more useful to study those provisions simply as a basis for pin-pointing the preoccupations of the Soviet government of the time.

The first thing that struck one about the 1979 decree was its internal inconsistency. The items listed under 6 seemed to pull the long-suffering ministries half in the direction of greater tautness, half in the direction of more slackness. On the same basis, 5 stood in flat contradiction to 7. Partial autonomization seemed to be back in vogue, with encouraging noises about wholesale fairs, and a slightly ambivalent statement about decentralized investment. At the same time the degree of centralization of the basic plan construction process was to increase, while the new full array of success indicators, if they were all to 'bite', would likewise have represented an increase in the overall level of centralization. More specifically, with profit pushed into the background and the position on NNO very non-committal, the success-indicator proposals to a great extent seemed to boil down to a return, directly or indirectly, to gross output – what else could 'output in natural terms' mean in a Soviet-type economic system? And when we saw formalization of the reintroduction of cost reduction as a success indicator – something which had been happening *de facto* since 1974 (Dyker 1983, p. 33) – we wondered whether the Soviet leadership could actually remember as far back as 1959.

The trend towards greater centralization highlighted the inconsistency of the decree by making a nonsense of the stated aims of killing the ratchet principle and improving medium- and long-term planning. How could planners with even more work to do eschew use of their tried and trusted rules of thumb? How could Gosplan, which had always notoriously neglected the long term because the short term made such impositions, possibly switch resources and manpower to five- and ten-year perspectives?

The reform decree did, in fact, bear all the marks of a compromise between different pressure groups. There was still a nod in the direction of the once-ascendant marketizers, but it was the 'perfect computationists', among the professionals, who were clearly holding the stage in the late 1970s. They believed that they could raise the number of centrally planned commodity groups from *c.* 15,000, presumably on the basis of computerization, though no Soviet input–output table had ever numbered more than a few hundred sectors. They must have believed that on the same basis the process of 'passportization' of Soviet industrial capacity could eventually make it possible to assess production capacity directly, without use of the ratchet principle. Certainly the 1970s witnessed some success in using computerized input-planning systems, in which the stage of indent (*zayavka*), the stage where the water is usually poured in, was dispensed with (Rabinovich 1976, pp. 209–10; Cave 1980, pp. 108–9). but as Martin Cave's detailed research has shown, the development of computer networks in the Soviet Union in the 1970s was hampered by general systemic problems as much as any other potential source of 'intensification'. So powerful, for example, was the imperative to organizational autarky that even mini-computers were being produced by handicraft methods in dwarf workshops (Conyngham 1982, p. 120).

*Figure 3.1* The organizational structure of the Soviet economy as envisaged by the 1979 planning decree and associated measures

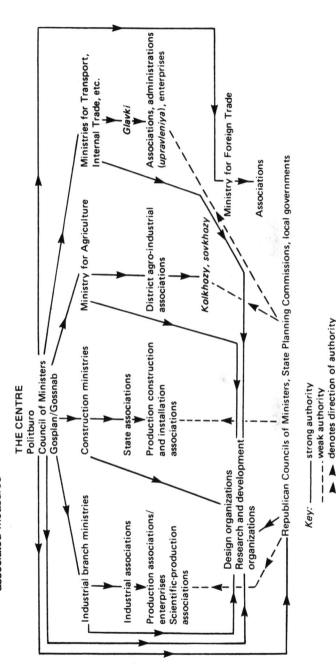

THE CENTRE
Politburo
Council of Ministers
Gosplan/Gossnab

Ministries for Transport, Internal Trade, etc.
*Glavki*
Associations, administrations (*upravleniya*), enterprises

Ministry for Foreign Trade
Associations

Ministry for Agriculture
District agro-industrial associations
*Kolkhozy, sovkhozy*

Construction ministries
State associations
Production construction and installation associations

Industrial branch ministries
Industrial associations
Production associations/ enterprises
Scientific-production associations

Design organizations
Research and development organizations

Republican Councils of Ministers, State Planning Commissions, local governments

Key:  ——— strong authority
      - - - weak authority
      ▶ denotes direction of authority

Where the marketizers and perfect computationists may not have been in substantial disagreement was on the question of the balance of tautness/slackness. It was surely the hand of an *apparatchik* that sketched in the bits about 'rate-busting' and 'no downwards adjustments'. The whole logic of the traditional crude growth maximization strategy does, of course lie precisely in the notion that when growth rates falter trouble-shooters can be sent out to 'chivvy people up'. It is a logic familiar to bureaucratic structures around the world, a logic which an *apparatchik* stratum threatened with the fate of the dinosaur may be politically bound to pursue. It is, of course, a false logic.

As we suggested earlier, not a great deal happened between the publication of the 1979 decree and the death of Brezhnev. By the end of 1980 NNO was being used as an actual output indicator in only a small proportion of the total number of industrial enterprises and the situation may not have changed a great deal by 1982 (Hanson 1983, p. 2; p. 12, n. 13). There was, as far as we can tell, no rapid extension of the Shchekino system, and indeed a follow-up decree on labour problems placed primary stress on labour discipline, looking forward to the Andropov era ('O dal'neishem . . .' 1980). The impetus to further rationalization of the price system implicit in the decree was sustained through a comprehensive price reform carried out in 1981–2, which brought energy prices into line with secular production cost trends, without abandoning the principle of average-cost pricing (Hanson 1983, p. 2). To the extent that use of value-added and profit as success indicators demands a consistent price system, this was of some importance. But of course nothing had happened to make producing units more responsive to prices. We can only speculate as to whether planners were becoming more sensitive to shadow-prices. As the Brezhnev era drew to an end, it was difficult to avoid the impression that, at least in relation to economic planning, the Soviets, like the Bourbons, never forgot anything and never learned anything.

# Chapter 4

# Gorbachev's *perestroika* programme

## ANDROPOV SETS THE SCENE

When the ex-KGB chief succeeded Leonid Brezhnev as General Secretary of the Soviet Communist Party on the latter's death in November 1982, few people expected radical changes. And indeed the formal measures promulgated during the short period of Yurii Andropov's leadership – with the possible exception of the anti-vodka campaign – sent no shock waves through Soviet society. It was easy to interpret Andropov's discipline drive as simply the obsession of a martinet, easy to dismiss his planning reforms (see points 1–9 below) as little more than a rerun of the failed Kosygin reform. But the new General Secretary's discipline theme was closely intertwined with another new theme – that of 'socialist self-management'. Now self-management, the child of Titoist revisionism, had always been anathema in the Soviet Union of Stalin, Khrushchev, and Brezhnev. Andropov certainly envisaged no transition to Yugoslav-style workers' councils – rather he saw self-management simply as the obverse of responsibility. But in his policies on alcohol-abuse, work ethic, and civic consciousness, Andropov evinced a deep understanding of the depths of socio-political crisis to which the Soviet Union had descended by the early 1980s. The slovenly egalitarianism of the Brezhnev era was on the way out, and its demise triggered off a reappraisal of all the sacred cows of Soviet socialism – job security, full employment, the immorality of private entrepreneurship. And on the economic planning side, Andropov's cautious measures were already under the dynamic management of Mikhail Gorbachev, newly promoted from the agriculture chair within the Communist Party secretariat to the position of economic policy overlord. Let us look now in more detail at the provisions of Andropov's 'industrial planning experiment', announced in mid-1983, and introduced at the beginning of 1984.

The main elements in the experiment were as follows:

1 As a general principle, the role of enterprises and production associations was to increase. That of industrial ministries and industrial associations was to decrease. Echoing one of the principal themes of Tatyana Zaslavskaya's famous 'secret' seminar paper of April 1983 (Zaslavskaya 1983), which had presented perhaps the first comprehensive Soviet critique of the existing planning system, the decree implicitly pinned much of the blame for planning shortcomings on too much bureaucratic interference from the intermediate administrative level. In moving the centre of gravity of the system towards the level of the primary production unit the planners sought to switch its functional emphasis away from commands and instructions, towards prices and norms – norms for materials utilization, for bonus-fund formation etc. That implied greater autonomy for enterprises and production associations, but also more rigorous assessment of plan fulfilment.

2 Key success indicators were to be sales/deliveries in accordance with contracts for all producing units, and where appropriate 'development of science and technology', quality, growth of labour productivity, and cost reduction or increase in profit. Profit would continue to be the main source of finance for incentive funds. Thus, while the experimental system aimed to give the enterprise/production association more autonomy, it was to be an autonomy strictly circumscribed by centrally determined targets or norms.

3 Stable norms for wage funds, incentive funds etc. were to be established on a five-year basis.

4 No bonuses would be paid to managerial workers unless plans for sales/deliveries according to contracts were met in full. In this way the drafters of the decree sought to shift the focus of the system away from the aggregate, quantitative, towards the satisfaction of specific, disaggregated demands, and to impress on managers that the easy-going, bonuses-for-everyone style of the Brezhnev period was gone for good.

5 Autonomous production association/enterprise control over

decentralized investment was to be re-established. Andropov's industrial planning experiment also predicated that production units should enjoy greater freedom in financing 'technical re-equipment' (*tekhnicheskoe perevooruzhenie*) or upgrading invest-ments from amortization allowances and credit.

6 Production associations and enterprises were to be permitted to use moneys from the association-level Unified Fund for the Development of Science and Technology to finance autonomous R&D work, and to compensate for increased costs in the period of assimilation of new products. Through this measure the Soviet planners aimed to consolidate the impact of the stable norms rule on the innovation process.

7 Production units would also be allowed more independence in deciding the allocation of the socio-cultural and housing fund. This element echoed Andropov's concern to develop meaningful socialist self-management, as well as the desire for financial decentralization.

8 Management was to be given greater freedom in the use of the bonus fund, and in the disposition of wages-fund economies accruing through job rationalization. This broadening of the application of the Shchekino system underlined the depth of concern felt by the Soviet authorities about the labour productivity variable.

9 Budgetary rules were to be changed so that production units could retain a larger proportion of profit on a regular basis. That meant that all three incentive funds – the production develop-ment fund, the socio-cultural and housing fund, and the bonus fund – would grow in size as well as independence.

It is easy to criticize the Andropov industrial planning experiment if we view it on its merits as a piece of policy legislation. Most obviously, it simply failed to attack the fundamental problem of general over-centralization. Its system of success indicators was if anything even fussier than the Kosygin system, and it soon became clear that enterprises on the experiment were to benefit from little in the way of relaxation of central control over prices and specification of contracts. In this key respect, then, the industrial planning experiment seemed to share the weakness of every Soviet planning reform proposal since the death of Stalin.

We can illustrate once again the crucial significance of general decentralization as a *sine qua non* of effective reform by placing the main elements in the experiment against that yardstick. It is all very well to strip the ministries of their power, but in an economy where the central planners are burdened with an impossible work load 'ministerial arbitrariness' may play an indispensable role – chopping and changing plans to ensure overall fulfilment against a background of generalized supply uncertainty. To a great extent it does, in fact, simply represent a form of continuous adjustment process, whereby consistency is eventually approximated through a series of iterations. It is certainly not an efficient way of doing the job. It requires an army of ministerial administrators, and at the end of the day the standard of coordination may still be rather poor. In particular, problems of intersectoral, interministerial and intraregional coordination may actually be exacerbated. The alternative, of course, is to introduce a more efficient continual adjustment process. But that can only mean some form of market mechanism, i.e. radical decentralization.

Exactly the same point emerges when we look at the success-indicator system of the industrial planning experiment. It is undeniable that one of the main weaknesses of the Soviet system in the past had been production for the plan rather than the customer. But the draconian rule on bonuses and fulfilment of contracts introduced by the 1983 decree seems to have rested on the supposition that low-quality or poorly specified deliveries are always the fault of the delivering enterprise. Certainly the traditional output-based success indicators had encouraged enterprises to go for quantity rather than quality. But failure to meet contractual obligations had more often than not been the result of supply breakdowns upstream – in turn largely the result of over-centralized planning. The lack of any powerful impetus within Andropov's planning experiment towards decentralization made it inevitable that that should continue to be the case, with the emasculation of ministerial 'wheeling and dealing' powers possibly making things worse rather than better. In that context the very best enterprises working under experimental conditions in 1984 found themselves severely penalized.

Where the industrial planning experiment really did seem to offer enterprises genuine new freedom of manoeuvre was in relation to disposition of profits and wages funds. But a close perusal of the history of the Kosygin reform might have warned the drafters of the 1983 decree to expect trouble here. Once again the absence of a consistent pattern of decentralization was the nub of the matter, once again the Soviet planners seem to have failed to perceive the crucial link between financial and supply planning parameters. Sure enough, early reports from enterprises transferred onto the experimental system on 1 January 1984 complained of serious difficulties in turning production development fund and sociocultural and housing fund money into concrete investment supplies (Ural'tsev 1984; Tsagaraev 1984). Whichever way one looked at it, then, Andropov's industrial planning experiment seemed to offer necessary – but not sufficient – conditions for effective reform.

## GORBACHEV IN COMMAND

Of minor significance in itself, the experiment did, however, represent an enormously important educational experience for Mikhail Gorbachev. Gorbachev had come to Moscow with a reputation as a highly efficient administrator, but with no outstanding radical credentials. His years as agriculture secretary marked him as a man seeking rationalization of the existing system, rather than revolutionary change. His broader economic policy remit under Andropov brought him face to face, for the first time, with the whole gamut of Soviet economic decline. His stewardship of the industrial planning experiment taught him the lesson so many Soviet leaders had sought to ignore – that there is no radical reform without radical decentralization. The brief interlude of the old Brezhnevite Konstantin Chernenko's General Secretaryship, following on Andropov's untimely death in 1984, seemed if anything to consolidate the development of Gorbachev's ideas. Still in charge of economic policy-making, and often chairing Politburo meetings in the absence through illness of the ailing Chernenko, the future Soviet President had plenty of opportunities in 1984 and early 1985 to view the futility of any return to Brezhnevite 'Party-mindedness'. At a more general level, increasing experience seemed to promote a process of continuous radicalization of Gorbachev's ideas which was to extend well beyond his own accession to supreme power.

When Gorbachev succeeded to the General Secretaryship on Chernenko's death in March 1985, he lost no time in publishing his own amplification of Andropov's industrial planning experiment. A decree of July 1985 'on the extension of the new economic methods and the strengthening of their effect on the acceleration of scientific and technical progress' highlighted the new Soviet leader's perception of the technology dimension as the nub of the productivity problem. But while the focus is sharp enough, and the trend unmistakable, the July 1985 decree evinced a strong aura of provisionality, of political muscle-flexing rather than definitive policy-making. The main respects in which it modified Andropov's measures were:

1 The key 'no bonuses unless all contracts met' provision of the 1983 decree was effectively emasculated. The difficulties mentioned above had, it seems, compounded to such an extent as to make the rule unworkable. Gorbachev's decree predicated that managers should receive a maximum of two months' salary for fulfilment of all deliveries according to contracts. Bonuses earned on other counts should not be dependent on prior fulfilment of the deliveries according to contract plan. We must assume that this backtracking represented a deepening understanding of the relationship between particular systems of planning indicators and different degrees of centralization.

2 New ground was broken in the area of price incentives for quality and technical dynamism. Under new experimental regulations, industrial products judged to be in the top quality category would now attract a wholesale price supplement of up to 30 per cent. Products in the lower quality category would suffer a price drop of 5 per cent in the first year, rising to 15 per cent in the third year. After that they should normally be taken out of production. The new rules ensured that the loss of revenue resulting from such price reductions would affect bonus funds. In the event of goods being returned to the manufacturer because of low quality or defects, the fines thus incurred or the cost of correcting the defects should likewise come partly out of the bonus fund. Exports of manufactured goods would attract a special price supplement of 20 per cent, and such supplements were to be paid into a special hard-currency fund, all this threatening a serious breach in the traditional monopoly over Soviet foreign trade enjoyed by the Ministry for Foreign Trade.

3 Gorbachev's decree considerably extended the provisions of the 1983 industrial planning experiment in relation to decentralized investment. Now all retooling or upgrading investments financed from the production development fund of estimated value up to 4 million roubles in heavy industry, and up to 2.5 million roubles

elsewhere, were to be planned independently by enterprises. Thus a whole category of medium-scale investment which had previously been the preserve of the ministries under the rubric of 'below-limit' centralized investment was now to be handed over, experimentally, to enterprises. Ministries were given a clear warning that interference in decentralized investment matters would in future not be tolerated. In this respect the July 1985 decree consolidated and concretized the anti-ministerial theme which had permeated the official and semi-official documents of 1983. Clearly enterprises could not be expected to finance all this investment from retained profits, and the new proposals envisaged large-scale borrowing from the State Bank and the Construction Bank into production development funds. It was emphasized in the decree that these new provisions were strictly for genuine upgrading investments. Just replacing existing equipment with similar equipment was forbidden.

This was certainly a much punchier package than the 1983 provisions had offered. But while the process of continuous radicalization is clearly signalled, it comes through at this stage mainly in the form of a sharpening of the inherent contradictions of Andropov's experiment. Let us look first at the price incentive issue. The aim of making prices more sensitive to the technology and quality dimension was certainly commendable. But we looked in vain among the clauses of the decree for any movement in the direction of flexible prices. It would still be the State Prices Committee which decided on the supplements and reductions, so that the approach could not but complicate further the lives of already hard-pressed Soviet planners. Again, it is all very well to insist that when goods are sent back to the manufacturer as sub-standard the bonus funds of the latter should suffer. In the absence of freedom of contract the client, with his own quarterly plan to fulfil, remains a 'captive' of the errant manufacturer, unless the former happens to be the Ministry of Defence. In that context, consignments are sent back by civilian clients only in the most extreme cases. Thus the biggest weakness of the 1983 decree – the absence of a significant movement towards general decentralization – was merely compounded by Gorbachev's 1985 measures.

We can make exactly the same point in relation to investment finance arrangements. Despite the manifold reports of difficulties with supply to decentralized investment through 1984, a much larger chunk of investment was now to be exposed to the same supply problems. As if to underline the point, a decree published a couple of months earlier, just after Gorbachev's accession, had made it possible for private citizens to purchase construction materials, including cement, for private building purposes – again without specifying the mechanism whereby the central material-supply network would, or could, make such supplies available (Medvedev 1986, p. 192).

The proposed transfer of the bulk of medium-scale investment to the enterprise/production association level also raised a whole range of questions relating to the actual allocation of investment. It is one thing to permit the development of autonomous enterprise investment as a basis for small-scale rationalization, in particular rationalization of the second economy, the dwarf workshops etc. But in extending the same principles to a large proportion of retooling and upgrading investments, the Soviet authorities seemed to be banking on the existence of stimuli at production-unit level which they had found to be lacking elsewhere in the planning and management hierarchy.

What were they looking for? The campaign in favour of reconstruction and re-equipment run in the 1970s had been signally unsuccessful in its aim of raising the rate of return on investment (Dyker 1983, pp. 43–5). The reasons for this piece of typically Brezhnevite ineffectuality were essentially twofold. On the one hand, reconstruction was often used as a cover-up for expansion of existing enterprises, involving complete redevelopment of sites – often inner-city sites, which were cramped and awkward to manage. On the other hand, the re-equipment rubric was heavily exploited as a basis for maximizing the flow of funds from the centre, with replacement equipment frequently representing no improvement whatsoever in technological level.

It was not surprising, then, that the new decree explicitly forbade 'simple replacement'. What is less clear is how this prohibition was to be translated into practice. Soviet managers had in the past put in requests for equipment they did not need because in a bureaucratic set-up the man who only asks for enough gets nothing. The ministerial administrator bent on survival had been constrained to follow the same tactical logic in seeking block-votes from the centre. The 1985 moves in the direction of a greater role for the production development fund, and for bank credit, should certainly have made Soviet managers count investment cost more carefully. But as long as quantitative plan fulfilment remained the overriding imperative, they would surely continue to endeavour to grab as many resources as possible, whatever the cost to the national economy. Thus while we could agree that in the past the ministries had often been the instrument of some of the more glaring misallocations in the Soviet economy, we had to question an approach which simply assumed that an enterprise manager would be more 'virtuous' than a ministerial bureaucrat. For the one as for the other, it is surely the general economic environment that is of overriding importance. It may in principle be easier to transform the environment for producing units than for sectoral administrations. In order to do so, however, you need a sustained and consistent policy of decentralization.

It would be unfair to suggest that the July 1985 decree ignored this fundamental issue. Tucked away in the third last paragraph was a poker-faced statement to the effect that the 'Commission for the General Management of the Economic Experiment' had been detailed to produce by the end of 1985 proposals for the 'development of forms of wholesale trade in the means of production', i.e. free trade in industrial supplies. Thus the drafters of the decree themselves seemed implicitly to recognize its transitional, even fleeting nature. Gorbachev's addendum to the industrial planning experiment was in the event never fully implemented (Aganbegyan 1986, p. 21). Like the 1983 decree, its main significance was as a milestone in the process of recognition of how much needed to be done to reform the Soviet economy.

As if to underline the point, another, more radical experiment had already been started by early 1985, at a time when the 1983 industrial planning experiment still covered only 12 per cent of total industrial production, and when, indeed, Chernenko was still General Secretary. The experiment was first set up at the Sumy machine-building scientific-production association, based on 'pre-experimental' experience going back over fifteen years (Lynev 1985).

The key feature of the Sumy experiment was that it developed further that aspect of the industrial planning experiment – the self-financing principle in investment – which was, indeed, to be specially featured in Gorbachev's decree of July 1985. But three qualitatively new elements were introduced. First, ministries and industrial associations were forbidden to redistribute funds between enterprises and production associations. (This had been a principle, largely honoured in the breach, of the 1965 reform.) Second, stable norms were fixed for the first time for deductions from profits back to the state budget. The same principle applied to payments from profits to the ministry. Third, the Sumy system was based on the principle that investments relating to retooling, upgrading, and expansion should be financeable only from the production development fund. The latter was to be in turn financed primarily from profits, but could be supplemented by Stroibank (Investment Bank) credits and the whole of amortization allowances. The principle of stable norms was also applied to deductions from profits into the three incentive funds – the production development fund, the bonus fund, and the socio-cultural and housing fund. Additional details ensured that a degree of planning pressure on the enterprise was kept up. While norms for deductions from profits into the state budget were initially known in advance up to 1990, they were programmed to rise steadily throughout the five-year period. Some scope for switching moneys between bonus and socio-cultural and housing funds was allowed. But if productivity failed to grow at least twice as fast as wages, part of the bonus fund was put into reserve, or indeed switched into the socio-cultural and housing fund (Moskalenko 1986; Luk'yanenko and Moskalenko 1985).

More than 70 per cent in all of total profit was planned to stay with the Sumy association in 1985. At one level, then, the experiment represented a vindication of Kosygin's principle from 1965 that profit should be the main success indicator and the main focus for incentives at the level of the production unit. But again there is a qualitative innovation. Under the 1965 regime, as we saw in Chapter 3, the role of profit had been obfuscated by an insistence that it should be planned in terms of rates – rates of profit on capital, rates of growth of profit. Under the Sumy experiment, the only thing that mattered was the absolute level of profit, which the association was invited to maximize.

In one respect, however, the Sumy experiment was just like every other planning reform or experiment promulgated in the Soviet Union since the death of Stalin. Its most positive features served merely to highlight what remained to be done and to heighten the tensions between different parameters of the economy. The key problem was prices. Again, as became clear after 1965, if you create incentives for profit without creating a flexible price system, you run the risk of encouraging profiteering. The Sumy management claimed that the deliveries according to contracts indicator solved this problem, but contemporary journalistic sources cast doubt on the claim (Ronichev 1985). Of course, the price issue goes far beyond that of profiteering. If prices are wrong, then not even the consciences of chosen experimenters can stop their organizations from producing the wrong things, or the wrong quantities.

As of the end of 1985 the price system imposed on the Sumy association was simply the system detailed in the July 1985 decree on the industrial planning experiment. Prices could vary according to quality, but in a way fixed by the State Committee for Prices (Moskalenko 1986, p. 33). Around the same time supply arrangements at the association were still a long way from free trade in industrial supplies, and the association management was suffering exactly the same problems in finding supplies for decentralized investment and housing construction as other enterprises on the industrial planning experiment. Basic production planning remained heavily tutored, with 76 (out of a total of 200!) plan indicators coming down from the ministry, including, for example, detailed figures on how much wood should be sawn up for packing. Perhaps even more telling, the new decentralized investment regime could not stop two-thirds of designers' time being wasted on paperwork and obtaining approvals (Lynev 1985). By early 1986 significant further decentralization had taken place, but an April 1986 report on the experiment still singled out over-centralization and supply problems as among the major obstacles to further progress ('Samofinansirovanie. . .' 1986, p. 14).

## THE FOREIGN TRADE REFORMS OF 1986–7

Over the period 1983–6, then, we witnessed very significant developments in the Soviet economic system. But there was still no clear break with the Brezhnev style of policy-making, a style that had continually fudged the distinction between experiments and generally legislated change in such a way as to make any monitoring of policy implementation almost impossible. Thus by the time the 1983 industrial planning experiment had been generalized throughout Soviet industry at the beginning of 1987, it had clearly been effectively superseded as a framework for policy articulation. But something happened in 1986 which was not just an experiment, which really did change the systemic framework of the Soviet economy in a way that neither Khrushchev nor

Brezhnev had ever contemplated. The classic, Leninist monopoly of foreign trade was abolished.

The arguments for and against the traditional rule that no Soviet enterprise could import or export except through the Ministry of Foreign Trade parallel the arguments for and against centralization and the command principle at the level of the domestic economy. The monopoly certainly gave the young Soviet state a *masse de manoeuvre* which was no doubt invaluable as it endeavoured to navigate the waters of a hostile capitalist environment. But while the Ministry of Foreign Trade was able to use its monopoly power over Soviet exports – and a degree of market power on the importing side too, particularly in relation to grain imports as the Soviet bread gap grew in the 1960s and 1970s – to drive hard bargains, it was less adept at ensuring that the Soviet Union obtained genuine value for money. For it is no use buying cheap and selling dear if you are buying and selling the wrong things. The Ministry proved particularly ineffective in relation to the dimensions of equipment import and technology transfer, which became so much more important in the 1970s and 1980s. A purely administrative organization, it had no basis on which to rank competing demands for equipment import except that of the political muscle of the client. Equally damaging, it had no way of ensuring that equipment, once purchased, would actually be efficiently assimilated by the client. As we saw, the weakness of that assimilation process lay at the bottom of the most serious economic miscalculation of the whole Brezhnev era – the notion that high oil prices could be a substitute for economic reform. This was one of the main reasons why Gorbachev's predecessor failed to reverse the tendency to slow-down.

In 1986 the Ministry of Foreign Trade lost most of its traditional directive powers. It was abolished altogether a couple of years later and replaced by a new Ministry for External Economic Affairs shorn of explicit powers of command, but still with substantial prerogatives both in relation to the vetting of organizations wishing to engage in foreign trade and to the complex system of 'coefficients' whereby world prices were converted into roubles for domestic accounting – and incentive – purposes. In addition, the new ministry was slated to place relatively greater emphasis on the area of long-term trade strategy articulation. Under the original legislation a specified group of ministries and enterprises gained the freedom to enter into direct contractual links with foreign companies. They would be at liberty to export goods, including equipment surplus to planned needs at home, at prices agreed by them with the foreign purchaser. They would also be permitted to retain a fixed proportion of their hard-currency export earnings to spend freely on imports of equipment, or indeed to lend at a fixed rate of interest to other Soviet organizations wanting to finance imports. Direct state control over the key strategic areas of energy exports and food imports was maintained, but by the first quarter of 1988 organizations operating under the new dispensation were accounting for 18 per cent of Soviet exports and 30 per cent of imports. A decree of December 1988 extended the right, in principle, to trade directly with world markets to all Soviet enterprises. A further decree of March 1989 laid down a tight procedure for registration of enterprises engaging in foreign trade, but did not qualify the principle of universal access as such.

An equally momentous piece of new basic legislation was passed in 1987. The joint venture law of that year permitted, for the first time, foreign ownership of equity in the Soviet Union. Here again we see Gorbachev at work dismantling the 'fortress Soviet Union' principle which had survived unquestioned through decades of would-be reform under his predecessors. The maximum foreign share in a joint venture was initially limited to 49 per cent, but was raised to 80 per cent at the end of 1988. Joint ventures are subject both to profits tax (basic rate 30 per cent) and repatriation tax (basic rate 20 per cent), but with a tax holiday for foreign partners for two years from the date on which profits are first generated. They are not subject to the authority of domestic Soviet planning bodies. By June 1990 about 1,830 joint ventures had been agreed with foreign partners, the bulk of them from western countries.

That these represented changes of enormous importance is beyond doubt. Yet once again they raised more questions than they answered. With the old Foreign Trade Ministry and the old Foreign Trade Bank (also abolished in 1988) out of the way, enterprises still found themselves frustrated in that year in their attempts to spend their retention quotas by the unrelenting drive on the part of the industrial ministries to pre-empt resources by making out import 'shopping lists' backed up by traditional indents. There were also problems on the financial side. Most Soviet exporters operating under the new regulations also manufacture for the domestic market so they are going to accumulate development and incentive funds in two parallel streams – one in hard currency, one in roubles. What formula should be used to ensure that employees working on export orders would be treated equitably in relation to those serving the 'softer' domestic market? What, in a word, is the rouble worth in terms of dollars and Deutschmarks?

## RESTRUCTURING THE CMEA

Or, indeed, what is a rouble worth in terms of zlotys, crowns, forints or leva? One of the enduring paradoxes of the USSR's position within the world economy has been the failure to develop a socialist division of labour, never mind a division of labour with capitalism. The CMEA (Warsaw Pact countries, plus Mongolia, Vietnam and Cuba) has in the past accounted for nearly 60 per cent of total Soviet exports, according to official data. True, the price formula whereby CMEA trade (largely settled on a bilateral, clearing-account basis) and hard-currency trade are aggregated in official Soviet statistics tends to exaggerate the CMEA component, but even so CMEA trade must have accounted through the 1980s for more than half of total Soviet trade. The trouble is that intra-CMEA trade has been concentrated largely in categories promising little prospect of expansion in the future. In essence, it consists of swapping Soviet oil and gas for second-rate EE-6 routine manufactures. As the constraints on Soviet hydrocarbon production tighten, and as Moscow increasingly shifts the priority to quality in consumption as well as production, these trading categories would have been set to stagnate, or even contract, irrespective of international political developments. There have been some CMEA successes at a deeper level of specialization – EE-6 countries have contributed men and materials to the big pipelines bringing oil and gas from the Soviet Union, and a sensible division of labour has been implemented in the area of transport equipment. The most striking feature of intra-CMEA trade has, however, been an almost total absence of high-tech commodity exchange.

Khrushchev was the first Soviet leader to try to breathe real life into the CMEA specialization framework. He failed, most obviously because of the autarkical intransigence of the Romanians, though the rest of the EE-6 showed little enthusiasm. Brezhnev let this matter, like so many others, lie, and it was left to Andropov and Gorbachev to reopen the whole issue of the socialist international division of labour. In 1984 the first CMEA summit for thirteen years was held in Moscow. Progress was initially hampered by a fundamental disagreement between the Soviet Union, on the one hand, and the EE-6 on the other. Moscow tended to see the future of the socialist division of labour in terms of joint enterprises. The others, fearing a loss of economic sovereignty and suspicious of Soviet pricing formulae, tended to favour increased marketization of intra-CMEA links. It was disagreements like these which condemned the Complex Programme for Scientific and Technical Cooperation, signed in 1985 and aimed at achieving meaningful integration in high-tech areas like electronics and robotization, to ineffectuality. But as Gorbachev's domestic *perestroika* programme grew in radicality, so the basis of the disagreement was rapidly eroded. A fresh consensus seemed to be emerging with the signing in 1988 of the Collective Concept of the International Division of Labour in the Period 1991–2005. The new document was based on the earlier Complex Programme, but sought to correct the latter's shortcomings by taking explicit account of reform trends and of the need for a degree of currency convertibility to help member-countries break free of the shackles of bilateralism; it also aimed to provide a universal *numéraire* for CMEA trade. But the Collective Concept envisaged the introduction of no concrete measures before 1991. In the event it was dramatically overtaken by the momentous events of 1989, which saw the demise of communism in many CMEA countries. A series of crisis meetings in 1990 produced agreement, in principle, that trade within the bloc, if such it could still be called, should be put onto a hard-currency, multilateral settlements basis from 1 January 1991. Practical difficulties are likely to delay full implementation of that principle, but by 1990 the CMEA had emphatically ceased to be in any sense an organization seeking to apply Soviet planning principles in the arena of international trade.

## THE PACE QUICKENS

Successful or unsuccessful (we leave final appraisal to a later stage), these reforms and policy initiatives in the foreign trade field did represent a crucial milestone in the history of *perestroika*. Up to 1986–7 Gorbachev basically continued the tinkering tradition of Kosygin and Andropov, albeit with a style and verve undreamt of by earlier leaders. But by the middle to late 1980s it was clear that a new watershed had been passed – as important, perhaps, as the death of Brezhnev had been. It was an essentially conceptual watershed, and it did, indeed, give *perestroika* a clear conceptual basis for the first time. Most importantly, the basic point which economists, east and west, have been making for decades – that the Soviet economy is fundamentally over-centralized, and that no reform programme will have any significant impact until this problem is solved – was 'officially' accepted. In more concrete terms a new package had emerged by 1988–9 based on the following interrelated key points:

1 It is not possible to run an industrial economy without a fully-fledged market mechanism. The fully restructured system of the future would therefore have to be, in some sense, a market (socialist) system. Elements of directive planning might be retained within the domain of industrial production and supply, but should be totally excised from the consumer good/retail sectors. The immediate practical result of this reappraisal was that from 1987 the traditional, quasi-military terminology of plan implementation was replaced by the notion of 'state order' (*gosudarstvennyi zakaz*) – order in the commercial rather than the directive sense. (We shall see in Chapter 7 how much difference this made in practice.) The new orientation was reinforced by the abolition of the industrial association, which had led an uncomfortable existence in between administrative and *khozraschet* levels in the Soviet economy.

2 Not only is it not possible for the centre to fix all prices, it is not even desirable. The market mechanism demands rational prices, and that means flexible prices. Prices of key commodities should continue to be centrally determined. The rest should be agreed between client and supplier.

3 A rational economic system demands pluralism in ownership and business forms, including cooperation, shareholding, lease-holding etc. That ultimately implies the creation of some kind of stock-market.

4 The principle of self-financing should be systematically extended. That means giving enterprise directors full control of profits (subject to a profits tax), and implicitly complete freedom to juggle the variables of plough-backs, wages, bonuses and labour force as they see fit. It also means giving republican governments control over 'their' industry, agriculture etc., on the understanding that they would seek no subsidies from Moscow.

5 The implementation of points 1–4 would in turn require the

development of an active banking system, capable of mobilizing and deploying savings, providing flexible financial support to market operators, and furnishing an institutional basis for a bond market.

These points are in the main self-explanatory, but some require a degree of institutional filling-out, namely:

## Privatization

After the promulgation in 1987 of a disappointing law on private enterprise as such (it bore all the marks of a political compromise), 1988 saw the appearance of a much more important piece of legislation on cooperatives. The new cooperatives would operate on a limited liability basis, would be allowed to employ non-cooperant labour, apparently without any upper limit, and with wages and working conditions subject to individual contract. Distribution of cooperative income would be decided exclusively by the members of the cooperative, and cooperatives would have complete freedom as regards sales and purchase contracts. They would, however, be subject to elements of central price control. Under the new legislation cooperatives may raise capital by issuing shares, but only for sale to their own members and employees. By mid-1988 cooperatives were employing between 100,000 and 200,000 people. By the first half of 1990 the figure had risen to 3.1 million (2.4 per cent of the work-force), with the cooperatives generating perhaps 3 per cent of Soviet GNP. Some Soviet economists have suggested that they could ultimately account for as much as 10–12 per cent of national income.

But the course of the new cooperation in the Soviet Union has not run smoothly. In December 1988 a decree was issued which sharply restricted cooperative activity in some areas. Cooperatives would no longer be allowed to trade in video films or produce alcohol. Their activities in areas such as publishing, medical care, and the production and sale of jewellery would be sharply restricted, and they would no longer be allowed to exchange foreign currency for cash. The authorities claimed that these new regulations would affect only 1 per cent of cooperatives, but cooperants expressed fears that this might be the thin end of the wedge. Those fears appeared better and better grounded as 1989 progressed. With the rate of open inflation starting to accelerate at the beginning of 1989, following on the partial price liberalization of 1988, the cooperatives were among the prime targets of emergency price control measures promulgated in January 1989.

There can be no doubt that the new cooperatives were initially welcomed by the long-suffering Soviet consumer. A 1988 survey conducted in Sverdlovsk found that cooperative prices were, on average, 1.5–2.0 times higher than state sector prices. But only 25 per cent of respondents thought that the coops were overcharging (Tatarkin et al. 1988). Fairly rapidly, however, public opinion started to turn against the cooperatives, particularly those involved in purely trading rather than production activities. By late spring 1989 it seemed fashionable in Moscow to blame the cooperatives for everything, particularly inflation. It was alleged, with a degree of justification, that some cooperatives were behaving like touts, exacerbating shortages by buying up products from state shops and reselling them at a much higher price. The Soviet public was also becoming increasingly worried about the relationship between the development of the cooperatives and the sharply rising Soviet crime rate. Cooperatives were, it was alleged, being used to launder dirty money from the criminal end of the black economy. What is clear is that they were tending to fall victim to protection rackets. (At mid-1990 there was not a cooperative restaurant in Moscow that was not in the clutches of protection racketeers, and arson attacks were becoming increasingly frequent.) Meanwhile, local authorities were increasingly using safety regulations as a pretext for stopping cooperatives offering real competition to state enterprises (Fedotov 1989).

By the autumn of 1989, despite the continued growth in cooperative turnover, the movement was at crisis point. Local Party chiefs in a number of regions, including Leningrad, had ordered the closure of retail cooperatives for alleged touting of goods bought up from state shops. Legislation passed by the Supreme Soviet in late October imposed a general ban on touting, tightened up on the tax regime for cooperatives, and threatened confiscation of profits for cooperatives breaking the law. Significantly, this in itself represented a compromise between a government anxious to maintain the impetus of *perestroika* and a (partially) democratically elected Supreme Soviet baying for the blood of the cooperatives. A government public opinion survey covering 101,000 people conducted at the end of 1989 found that some 30 per cent of the sample gave a negative evaluation of coops, and only 15 per cent a positive one. The number of 'don't knows' apart, perhaps the most significant detail of the survey results was the fact that in Estonia, on the Baltic, only 8 per cent of those interviewed condemned the cooperatives. (Glushetskii 1990). For how much longer, one wondered, would we be able to talk about 'Soviet reforms'?

Privatization of a type more familiar in the west was meanwhile progressing steadily. In December 1988 the government authorized the sale of state-owned homes to sitting tenants. Buyers would have to make a down-payment of 50 per cent, and pay the rest off over ten years. A small two-room flat would cost 10,000–12,000 roubles. This is a hefty proportion of a Soviet wage packet, but compares realistically with the average savings bank deposit in the Soviet Union – some 1,500 roubles – bearing in mind that many Soviet families have more than one savings account. (We discuss the crucially important issue of privatization in agriculture in Chapter 5.) On a rather different tack, mid-1990 witnessed the passing of legislation permitting the setting up of joint-stock companies, empowered to make public share issues. The model was the giant Siberian lorry plant KamAZ, which was transformed into a joint-stock company in June 1990. The idea is that the state should keep 51 per cent of the shares, with the rest being marketed. First refusal in the sell-off would go to KamAZ employees, who would in any case be guaranteed a 25.5 per cent block vote in the shareholders' meeting. But the KamAZ management is targeting the international share market as the only one that can provide the bulk of the 6 billion roubles which the plant needs for thoroughgoing modernization (Korotkov and Ul'yanov 1990).

## Reform of the banking system

The traditional Soviet banking system fulfilled an essentially passive, accounting role. The supply of money was divided into two distinct 'pools' – cash for the population and bank-account money for enterprises and other organizations of the state – with no direct connecting channel. There was no credit creation mechanism, and no hierarchy of central bank and commercial banks; Gosbank (the State Bank) performed central bank functions and also financed all short-term credit. Stroibank (the Investment Bank) financed investment, and the Foreign Trade Bank financed the foreign trade monopoly. But none of these banks concerned itself systematically with the *ex ante* assessment of the worthiness of particular projects or deals. Rather, the banks' remit was to try to ensure, *ex post*, that projects had been implemented as detailed in the plan, and subject to the cost constraints laid out in the plan. Soviet policy-makers are now seeking to refashion their banking system in an essentially western mould. Gosbank should be relieved of all commercial banking work, and should operate purely as a central, issuing bank. A wide range of specialized, commercial banks should be set up on a shareholding basis, empowered to pursue active credit policies and thus effectively to take over part of the Soviet planning process. Under such a system, the classical principle that 'loans create deposits' would re-emerge, so that relations between the State Bank and the commercial banks would develop in terms of a relationship between the supply of high-powered money and total credit, in turn permitting the central bank to use conventional monetary policy measures to control the aggregate level of credit.

These ideas have been slow to take institutional shape, and in 1989 only a tiny proportion of total investment finance – less than in 1972 – came through bank loans. Budgetary grants still accounted for some 40 per cent (it was planned to fall to 30 per cent in 1990) (Pavlov 1989, p. 12). Projections for a definitive transition to a fully credit-based system by the beginning of the 1990s seemed frankly unrealistic. But progress with the creation of a network of new specialized lending banks has been swift. By 1 July 1989 the number of Soviet commercial banks operating on a shareholding basis had risen to 125, including a special bank to service the cooperative sector and banks like the Leningrad Innovation Bank which models itself on western venture capital institutions by lending exclusively for R&D projects. But of course these new banks would only be able to operate properly once the basic issues of the money and credit system had been resolved.

## *PERESTROIKA* AND THE PLANNING SYSTEM

Where did all this leave socialist planning in the Soviet Union? If current production is to be market led, what role is left for Gosplan and Gossnab? If the banking system is to take on an active role in the allocation of investment, what active role will remain for the centre? One radical economist, Vasilii Selyunin, had no doubts about the answer:

And planning? It was quite simply an invention that did not work. . . . We have to get rid of planning and the command principle completely, and make the transition to normal management. Not a single one of the five-year plans has ever been fulfilled, and there is no prospect that the 1986–90 one will be. . . . Anyway, it is impossible to put together a plan for five years and then live by it, especially in our age of rapid technical progress, when needs are changing all the time in ways you would never guess. Not for five years, not even for one. Only consumer demand can do this – and that's the market.

*Interviewer:* Vasilii Illiarionovich, what then is left of socialism?

Don't ask me that question. I'm not even interested in these things. I'm not concerned to distinguish one 'ism' from another. . . . Let's forget about the concepts 'capitalism' and 'socialism', and let's concentrate on one simple thing – 'market production'. If contemporary market production is only conceivable in the context of a western economic system – then we've got big problems. If it is conceivable with our set-up – then let's get on with it. And if it turns out that we have been going in the wrong direction. . ., then let's follow the advice of the classics. Remember Mozart's words: 'What shall I say? When the great Gluck appeared on the scene and opened up new secrets (deep, captivating secrets), did I not throw out everything that I had known before, that I had loved, that I had so passionately believed in, and did I not follow on boldly behind him, as one who had lost his way. . . ?'

(Selyunin 1989, pp. 102, 105, 111)

This is an extreme formulation. Yet we find echoes of Selyunin's vivid analysis at all levels of the Soviet economics profession. By 1989 there was general agreement that the 1986–90 plan was a dead letter. Radical economist and Member of Parliament Nikolai Shmelev proclaimed that the five-year plan has been a hindrance rather than a help to restructuring policies (Shmelev 1989a). N. Lagutin of Gosplan revealed that the series for net material product (NMP) in 1983 prices, in terms of which the aggregate targets of the 1986–90 plan were couched, 'was reclassified as an official secret in 1986. Thus no one can say how the fulfilment of the plan is going.' ('Sotsial'nye garantii' 1989).

But if the old kind of five-year plan was now simply *passé*, what of future medium-term and long-term plans? There exists an official set of guidelines for the period to the year 2000, which includes specific, fairly ambitious quantitative targets (Dyker 1987a). By the late 1980s, however, these seemed increasingly unrealistic, even inappropriate in the context of the essentially qualitative and structural priorities facing the Soviet government. They stood, indeed, as a monument to that earlier stage of *perestroika*, when Gorbachev still believed, like so many of his predecessors, that planning reform was about improving rather than replacing the system. Around 1988–9 they seem to have been superseded by a 'Concept of Socio-Economic Development of the Country to the Year 2005'. This document was discussed by the Politburo in 1988 (Aganbegyan 1989), though it does not appear to have been adopted on any official basis. The Concept stressed the importance of systemic reform and 'intensification' – nothing new in themselves. The novelty of the new long-term programme was the way in which those elements were combined with a new stress on 'social orientation'. In the words of Abel Aganbegyan, till 1989 Gorbachev's senior economic adviser, 'The key feature of the new social policy lies in the demand for total abandonment of the so-called residual principle, and for guaranteed *priority* [emphasis added] development for all sectors and spheres connected with the satisfaction of the needs of the population.' The implication of a new priority for social goals is that the old principle of expressing production priorities through output targets must finally go.

In an article devoted more specifically to the 1991–5 five-year period, Leonid Abalkin, who in 1989 displaced Aganbegyan as senior economic advisor with his appointment as deputy prime minister and chairman of the new State Committee for Economic Reform, confirmed that the social orientation was to be embodied in the new medium-term plan. Abalkin went on to argue that in working out the plan, Gosplan should, indeed, completely abandon quantitative production targets – 'the most unreliable way of controlling an economy' (Abalkin 1989a, p. 15). How, for instance, Abalkin asked, could conversion of military production capacities be implemented if everyone was still desperately trying to fulfil output targets? Rather the plan should consist of a series of key priority goals, backed up, where necessary, by specific, budget-financed programmes.

The picture painted by Aganbegyan and Abalkin was, then, one of a form of medium- and long-term planning which would largely eschew the most traditional of Soviet plan indicators, which would render the plan-fulfilment report meaningless in its traditional form, and would mark the transition to an essentially indicative planning system. And there were echoes of such (in Soviet terms) radical thinking at the level of operational, sectoral planning. Professor D. Aksenov of the Gubkin Oil and Gas Institute argued in 1989 that the energy strategy embodied in existing plans was completely misconceived, in that it focused exclusively on gross energy production rather than net, taking account of the massive energy requirements of the Siberian fuel industry itself (Aksenov 1989). Aksenov demonstrated that existing plans for gross gas output to peak in the year 2005, for instance, actually implied a peaking of net gas output as early as 1990. He suggested that gross gas output should be held at the 1990 level, that some of the investment funds thus saved should be invested in energy-saving technology, and that the package would yield an economy of more than 150 billion roubles in terms of capital investment. In effect, Aksenov was suggesting a total abandonment of output planning as it has been traditionally practised in a sector which in the past had epitomized the strengths as well as the weaknesses of traditional, output-based planning.

The tone of Aksenov's reasoned radicalism was echoed in an article by economists V. Shcherbakov and Ye. Yasin (1989). They posed a crucial question: if the Soviet Union moves towards a more decentralized, market-based system what role, if any, is left for the ministries? As we have seen, the industrial ministries and their sub-divisions had been the linchpin of plan implementation in the energy sectors and in manufacturing proper. Precisely for that reason they had been the prime targets of reforming economists like Zaslavskaya in the 1980s. Shcherbakov and Yasin began their treatment of the problem by reporting an opinion poll amongst industrial managers which suggested that the majority of Soviet executives would like to see the ministries abolished altogether, or transformed into commercial consultancy organizations. No, said the authors, that would not do because the ministries must retain their role as 'executors of the policy of the state'. But they rightly warned against the idea of putting all ministries onto a system of *khozraschet*; the principle of business accounting, they argued forcibly, could be established at only one level, and a 'hierarchy of *khozraschet*' would just intensify the arbitrariness and deparmental narrowness of the old system. So the ministries should be wholly freed from their brief to supervise enterprise plan fulfilment. The web of output targets would be broken at a key place. The ministries would continue to distribute and place orders for commodities still subject to centralized allocation, but on a non-directive basis. Operational planning, presumably including output planning, would be devolved to 'large-scale production-business complexes', including, no doubt, self-financing republics. The ministries should, however, take responsibility for overall investment policy, including the setting-up of new enterprises and the liquidation of old ones, and for science and technology policy.

In their cautious radicalism, Shcherbakov and Yasin very much echoed the style of Leonid Abalkin, and their ideas fitted in rather neatly with the Aganbegyan/Abalkin thesis. But was the Aganbegyan/Abalkin thesis a programme or just the dream of two economists – admittedly, each in his turn, the most influential at Politburo level? In calling for a 'new concept of centralism, a new philosophy of centralized state regulation of the economy' (Abalkin 1989c, p. 3), Abalkin himself seemed implicitly sceptical about the chances of totally overturning the command planning system. While arguing emphatically against the use of output targets, he also estimated that in real terms the transition to a 'socialist market' in industrial goods and services would be a difficult one, unlikely to be achieved before 1993 (Abalkin 1989c, p. 4). But you cannot get rid of output targets unless you also get rid of centralized allocation of supplies through the *naryad* (allocation certificate) system. And in arguing in favour of the 'balanced economy' Abalkin averred that 'if it is not introduced, then return to the administrative [i.e. command] system, with all the consequences that implies, is inevitable. That is what the argument about what kind of plan we want under the new system comes down to' (Abalkin 1989a, p. 17). But there is another problem, perhaps even more basic, with the Aganbegyan/Abalkin concept of socialist indicative planning as elaborated in 1989. Both economists placed great stress on the need for priority on social goals. But the analysis of our earlier chapters suggested that the priority principle as it has been known in the past is inextricably bound up with the whole essence of centralized, command planning. What kind of new priority principle did Aganbegyan and Abalkin envisage for the future? We will return to this, and other fundamental questions of the future of the Soviet planning system, in Chapter 7.

# Chapter 5

# The special problem of agriculture

## GENERAL ASSESSMENT

Soviet agricultural performance over the last fifteen years or so has been disastrous. With over 18 per cent of the work-force still employed in the sector, this must obviously have had a serious direct effect on national income performance, quite apart from any dislocations that may have occurred when agricultural deliveries to industry have fallen below the planned level. Most important of all, despite massive levels of food import (worth more than US$15 billion in 1987 and nearly US$19 billion in 1989), food supply to the population has been, and remains, a chronic crisis point. Leading Soviet agricultural specialist V. Tikhonov has predicted that if something really radical is not done soon, there is a real danger of famine coming to some parts of the Soviet Union ('Deputaty-ekonomisty. . .' 1989, p. 6). There cannot be the slightest doubt that bad luck with the weather has had something to do with the crisis situation. It is, furthermore, quite clear that in Soviet natural conditions North American yields are simply unattainable. But the extent of failure in the agricultural policies of the Brezhnev government must incline us to suspect that organizational problems have been at least as important as acts of God in inducing the generally dismal production and productivity record displayed in Table 5.1.

Even more striking is the failure of post-Brezhnev governments to do very much better. It was Mikhail Gorbachev who was brought to Moscow from his native Stavropol' province in 1978 to take charge of agriculture within the Communist Party secretariat. He came with the reputation of having been a forceful, pragmatic, highly effective Party boss in a predominantly agricultural region,

*Table 5.1* Rates of growth of Soviet agricultural output and productivity, 1966–89

| Year | Output | Output per agricultural worker |
|---|---|---|
| 1966–70 average | 4.0 | 6.7 |
| 1971 | 1.1 | 1.8 |
| 1972 | −4.6 | −4.2 |
| 1973 | 16.1 | 15.6 |
| 1974 | −2.7 | −3.1 |
| 1975 | −6.3 | −5.4 |
| 1976 | 6.5 | 6.5 |
| 1977 | 4.0 | 4.4 |
| 1978 | 2.7 | 3.1 |
| 1979 | −3.1 | −2.4 |
| 1980 | −2.5 | −2.0 |
| 1981 | −1.0 | −0.6 |
| 1982 | 4.0 | 3.6 |
| 1983 | 5.0 | 4.8 |
| 1984 | −0.1 | −0.3 |
| 1985 | 0.0 | 0.8 |
| 1986 | 5.0 | 5.9 |
| 1987 | −0.5 | 0.8 |
| 1988 | 1.7 | 0.4 |
| 1989 | 1.0 | – |

*Source:* Official Soviet and UN statistics.

able to mix centralization with decentralization – and even to introduce a bit of unofficial privatization – in the cause of improved output and efficiency (see Dyker 1987b, pp. 96–8). He was the architect of the major agricultural policy measures of Brezhnev's last years, and retained the agricultural portfolio within the secretariat until he took over as General Secretary on the death of Konstantin Chernenko in 1985. As General Secretary and then President he has continued to maintain a high profile in relation to agricultural policy-making; but all, apparently, to little avail. Why so? Before trying to answer that question, let us review agricultural policy developments during the Brezhnev period.

## STRATEGY AND STAGNATION 1964–82

The new regime of 1964 seemed to start off by doing all the right things. During Khrushchev's last years price policies were less favourable to agriculture than they had been in the 1950s, and this,

combined with other policies, had conspired to halt the movement
towards more investment and better incomes on the *kolkhozy*.
Brezhnev and Kosygin re-established the earlier trend, and by
1975 collective farmer income from work on the *kolkhoz* alone was
approaching 60 per cent of the average for non-farm workers, with
*sovkhoz* incomes very nearly at the level of those of non-farm
workers by that year (Schroeder and Severin 1976, p. 629). Taking
the private sector into account, by the latter part of the Brezhnev
era the gap between farm and non-farm incomes in the Soviet
Union was no greater than it is in many western countries.
Between 1966 and 1969 the great majority of *kolkhozy* were able to
abandon the traditional labour-day basis for remuneration and
substitute a standard minimum monthly wage (Dyker 1976,
p. 136). Investment inputs into collective agriculture, and indeed
into agriculture as a whole, also rose steadily throughout the post-
1965 period, and agricultural investment as a proportion of total
investment held at the extraordinarily high figure of 20 per cent
throughout the 1970s (Economic Commission for Europe 1977b,
p. 100; 1983, p. 140).

We saw in Chapter 3 that the late 1960s and early 1970s was a
period of refreshingly flexible attitudes to subsidiary industrial
activity in the countryside, and this flexibility was mirrored in
approaches to the internal organization of the farm. The tradition
of arbitrary Communist Party interference in *kolkhoz* and *sovkhoz*
affairs through the medium of a special breed of trouble-shooter
who might descend on a particular farm at any time was laid to
rest, for the time being at least, with the declaration that 'the
plenipotentiary has been abolished' (Yagodin 1968, p. 26). The
number of products carrying a compulsory procurement target for
each farm was reduced, permitting farm managements to take a
much more positive policy line on specialization (Gray 1979,
p. 546). But the reaction which caught up subsidiary industrial
production in the early 1970s could not fail to touch agriculture
itself. The initiation of vast land improvement schemes like the
non-Black Earth Programme, inaugurated in 1974, inevitably
meant renewed interference in farm affairs, with blueprints for new
field systems and crop rotations coming from 'specialist' design
organizations rather than from the farms themselves (Kopteva
1983). The development of various kinds of inter-*kolkhoz* and mixed
*sovkhoz/kolkhoz* associations facilitated the development of a new

*dirigisme* in relation to basic agricultural as well as subsidiary industrial activities.

By the early 1980s production trends were calling into question the wisdom of this, as of every other aspect of Brezhnev's agricultural strategy. It had become clear that the impressive figures on aggregate investment in agriculture presented a fundamentally misleading picture of resource inputs into the sector. The fact is that most of the money was wasted on zero- or negative-return land improvement projects, while peasants continued to want for the simplest pieces of equipment. Here, indeed, was one area where the traditional tactic of using capital investment to create mobilizatory impetus, to forge 'creative' imbalances, would probably never have worked, even in a period when it was working quite well in industry. Under conditions of 'developed socialism' it was little short of a disaster. On the consumption side too, increases in agricultural wages during the 1970s had merely served to highlight the chronic inadequacies of a rural distribution network that could only be counted on to supply vodka – not always the best aid to high productivity.

Finally, the ageing leader seems to have perceived the need for a radical shift in direction. Operational strategy for the future was, however, now firmly in the hands of the newly promoted Gorbachev. Decrees of November 1980 ('Ob uluchshenii. . .' 1980), and 1982 ('V Tsentral'nom Komitete KPSS. . .' 1982), the latter published simultaneously with the Food Programme for the Period up to 1990, laid out a new planning structure for the sector, and gave Gorbachev the chance to make his first mark on the Soviet system at national level.

The 1982 decree singled out three major flaws in the existing system of agricultural planning and management. First, it was top-heavy, overstaffed, and fragmented. Second, and partly flowing from that, it had failed to marry up sectoral and territorial aspects of planning. Third, there was too much administrative interference in the running of actual farms. The decree set out the following basic elements to a new approach:

1 The independence and scope for initiative allowed to farm managements should be increased. *Kolkhozy* and *sovkhozy* should be viewed as the key links in the system of socialist agriculture. Specifically, a consolidation and expansion fund, distinct from the production development fund, was to be created at state

farm level for the finance of decentralized investment on the basis of a 5 per cent rate of deduction from profits.

2 With a view to improving the link-up between territorial and sectoral planning, and to slimming down administrative staffs, district agro-industrial associations (RAPOs) should be created. These would include not only farms, but also enterprises involved in the supply of inputs to agriculture, agricultural processing, etc. They would thus cut across existing lines of departmental subordination. They would not have independent staffs, but would use the apparatus of the district agricultural administration, a routine local government body. Agro-industrial associations would also be created at the provincial/autonomous republic level.

3 By contrast with the situation in at least some of the older types of agricultural association, the constituent farms and enterprises of the RAPOs would, in conformity with 1 above, retain their *khozraschet* status. Nevertheless the RAPO would take over a number of operational planning roles, namely:

(a) Break down aggregate control figures into specific procurement targets for state and collective farms; check draft plans of other organizations, and present any suggested modifications to the appropriate hierarchical superior.

(b) Distribute investment votes, budgetary grants and credits, equipment and other supplies, to farms; reallocate, subject to the agreement of the organizations concerned, 10–15 per cent of the production inputs allocated to other enterprises etc. attached to the association.

(c) Centralize, on the initiative of farm or enterprise managements, specific production and business functions; subcontract such functions to specialist organizations, irrespective of administrative subordination, or create subdivisions for their execution.

(d) Set prices for intra-association transactions, irrespective of administrative subordination.

(e) By agreement with the appropriate hierarchical superior, reallocate unused capital investments (it was left unclear whether this meant funds or equipment) between state organizations within the association.

(f) Create centralized incentive funds on the pattern established by the 1965 planning decree, these presumably to operate in parallel with farm and enterprise incentive funds;

sanction farm and enterprise rules for the distribution of bonuses to management.

(g) Work out medium-term development plans.

The provincial/autonomous republic agro-industrial associations were programmed for a much less operational role in relation to short-term planning. They would only 'examine' (*rassmatrivat'*) basic production indicators, while being empowered, with the agreement of republican ministries, to reallocate investment resources and production inputs. Like the RAPOs they would have the right to centralize specific but unspecified planning and management functions and subcontract them. Beyond that, their main area of interest would be medium-term development plans.

4 A network of agricultural scientific-production associations was to be developed, dedicated to the design of management systems and incentive schemes as well as to strictly agronomic research.

5 Following up the general principle enunciated in the 1979 planning decree, stable five-year fund-forming norms were specified as the basis of agricultural planning.

6 The procurement price system was to be reviewed, with the introduction of improved prices for cattle, pigs, sheep, milk, grain, sugar-beet, potatoes and vegetables as from 1 January 1983.

7 Financially weak collective farms would now be eligible for budgetary grants to finance infrastructural investment, and also to help meet insurance claims. (Hitherto only state farms had enjoyed this privilege.)

8 A total of 9.7 billion roubles' worth of debts owed by weak *kolkhozy* to Gosbank was to be written off, and interest payments lifted and a ten-year moratorium declared on repayment of a further 11 billion roubles' worth.

9 Farm directors would have the right to autonomize the activity of peasant work teams on the basis of a 'collective contract'.

In some ways this package simply represented an extrapolation of the policies of the early Brezhnev period – improving procurement prices, facilitating investment flows, seeking to allow farms greater independence in relation to day-to-day production decisions. Layered on top of that was an attempt to improve the coordination of sectoral and territorial planning (one of Khrushchev's old themes), and to create a new locus of price and investment planning activity at local level. But there were plenty of contradictions in the package as well. As usual in this period, the partial autonomization of farm investment finance was backed up by no corresponding measures in the sphere of supply of investment inputs. While the decree predicated more independence on crop choice to the farm, RAPOs quickly began to distinguish themselves by the number of procurement targets they imposed on farms (Kopteva 1983). The massive writing-off of *kolkhoz* debt and the extension of budgetary grants to the collective sector reflected a proper recognition of the investment errors of the past (see pp. 105–6), but did nothing to improve the climate of financial discipline amongst farms. The difficulty with credit amnesties is, of course, that they tend to create expectations of further credit amnesties. Perhaps more serious, these massive financial manoeuvrings in the early 1980s were a grim portent of the colossal state budgetary problems of the late 1980s (see Chapter 7).

Point by point, then, the 1982 legislation seemed on the whole sensible enough, give or take one or two *non sequiturs*. Viewed as a whole, however, it was an impossibly and ludicrously over-complex structure, still hopelessly top-heavy, and architect-designed to make heavy weather of the most trivial problems. It failed, for example, to make any real impact on the perennial problem of industrial supply to farms.

In this connection the work of the Sel'khozkhimiya association which serves the farms of the district within the framework of the RAPO is in very poor order. Unloading of wagons goes on in the open air, often when it is raining, in places where various other things are lying around. More than once it has happened that nitro-ammophos has been rained on and spoiled before it could be picked up, or delivered mixed up with dolomite powder and broken the spreading apparatus. In a word, it simply will not do for us or our partners in the RAPO to treat fertilizer so carelessly and negligently. . . . Lorries and combine harvesters are frequently out of service because of the acute shortage of particular components. Indents for cultivators, equipment for working the surface of the soil and mowers are anything but satisfied. It would appear that these headaches do not particularly worry our RAPO partner, Sel'khoztekhnika.

(Filippov 1983)

The fact, is, however, that there was often little enough that Sel'khoztekhnika could do about supply problems in the face of an industrial structure peculiarly inimical to the satisfaction of the more subtle, organic requirements of agriculture, a structure which had, of course, formed during a period when agriculture enjoyed no priority whatsoever.

For all that, however, the new rights in relation to autonomous work teams conceded to farm directors by the 1982 legislation were a genuine ray of light amidst the bureaucratic fog. So important is this theme in relation to subsequent developments that we now pause to examine the history of the link (*zveno*) system over the post-Stalin decades.

## INTRA-FARM CENTRALIZATION AND DECENTRALIZATION

The essence of the traditional collective or state farm was summed up in the institution of the brigade. Up to a hundred strong, performing general agricultural tasks under orders which might change from day to day, the brigade system epitomized the extensive utilization of unskilled labour and the total alienation of the agricultural worker from the decision-making process. Thus the brigade had symbolic as well as organizational importance, and exactly the same can be said about its antithesis – the link. The link is a small unit, often of less than ten people, which is allocated a particular piece of land to work or given a particular, specialized function. The link was in favour with Stalin himself in the late 1940s, but fell sharply into disfavour in 1950. In the late 1950s and early 1960s Khrushchev ran a link campaign without great success – perhaps because he placed emphasis on the 'crop-attached' link, which has to move from one piece of land to the next with the crop rotation (Pospielovsky 1970, pp. 425–6). The autonomous, or 'normless' (*beznaryadnoe*) link, which came to the fore in the late 1960s and early 1970s, is simply given a small piece of land, the necessary supplies and equipment if it is lucky, and left to get on with it. No specific set tasks are handed down, only an aggregate sales plan, and members share on the basis of stable norms in the profits of over-plan sales (Kolesnevov 1971, p. 23). The emphasis in the early Brezhnev period on the 'land-attached' link represented a clear recognition of the tremendous psychological importance of giving, or rather returning, some real sense of 'mastery' of the land to the peasants (Kopysov 1968, p. 10).

Yet in 1971 I. Khudenko, architect of the highly successful Achki integrated link system, one of the most advanced decentralized forms, was imprisoned on trumped-up charges. He later died in jail (Katsenelinboigen 1978, p. 66). This by no means spelt the end of the link, but it did represent a reassertion of the power of the Communist Party apparatus men (in this case the rural Party secretaries) exactly paralleling the elements of general economic policy reaction we discussed in Chapter 3 and the trend towards more interference at farm level discussed earlier in this chapter. Rural *apparatchiki* clearly felt that autonomization was going too far, and they were also worried about the fact that many autonomous links were being operated by family groups (Ivanov 1968).

Just as the oil price hike of 1973–4 strengthened the hand of the conservatives in relation to planning as a whole, so the bumper harvest of 1973, following on a couple of poor years, gave confidence to rural reaction and seemed to indicate that the clamp-down on autonomous links and subsidiary industrial production was paying dividends. The result was that the 'normless' idea became distorted out of all recognition in the mid-1970s, with norms, indeed, re-encroaching with a vengeance on the activity of agricultural work-teams. Emphasis shifted towards the 'autonomous' brigade. In principle, under this system, the brigade council administered, and could modify, the pattern of incentive payments to members, with direct farm–peasant relationships being reduced to a minimum (Bakhtaryshev 1980). Under full brigade *khozraschet*, the primary production unit was supposed to operate as a quasi-independent mini-enterprise, with sales, wages fund and material costs the only planned indicators coming down from farm level (Revenok and Pichugin 1981). The autonomous link, it should be remembered, does not normally even have wages fund and cost plans, and the size of the brigade must in any case have meant less effective freedom of action for the individual peasant than under the link system. But the trend back to more bureaucracy and more interference in the late 1970s tended to neutralize the autonomous content of link and brigade systems alike. Even where the link pattern survived, it tended to become over-bureaucratized and over-complex (Aksenov 1980). Farm incentive schemes in general became so complex and confused in this period that actual payments had in many cases to be made on the basis of 'common sense' – no prizes for guessing whose common sense!

More seriously, the ratchet principle reasserted itself emphatically in the relationships between centre and farm and between farm and work-team, with peasants' wages in some cases actually falling as productivity rose (Aliev 1980). If we glance back at Table 5.1 it is not difficult to see why this happened. The hopes raised high in 1973 were dashed in the succeeding years, and, as we reasoned in Chapter 3, the instinctive *apparatchik* reaction to a growth crisis is to go back to crude growth-maximizing tactics. But with the consequent re-establishment of the incentive to hold back production levels, so that succeeding years' plan targets would not be too demanding, the basic rationale of the autonomous work-team – that members should in some sense be profit-sharers – was destroyed. As we saw, the agricultural decrees of the early 1980s professed to be anti-ratchet. In reality the achieved level remained a key planning parameter, though there were reports from the early 1980s of brigades working on a system of three-year norms (Bogomolov 1982).

However sceptical we may be about self-denying ordinances from the Brezhnevite apparatus in relation to the ratchet, there can be no doubt that there was a change in attitudes towards autonomous work-teams as early as 1980. The most striking development was the so-called 'hectarer' (*gektarshchik*) system, introduced in tobacco- and tea-growing, viticulture and potato farming in Azerbaidzhan. The hectarer system went beyond the autonomous link idea in that it organized work on the basis of individual land attachment. Manuring, irrigation, application of pesticides etc. were done at brigade or farm level. Hectarers were allotted a hectare and left to organize tending of crops on a personal basis, perhaps with some help from the family but with no interference from above – though crop pattern was, of course, still centrally determined. There appear to have been no formal norms at all. *Gektarshchiki* were simply paid a uniform price per kilogram, however much they turned in, and annual earnings of as much as 3,500 roubles – at least double the average agricultural wage – were being reported in the early 1980s (Agaev 1981). Clearly this verged on the supersession, in all but name, of the *kolkhoz/sovkhoz* system as such.

There was to be no swift generalization of the hectarer system outside Transcaucasia, but from 1982 more genuinely normless interpretations of the link system soon started to appear in the Soviet press again. Under the rubric of the collective contract (see discussion of the 1982 decree, p. 108), links were to be formed voluntarily, with an elected link leader (*zven'evoi*), and all forms of bonus distributed on a democratic basis. The farm was to make cash advances to the link, and undertake not to reallocate equipment and men (Petrov 1982). Thus as the Brezhnev era came to an end, the prospects for a lifting of the dead hand of the collective farm system seemed reasonably bright.

## GORBACHEV AND CHERNENKO

During Andropov's brief tenure of the General Secretaryship agricultural policy continued along the lines set by the 1982 agenda. But with the reversion in 1984 to geriatric Brezhnevism, on the succession of Konstantin Chernenko to the Party leadership, agricultural policy took a step backwards again. Normless link and hectarer systems came in for substantial public criticism, and Chernenko, the old ideology (i.e. Communist Party control) hack, expressed serious worries about the loss of 'collective' spirit (Dyker 1987b, pp. 100–1). More positively, but no less mistakenly, Chernenko reverted to Brezhnev's policy of trying to spend the Soviet Union out of trouble on the agricultural front. 'We will, of course,' he averred, 'continue in the future to increase capital investment in agriculture, to saturate it with technology and other material inputs' (Chernenko 1984, p. 3). Chernenko was aware of the colossal waste of resources which his erstwhile patron's grand schemes had occasioned. But his proposals for countering such waste were hopelessly underpowered. The notorious Ministry for Irrigation and Drainage (Minvodkhoz), which in the words of radical economist and member of parliament Nikolai Shmelev 'has done nothing but harm [to the Soviet Union]' (Shmelev 1989b, p. 271), was to undergo yet another reorganization, but nothing was done to attack the basic problem – Minvodkhoz's inherent, system-induced antipathy towards the requirements of farmers and the well-being of the land – beyond a weary expression of faith in the Party mobilizatory tactics of the past.

Agricultural reform made no progress, then, during the Chernenko interregnum. But Brezhnev's old crony was too weak a leader to make much of an impact at the operational level. Despite public criticism, the collective contract system did continue to develop in some areas (Dyker 1987b, pp. 101–2). Elsewhere the 1982 package – with its strengths and weaknesses – remained in force. Gorbachev adopted a fairly low profile on agricultural management during Chernenko's General Secretaryship, though he did publicly dissociate himself from the big spending approach. When he succeeded as Party chief in 1985 he was able more or less to pick up where he had left off in 1983.

## THE EVOLUTION OF ADMINISTRATIVE STRUCTURE 1985–6

The first major agricultural legislative measure of Gorbachev in power came in November 1985 when he announced the creation of a new 'super-ministry' for agriculture, with full executive powers, to be called the USSR State Agro-Industrial Committee – Gosagroprom ('V Tsentral'nom Komitete...' 1985, pp. 17–18). Gosagroprom was to take over the competences of the Ministry for Agriculture, the Ministry for Fruit and Vegetable Production, the Ministry for the Meat and Dairy Industry, the Ministry for the Food Industry, the Ministry for Rural Construction, and Sel'khoztekhnika, the machinery for agriculture organization. *Gosagropromy* were also to be created at republican and provincial level, forming a hierarchical system which would dovetail in with the existing system of RAPOs at district level.

The main duties of the new committee were to be as follows:

1  To reorganize the RAPO system with a view to creating a rationalised pattern of specialization and concentration.
2  To assume overall responsibility for the entire agro-industrial complex. This would mean taking on a quality-control role in relation to the work of the new Ministry for Bread Products, and of Minvodkhoz. It would also involve 'close co-ordination' with the Artificial Fertilizer Ministry and the engineering ministries producing equipment for agriculture. The ministers from all these ministries would themselves sit on Gosagroprom USSR.
3  To rationalize the administration of agriculture, with systematic redundancy for supernumerary agricultural administrators and a performance-related incentive scheme for Gosagroprom managerial workers.
4  To take responsibility for the supply of industrial inputs to agriculture, for relevant areas of price formation, and for the

'perfecting of economic methods of carrying on business and *khozraschet* relations'.

5 To play a major role *vis-à-vis* agriculture-oriented research and development, and in relation to agricultural training.

6 To develop the collective contract, the general principle of payment-by-results, and to improve financial and credit mechanisms as they affect agriculture.

7 To develop subsidiary agricultural activity in all its forms – peasants' private plots, allotments, and subsidiary agricultural operations run by industrial enterprises.

8 To maintain unconditional fulfilment of procurement targets (but in the form of *zakazy* – strictly commercial orders) as the main instrument of agricultural planning.

These points were developed, to some extent modified, in the decree 'on the further improvement of the economic mechanism in the agro-industrial complex of the country' published on 29 March 1986 ('V Tsentral'nom Komitete. . .' 1986). The new decree spelled out, first, the details of a new, more flexible, agricultural price system. Republican and local Gosagroprom bodies would now have substantial freedom to fix 'incentive prices' for some up-market categories of produce. Republican authorities were conceded the right to vary a broader range of procurement prices with the agreement of the central authorities. Farms would now be allowed to sell up to 30 per cent of their planned level of procurement of fruit and vegetables and table wine to consumer cooperatives and on the *kolkhoz* market – at freely negotiated prices. (Previously they had been allowed to do this only with overplan production.)

There was also a good deal in the new legislation on how the collective contract was expected to shape up through the rest of the decade. Immediately striking was the endorsement of family and individual contracts as forms of collective contract, signalling a complete rejection of the Chernenko line on the hectarer system. But the decree was vague on the crucial question of exactly how work-team remuneration systems should be organized.

For Gorbachev, as for Andropov, incentives have always been but the flip side of responsibility, and the March 1986 decree reiterated the stress on financial levers and financial correctness that was already showing strongly on the industrial side through the Sumy experiment. As a general rule, farms and enterprises belonging to the agro-industrial complex should, it was now predicated, move towards self-financing (*samookupaemost'*) in terms of capital needs. The decree extended Brezhnev's 1982 moratorium on debt repayment and interest for a number of farms and enterprises. At the same time it sought to attack the underlying causes of financial weakness in two ways. First, a degree of automaticity in the adjustment of agricultural procurement prices to increases in prices of supplies to agriculture was introduced. Second, the decree took a bite at the fundamental problem of land rent. The Soviet agricultural system had never levied any systematic differentiated charge for land of varying qualities. This had been a major source of operational inefficiency in the sector. Perhaps more important, it had made it almost impossible for the authorities to pin-point the locus of such inefficiency. From 1987 there would now be special supplements to procurement prices for deliveries from low-profit and loss-making farms. This simply represented an extension of the traditional principle of zoned procurement prices, which had, certainly, never been particularly effective. Rather more radical was the proposal to levy an income tax on all farms (it would be called 'payment to the state budget' for state farms), the rates of which should vary in accordance with land endowment and quasi-rental elements like capital stock. Overall, however, the rent package was rather underpowered.

The legislation of March 1986 clearly stated that the number of plan indicators imposed on farms should be reduced, thus in principle reversing the *de facto* trend since 1982 for RAPOs to set farms more detailed plans. But what about the nature of key plan indicators? There was certainly a terminological change – a tendency to talk (as far as farms were concerned) of plans for sales (*prodazha*) rather than the more Stalinist-sounding procurement (*zagotovka, zakupka*). On the administrative side, the planning of procurement of non-grain/pulse produce was to be decentralized to the republican and provincial level. More significant, however, was the projected change in the style of planning. True to the philosophy of stable norms, procurement levels of grain and pulses, and inter-republican and inter-provincial deliveries of other categories of produce, would be fixed for the five-year period as a whole. Targets would, furthermore, be held at the level of the plan for 1986 throughout the period up to 1990, though any farm delivering more than the average level for 1981–5 would receive an incentive price 50 per cent above the standard price, even if they failed to fulfil the plan. (If they did manage to fulfil the plan, the incentive price would be double the standard price.) Thus the plan as it came through at farm level would now represent very much a minimum plan, and farms might still receive a pat on the back even it it were not fulfilled. Indeed the whole approach was described at the 27th Congress of the CPSU in terms of a Leninist 'tax in kind'. Thus Soviet agricultural planners seemed to be envisaging transition to a form of 'slack' planning, under which the purpose of targets would be to build in a safeguard against extreme fluctuations in output levels, leaving it to the structure of procurement prices to ensure fulfilment of the five-year production target. In making this step towards parametric planning, the March 1986 decree moved on a good deal from the positions of the November 1985 legislation.

Finally, there were important innovations in the province of investment planning and finance. These added up to a significant extension of the farm's autonomy in relation to medium-scale investment projects, especially technical re-equipment (upgrading) projects, paralleling the provisions of the 1985 decree on the industrial planning experiment. Farms and enterprises would now be empowered to approve the title list (see Chapter 6) for investment undertakings up to a value of 1 million roubles. They would also be allowed to do their own design work on some categories of upgrading investments. To help with the problem of supply of investment inputs, farms which overfulfilled their targets would be offered payment in motor vehicles, tractors etc, with Gosagroprom setting up a special supply reserve for this purpose.

In sum, then, the March 1986 legislation on agriculture seemed to mark another significant step away from the crude target planning of the past, towards a system based much more on the price mechanism, a system under which farms and farmers could finally secure the right to manage the land themselves. On a number of key points – the development of the collective contract, the role of the private sector, the precise division of labour between targets and prices in agricultural planning, the vexed question of industrial supplies to agriculture – the decree left many questions unanswered. But as a milestone in the process of agricultural *perestroika* it seemed irreproachable. Why, then, was it necessary, within barely three years, to turn the whole system of agricultural administration upside-down again?

## THE PRICE OF DECENTRALIZATION

The first part of the answer is that Gosagroprom turned into a monster, exhibiting all the worst characteristics of traditional Soviet bureaucracy – interfering without helping, commanding without planning, and, above all, wasting money. At the local level the RAPOs were just as bad, but with a cast-iron excuse:

> The multitude of planning indicators, the diverse requests, the paper work – it's not our idea. The RAPO receives just as many instructions from the provincial agro-industrial committee, and we are obliged, in our turn, to pass them on to the collective and state farms. . . . That committee itself receives a fair number of regulatory documents from above. Thus there are daily at least 200 'incoming papers' alone.
>
> (Vasil′ev 1986)

So whatever the 1985–6 legislation achieved, it did not succeed in breaking up the treadmill of hierarchy, meddling, and petty tutelage. Far from eschewing procurement targets, many RAPOs were still trying to impose sowing targets in 1986. This no doubt reflected in part an element of bureaucratic stubbornness, an unwillingness to give up habitual prerogatives. But there were other, more technical factors. This example from the Baltic region nicely illustrates the problem:

> Natural and economic conditions in the Estonian republic are most suitable for the development of the beef and dairy industry and the cultivation of potatoes. But with the present structure of procurement prices, production of these relatively capital- and labour-intensive lines is not profitable enough – you can make much higher profits per unit costs, and with a lot less trouble, if you stick to pork and egg production, using fodder brought in from other regions. The only way to maintain output levels of less profitable categories is through administrative measures, setting targets for sales of all product lines, profitable and unprofitable, to the state. *That is why sowing plans and plans for head of livestock are still being imposed in some parts of the country, despite a number of government pronouncements condemning the practice* [emphasis added].
>
> (Bronshtein 1986, p. 81)

In agriculture, then, as in industry, you do not dare decentralize until you have got your prices right. And here the problem is compounded by the continued absence of a comprehensive system of land rent. As we saw, that makes it virtually impossible in practice for the planning authorities to isolate organizational inefficiency as a cause of loss-making. Going one step further, systematic loss-making mollified by handouts disguised as credits, a practice condoned by the 1985–6 legislation, provided another reason for the persistence of 'administrative methods', as the authorities sought ways to cut their own losses (Nefedov 1986, p. 71). In turn, the more detailed the instructions from above, the less freedom was left to the farm in the area of investment decision-making and the more difficult it was to to blame the farm for misallocations of resources. Thus defects in the basic agricultural price system set up a vicious circle of loss-making → administrative interference → distortion of price signals → failure to identify inefficiences → loss-making. The decrees of 1985 and 1986 nibbled at that vicious circle, but failed to break it.

The second major area in which the 1985–6 measures failed to have real impact was in that of industrial supplies to agriculture. Precisely one of the main purposes of giving Gosagroprom such a wide-ranging remit was to provide it with a base from which to marshal the off-farm inputs on which agriculture depends so crucially. But the operational style of local agricultural supply organizations changed little:

> They come along with arguments based on the principle that the customer is always wrong. Most of our suppliers try to pass off the delivery plan of the old pre-reform supply organization as the document determining delivery dates. Well, they say, our plan is broken down by quarters, and we will do loads of spare parts also on a quarterly basis (when we feel like it). The amazing thing is that the State Arbitration Commission in some provinces has gone along with these arguments.
>
> (Izrailev 1986, p. 10)

Sad, perhaps, but 'amazing' surely not. The creation of Gosagroprom had not broken the mould of hierarchical planning. It had simply sought to modify it, while making it more complex. It did nothing to change the behavioural pattern of Soviet bureaucrats, be they enterprise directors or inspectors, merely creating more avenues for administrative obfuscation. In a word, it was a measure peculiarly reminiscent of the style of Khrushchev. In any case, of course, the best Gosagroprom in the world would eventually have come up against the problem that as of 1986 Soviet industrial planning remained largely unreformed, and therefore still peculiarly insensitive to the true needs of agriculture.

Finally, and most important of all, the 1985–6 legislation failed to abolish the collective and state farms. It encouraged the family-based work-team within the socialized farm, but failed to provide that work-team with the kind of sympathetic environment in which it could 'take'. It simply did not address the problem of the motivational canker – the alienation, passivity and dependence – at the heart of Stalin's socialist farm. It failed, in a word, to look for *radical* alternative models of Soviet agriculture. But there is a radical alternative model, one which has coexisted with the collectivized model throughout most of the history of the Soviet Union. It is to that alternative model – the private subsidiary sector – that we now turn.

## PRIVATE AGRICULTURE: ANOTHER ROAD

The history of the private plot – on average 0.5 to 1.0 hectare – has been a chequered one. Stalin conceded this 'privilege' to the peasantry in the 1930s, mainly to stop them starving to death. In practice, the private plot developed as much as a supplier of specific product lines (e.g. eggs) to the urban population, as through autoconsumption. It also developed as a model of hard work, commitment, and high productivity. Khrushchev did not like the plot, believing, with some justification, that it distracted the peasants from their commitments to socialist agriculture, and persecuted it. Brezhnev was more tolerant, and indeed the 1982 Programme called for 'obligatory and systematic aid' from the state and collective agricultural sectors to the private, which was at that time still accounting for over one-quarter of total agricultural output. The early 1980s were, in fact, marked by the development of a number of forms of state/collective/private cooperation based on the 'putting out' or 'share-cropping' principles. On taking power Andropov pledged to continue the positive policy line on the private sector, and Gorbachev maintained and developed this orientation.

Here, as elsewhere, we see the Soviet President showing an un-Soviet capacity to learn from experience. The 1985–6 model was very much one of cooperation between socialist and private sectors, and success stories continued to be reported on this dimension through the middle to late 1980s, particularly in the fodder/ livestock-fattening nexus. But the new approach, based on the principles of planning and integration, served if anything merely to highlight the essential contradictions of agriculture's dual system. The good news in the area of livestock fattening was tempered by reports of serious misallocations of resources induced by these same positive developments. With common pasture a thing of the past on many collective and state farms, private sector cows now had to be pastured by the roadside. Therefore they had to be tended constantly, with the resultant problem of peasants taking time off from *kolkhoz/sovkhoz* work to look after their private assets becoming increasingly serious (Kozlov 1986), as did difficulties with the provision of ploughing and other services to the private subsidiary sector. Local authorities reacted to the latter problem by instructing farms to help with private plot ploughing, in some cases through the medium of a kind of collective contract. This was very laudable, yet at the same time it once again summed up the essential dilemma of the given institutional structure in agriculture – how to get *anything* done without handing out orders, how to bring any notion of planning to the private subsidiary sector except on the basis of the very model of traditional command planning which the reform programme as a whole aimed to abolish?

## THE CONCEPTUAL BREAKTHROUGH

In 1988 Gorbachev seems to have gone through one of the most important pieces of reappraisal of the whole *perestroika* period. The idea of bringing planning, even socialism, to the private sector had been tried. It had shown results, but it had highlighted more problems than solutions. Perhaps it was time to try the opposite tack, to bring the logic of the private sector to the collective and state farms, the logic of an embryo capitalism to the socialist sector.

The principle of lease-holding (*arenda*), whereby peasants are permitted to lease 50–100 hectare blocks of land and farm them on an independent basis, had been around for some time on an experimental basis. But in a Kremlin speech in October 1988 Gorbachev put forward the system as a blueprint for root-and-branch reform of Soviet agriculture, a blueprint for the effective reprivatization of the land. Leases would be long term, farmers should be permitted to pass their leases on to their children, collective and state farm staffs would have to join the leaseholders, set up as consultants, or go to the wall. With this momentous development, then, a new vision of an integrated Soviet agriculture was put forward, a vision owing much to the post-Mao Chinese responsibility system, a vision based on a fusion of the tradition of the private subsidiary sector and the experience with link- and collective contract-based experiments within the *kolkhozy* and *sovkhozy*. A few months after Gorbachev's speech the influential economics journal *Ekonomika i Organizatsiya Promyshlennogo Proizvodstva* ran a special feature (No.4, 1989) on the legacy and memory of I. Khudenko, the ill-fated pioneer of the link system.

## THE NEW LEGISLATIVE FRAMEWORK OF 1989

The Central Committee Plenum of March 1989 abolished Gosagroprom, to the relief of all. Follow-up decrees of 5 April sought, once again, to map out an organizational structure and a strategy for agriculture. Their main elements were as follows:

1 The majority of Gosagroprom's subordinate enterprises were transferred to republican jurisdiction.
2 The ill-reputed Ministry for Irrigation and Drainage was finally abolished. Irrigation and drainage work would now be taken over by the farms themselves.
3 A new system of wholesale prices was to be introduced in 1990.
4 The number of price zones (see earlier discussion of the land rent problem on pp. 116–19) was to be cut, but farms were to be allowed more freedom to chose their crop pattern to suit local conditions.
5 The incidence of agricultural subsidization was to be shifted from the procurement to the wholesale/retail stage, with subsidies henceforth to be financed by republican and local governments. The system of subsidization for dairy products was to be abolished.
6 The grain harvest was henceforth to be measured net of all transportation and storage losses, estimated to account for anything up to 30 per cent of gross production.
7 A Central Grain Fund for Inter-Republican Deliveries was to

be set up at a minimum level of 77 million tons, on the semi-directive basis of state orders. Beyond that, distribution would be handled by the republics.

8 Over the period 1991–5 total output of foodstuffs should grow by 26–30 per cent, i.e. at an average rate of 4.7–5.4 per cent per annum.

9 Investment in rural infrastructure was to increase by 50 per cent in the period 1991–5 by comparison with 1986–90. There would be a corresponding increase in funds for road construction of 180 per cent.

10 Increased productivity was to provide 60 per cent of total output increases during the period 1991–5.

A few days later, a decree on leaseholding was promulgated. It specified that land might be leased out on *arenda* by local governments, *kolkhozy*, *sovkhozy*, or even private individuals. More specifically, local governments would be empowered to take over unused or poorly used land from collective and state farms, with a view to leasing it out. Leaseholders would be under the obligation to maintain the property leased in good condition, but would also be entitled to compensation for any improvements they made. Leases should normally be for a period of 5–50 years, but might in exceptional cases be shorter or longer. On the expiry of a lease, first refusal on the new lease should be offered to the members of the family of the old leaseholder, always provided that they were living in the same house. The family could in any case retain the house and garden. Rents might only be raised by mutual agreement, and even then not more often than once in five years. The leaser would have the right to retain from the rent what is required to maintain capital stock and infrastructure on the land. The rest would go to the local government.

Once again we have to applaud the general sensibleness of the package: the provision of a stable legislative basis for leaseholding, the killing-off of bureaucratic leviathans, the refinement of reporting practices, the emphasis on productivity, the devolution of administration, and the emphasis on infrastructural investment. Once again we have to note that in practice the impact on agricultural performance seems to have been minimal, that there has still been no break with the pattern of stagnation in production and productivity inherited from Brezhnev. What went wrong?

## THE NEW POLICY BLOCKAGE OF THE 1990s

We have to say, straight off, that the 1989 legislative package was hardly free of the kinds of contradictions and ambivalences which have characterized Soviet agricultural programmes in the past. On the one hand, the leaseholding system was being featured as the key to the future. At the same time, the collective and state farms remained the institutional corner-stones of the system. Marketization was strongly implied, yet old-style output plans were also featured, albeit in terms of a 'purer' indicator. The price system was to be reviewed, but the central problem of land rent was side-stepped rather than addressed. And while the decrees were clear on the transfer of authority from the centre to the republics and localities, they said nothing about how that devolved authority was to be exercised. Would the rules of business accounting provide the framework, or would the Soviet Union simply end up with a mass of mini-Gosagroproms? By mid-1989 the answer was clear: 'Collective and state farms are set not only obligatory targets for deliveries to the state, but also detailed plans for the areas to be sown to different cultures, and for herd sizes' (Radaev 1989, p. 48).

The new leaseholding legislation also flattered to deceive. For while the principle was laid down that leases might be taken out from a number of different legal personalities, it soon became clear that in practice the great majority of leases would be taken out from *kolkhozy* and *sovkhozy*. Why, after sixty years of arbitrariness and tutelage, should Soviet peasants trust collective and state farm managements to be good landlords? Old habits and ingrained distrust apart, the fact is that the agricultural legislation of 1989 only modified further the principle of the obligatory procurement target, while in practice the status of that principle remained largely unchanged. If farms still have their own targets to fulfil, who could be quite sure that they would always manage to resist the temptation to impose informal procurement targets on 'their' leaseholders? However justified or unjustified these suspicions might be, they seemed to prevail amongst the peasantry. At the beginning of 1990 fewer than 10 per cent of all collective and state farms had introduced leaseholding. Only in the Baltic republics had there been a transition to a system of family farms as such (*Plan Fulfilment Report* for 1989). Against the background of increasingly militant independence movements in those republics, this looked very much like the exception that proved the rule.

Despite Gorbachev's emphatic conversion to the principle of privatization in agriculture, then, policy-making on this key sector remains as ambivalent, as top-heavy, and as ineffectual as ever. Why so? A good part of the explanation must be sought in the peculiarities of the Soviet political system as it existed up until the great watershed of mid-1990.

The Politburo was the nearest thing the Soviet Union had to a cabinet prior to the creation of the new Presidential Council in 1990, and the Party secretariat has in the past provided much of the muscle behind policy formation. But both organs form part of the pattern of cooptive oligarchy which has dominated Soviet politics. Thus when Gorbachev was elected General Secretary in 1985 he was merely being invited to fill the position of chairman of the oligarchs, not, to use Gladstone's phrase, to reach for the butcher's knife. As a result, policy generation and implementation was continually hampered after 1985 by the presence of men with at best an ambivalent commitment to *perestroika* in the two key bodies. The most important of these was Yegor Ligachev. An impressive and articulate man, Ligachev put himself at the head of the tendency within the Communist Party which saw a serious threat to the traditional Soviet notion of egalitarianism, indeed to socialism itself, in the implications of *perestroika*. He had considerable success in reforging Brezhnev's alliance between Party apparatus and working class, two groups whose employment prospects are equally threatened by Gorbachev's reform programme. Unable to get rid of Ligachev, the Soviet number one had to be content to demote him. This he managed to do in the autumn of 1988, when Ligachev was moved from the prestigious ideology portfolio within the secretariat to the agriculture one – ironically Gorbachev's old portfolio.

But if the agriculture brief was meant to be a poisoned chalice for Ligachev, the move backfired. A few months after Gorbachev's epoch-making speech on the leaseholding system, Ligachev went on Soviet television to pledge his commitment to a rejuvenated collective and state farm system as the proper basis for the development of a modern food industry. In an interview for British television in early 1990 he reiterated that Soviet agriculture would be decollectivized 'over his dead body'. It was in July 1990, at the 29th Congress of the Soviet Communist Party, that Ligachev finally overreached himself – not in relation to agriculture, but in an attempt to rally the conservatives behind his bid for the newly created Deputy General Secretaryship. The bid failed dramatically, and Ligachev's political career was over. The last obstacle to a genuine transformation of Soviet agriculture seemed to have been removed.

## FROM BLOCKAGE TO BLUEPRINT

We need radical change, and the Central Committee of the Party and the government consider that leaseholding within the structure of the collective and state farm represents just that. This is a myth, an illusion. You will never have *arenda* and independence for the peasant within the *kolkhoz*. The contemporary situation is similar to that which prevailed in 1861–3 [the liberation of the serfs]. They gave the peasant freedom, but not land. The land remained with the landlord. Today's landlord – the chairman of the collective farm or director of the state farm – is not going to give the land to the peasant on leasehold. Or if he does, experience suggests that he will do so on crudely exploitative conditions on which no one would want to lease the land.

We need a land reform. But a land reform is possible only if the government can find the strength to break up the prevailing system of monopolism, one of the main elements of which is the monopoly in ownership of land. . . . In the Baltic republics they asked me the question: 'How would you feel if someone stole your car, and you looked for it everywhere and couldn't find it. Then after a while someone came up to you and offered you your car back to you – on leasehold.'

('Deputaty-ekonomisty. . .' 1989, pp. 6–7)

Now that Ligachev is gone, we can finally pose the central question. Would reprivatization of the land, whether *de jure* or *de facto*, solve all of the Soviet Union's agricultural problems? Surely not. First, there is the problem of prices. The existing system of agricultural prices gives the wrong signals to collective and state farms. It would give exactly the same wrong signals to independent farmers, and those would operate more powerfully to the extent that they could not be corrected through the imposition of formal or informal procurement targets. Thus any notion that Soviet agriculture could be radically reformed in isolation from reform trends in the rest of the Soviet economy is dangerously mistaken.

There are, though, other problems with the leaseholding initiative perhaps structurally more fundamental. The 50–100 hectare family farm does not present a universal model of success in the west. Most American farms – even family farms – are much bigger, and there is a trend in the USA for the family farm to lose ground to the agricultural corporation. In any case, agriculture is often a relatively small contributor to total income on US family farms, as indeed was also the case in the private agricultural system of socialist Yugoslavia. The pattern of farm size in western Europe is very mixed, with Denmark justly famous for the commercial viability of its smallholdings, while crofters in Scotland and their counterparts in the South of France struggle. There *are* very significant economies of scale in many subsectors of agriculture, most notable in the growing of grain. However fundamental the idea of leaseholding may be as a political signal, as a symbol of liberation for the peasant, it does not exempt us from the need to look at the issue of economies of scale in different agricultural activities in a sober and sensible fashion.

No more can we simply ignore the fact that the structure of Soviet agriculture, like that of the rest of the Soviet economy, has been systematically distorted over a period of some sixty years. Perhaps the best illustration of this point comes from central Asia. The classically Stalinist policy of seeking to maximize output (in this case of cotton) by throwing in available resources (labour and irrigation water) *en masse* had worked well through the pre-war and early post-war periods, and had indeed given the central Asian peasantry a much higher standard of living than that enjoyed by the Russian peasantry under high Stalinism. But by the 1980s the price of extensive development extended too far was beginning to be apparent in a quite dramatic fashion in central Asia. While the local population complained with increasing impatience about the impact of monoculture on local food supply, and indeed also social conditions, much more momentous matters were coming to public attention. The irrigation systems of central Asia, a tribute to the late, unlamented Ministry for Irrigation and Drainage, had been founded on the diversion of the waters of the Syr-Darya and Amu-Darya rivers. Both these rivers flow into the Aral Sea, a great inland lake the size of Ireland. But under the pressure of this diversion the Aral Sea is drying up. On present trends it will have dried up altogether by the early decades of the next century. Water apart, this is causing the release of noxious salts into the atmosphere in the Aral region which are creating grave public health problems akin to the effects of nuclear radiation. The leaseholding system is not going to solve the problems of the Aral Sea. We will return to this theme in Chapter 7.

In July 1990 a draft law was published in the Soviet Union which seemed finally to offer the possibility of a farming system free to 'shake down' and find its own optimal organizational pattern, with cooperative farms, leaseholders, and family farmers free of any tutelage from the socialist sector, invited to compete to the benefit of the Soviet people. But it was not Gorbachev's draft law. It came from the parliament of the Russian Federation, and bore all the hallmarks of the thinking of Gorbachev's erstwhile political *bête noire*, whom he had sacked from the Politburo in 1987, arch-radical Boris Yeltsin. Yeltsin had made a dramatic political comeback in May 1990 when he secured the presidency of the Russian Federation. Even before the challenge of the conservative Ligachev had faded, then, Gorbachev was faced with a much more formidable challenge – the challenge of a Russian political leadership prepared to go its own way, and push through its own reforms in agriculture and elsewhere, regardless of what the Soviet government was doing. To this theme also we will return in our concluding chapter.

# Chapter 6

# The special problem of construction and investment

In Chapter 1 we pin-pointed fixed investment as a key instrument of mobilization in the early period of Soviet economic development, and specified the characteristic problems of excessive lead-times and capital cost escalation as flowing essentially from the strategy – 'wrong-headed' in neo-classical terms – of ample utilization of capital. It is time now to put more institutional and operational flesh on this sketch, and to go on to study how the Soviet authorities have tried to reconstruct the investment sector. We start by identifying the major actors in the investment process under the traditional, command system.

## THE HIERARCHY OF INVESTMENT PLANNING FROM STALIN TO BREZHNEV

### The central planners and the ministries and their sub-divisions

The key document of overall centralized investment planning, the title list, is a surprisingly brief document, normally about six pages, covering the basic technical, locational, and cost characteristics of a given project. The 1979 planning decree sought, for the first time, to give title lists some kind of binding force, for suppliers as well as construction organizations (Boldyrev 1979). This underlines the extent to which investment plans, under the traditional system, lacked the true command element characteristic of short-term output plans. As we shall see in the detailed discussion that follows (pp. 130–41), there was very little in the way of parametric elements to fill this gap. But the title list is, nevertheless, the document which has given an authority the legal right to proceed with a project. In the Brezhnev period, investment undertakings worth more than 3 million roubles were characterized as above-limit, which meant that the title list had to be specifically approved at the centre. For below-limit investment, block votes went to ministries (for the bulk of production investment) and republican authorities (for the bulk of infrastructural investment), and it was those intermediate bodies which approved the corresponding individual title lists. As we saw, the planning decree of 1979 aimed to increase the specificity of the title list by laying down that it should henceforth include breakdowns of volumes of construction work by year.

The weakness of the traditional Soviet planning system in relation to lead-times is underlined by the curious anomaly whereby the centre has issued *norms* for gestation periods, while ministries and republican governments have specified *plans* for the same, even in the case of above-limit projects. Table 6.1 demonstrates the extraordinary divergences to which this has led. Thus when we talk of traditional Soviet investment planning, we are clearly talking about something which is really, by Stalinist standards, rather nebulous. We should, of course, always bear in mind the elements of decentralized, i.e. strictly non-planned investment, which as we have seen was of substantial importance at certain times in Soviet economic history even before the advent of *perestroika*.

Only in the case of the 'most important' projects (defined in the Khrushchev period as those worth more than 150 million roubles) were the actual detailed designs confirmed by the central authorities. Even ministries and republican governments delegated much of the checking of designs to lower-level bodies. Specific issues like lead-times apart, then, how did the Soviet authorities (central and intermediate), go about ensuring that the design organizations which did the detailed drafting abided by some kind of basic efficiency rules in their choice of technology etc.? Although notions of rate of interest, rate of return, etc. were formally outlawed during the Stalin period, Soviet engineers fairly quickly developed a simple, but serviceable formula for assessing the relative merits of technologies with differing capital intensities in given production lines.

What they did was to compare the difference in capital costs to the difference (in the opposite direction) in running costs with a view to ascertaining how many years it would take the variant with

*Table 6.1* Normed and planned lead-times from inception to full-scale production, by ministry (in years)

| Ministry | Average normed lead-time | Average planned lead-time |
|---|---|---|
| Construction and road-laying machine-building | 1.9 | 10.7 |
| Machine building for light industry and the food industry | 1.8 | 8.2 |
| Chemical machine building | 2.3 | 9.6 |
| Heavy machine building | 3.1 | 11.7 |
| Heavy electrical machine building | 2.0 | 7.6 |
| Instrument-making | 2.4 | 8.0 |
| Machine-tool industry | 2.5 | 7.1 |
| Vehicle industry | 3.1 | 8.4 |
| Heavy-industrial construction | 1.9 | 5.0 |
| Industrial construction | 2.0 | 4.9 |
| Building materials | 2.4 | 5.2 |
| Dairy industry | 1.8 | 3.9 |
| Food industry | 2.1 | 4.4 |
| Coal industry | 4.8 | 9.6 |
| Petro-chemicals industry | 4.3 | 7.3 |
| Power industry | 5.8 | 9.0 |
| Light industry | 2.7 | 4.2 |

*Source:* Bronshtein 1970, p. 40.

lower running costs to pay off its higher capital costs. The approach was therefore a kind of marginal pay-off period approach, which can be stated formally thus:

$$t = \frac{K_1 - K_2}{C_2 - C_2}$$

where K is capital expenditure, C is running costs, including depreciation, and subscripts denote projects with identical output characteristics to be compared. The subscript $_1$ is used for the more capital-intensive, the subscript $_2$ for the less capital-intensive project. The more capital-intensive variant is considered preferable if $t$ is less than a normative $T$. It has been common Soviet practice to formulate the criterion in terms of a coefficient of relative effectiveness (CRE), defined as

$$e = \frac{C_2 - C_1}{K_1 - K_2}$$

the more capital-intensive variant being considered preferable if $e$ is greater than a normative $E$. This is, of course, simply the reciprocal of the primary formulation. A more general formulation, permitting comparison of more than two projects, is

$$C + EK = \text{minimum}.$$

Thus the coefficient of relative effectiveness can be made to serve the purpose of a general investment criterion, as long as we are concerned with strictly efficiency considerations – how to do a given thing at least cost – rather than welfare considerations. In the *Standard Methodology for Determining the Economic Effectiveness of Capital Investment and New Technology in the National Economy of the USSR*, published in 1960 and the first official formulation of the CRE, it was the sole basic criterion presented, as it was in the revised 1969 version of the *Standard Methodology* (*Tipovaya Metodika. . . 1960, 1969*). Those two editions did make some vague reference to a concept of absolute effectiveness, but it was only in the subsequent 1981 edition that the coefficient of absolute effectiveness was clearly specified as the increment in national income, value added or NNO against investment (Y/K, or if you like, the incremental output–capital ratio) for the economy as a whole, branches thereof or republics; and in terms of increment in profit or cost reduction against investment for associations, enterprises etc.

The 1981 *Methodology* (*Metodika Opredeleniya. . . 1981*) laid down norms for levels of absolute effectiveness which were to operate as 'gateways' through which blocks of investment projects would have to pass. The principle on which this norm was to be set for the whole economy for each five-year period was 'not lower than the average actual ratio for the previous five-year period'. For the period 1981–5 the reported aggregate relationship for 1976–80 – 0.14 – was applied more or less unmodified. Sectoral norms for the same period varied widely – 0.16 for industry, 0.07 for agriculture, 0.05 for transport and communications, 0.22 for construction, and 0.25 for internal trade, industrial supply etc. Because it was couched in terms of average returns on tranches of investment expenditure, rather than returns on specific increments to the capital stock, this indicator could not operate as a general criterion for individual investment projects. Rather, it simply provided a check on whether the economy as a whole, a specific sector or association etc. was holding to the policy aims of the authorities in relation to the overall capital–output ratio. It did not by itself provide a guide to action in cases where a divergence from those aims was indeed diagnosed. With the benefit of hindsight we can see in it a late Brezhnevist attempt to stem the tide of rising capital–output ratios, a kind of ratchet principle in reverse, condemned to ineffectuality by the macroeconomic trends within which it was supposed to operate.

If we want to assess the role of formal investment appraisal formulae at the level of individual projects, then, we must concentrate on the CRE. Before looking at how it was actually applied in the pre-*perestroika* Soviet economy, let us examine some peculiarites in its technical specification. First, it ignores the possibility of capital expenditures occurring in more than one time period. Second, it ignores the possibility of variation in running costs over time. Third, it includes depreciation in running costs. In fact, this last peculiarity works out as an advantage in the case of projects which do have once-and-for-all capital outlays and constant operating costs, and brings the CRE more or less into correspondence with the standard Present Value test (Dyker 1983, p. 105).

Where capital expenditures occur over a number of years, and/ or where operating costs vary, the CRE may clearly be a rather inaccurate guide to efficient investment decision-making. Given the special difficulties involved in precisely specifying all the parameters of an investment project, however, we should perhaps be a little cautious in criticizing a criterion which has the great merit of simplicity. The *Methodologies* do, in any case, give a formulation which can, in principle, be used to take account of those two complications, and which again almost reduces to the Present Value criterion (Dyker 1983, pp. 106–7).

Rather more serious, from the point of view of divergence from conventional approaches, is the fact that $E$ tended to be set at sub-clearing levels. The 1981 *Methodology* predicated a norm for the whole economy during the period 1981–5 of 0.12, as against estimates of the marginal product of capital (assuming lead-times as 'normed' etc.) varying from 0.15 to 0.25 (Vaag 1965; Trapeznikov 1970; Kantorovich and Vainshtein 1967 and 1970). The range of variation in $E$ by sector was as great as 0.1–0.33 in the 1960s, and the 1981 *Methodology* narrowed this only slightly to 0.08–0.25. As we might have expected, it was heavy industry which benefited from low $E$s, with a figure as low as 0.06 reported for power in the late 1950s (Dyker 1983, pp. 107–8). Thus the Soviet planners showed systematic preference to their favourite sectors in the structure of $E$ by sector. In addition, by keeping the average level of $E$ below clearing, they ensured that rationing, i.e. essentially bureaucratic arbitrariness, would always be a necessary element in shaping the investment front.

In any case, the status of the CRE, as an element in a command planning system, remained as ambiguous through the Stalin, Khrushchev and Brezhnev periods as that of the title list. Under Stalin it simply had no official status at all. The 1960 *Standard Methodology* was not made obligatory for design organizations (Bergson 1964, p. 252), and one of the authors of the 1969 version noted at the time that

> much work remains to be done before these principles can be transformed into working instructions for each sector, ministry, department and their subordinate institutions. It is necessary to finish this work quickly, so that instructions for the different sectors can be properly confirmed this year.
>
> (Mitrofanov 1969)

No confirmation that this work was carried through satisfactorily has ever come to hand. The 1981 *Methodology* was not even vouchsafed the epithet *Standard*, and its preface emphasized its provisional status. All our qualifications about the planning role of the CRE also apply to the special criteria, methodologically similar to the CRE, which covered the import of equipment (Dyker 1983, Appendix).

Thus, while parametric elements were present in the traditional system for the elaboration of investment plans, they were certainly not predominant. CRE-based calculations, one suspects, were cited when they suited the bureaucrats, ignored when they did not suit. In order to fully understand the origin of the investment patterns which developed in the Soviet economy under Gorbachev's predecessors we must, then, study the organizational pattern of the investment scene in some detail in order to put some flesh on the notion of 'bureaucratic arbitrariness'.

### Design organizations

Towards the end of the Brezhnev era there were around 1,800 design organizations, employing about 800,000 people. Strictly backroom organizations with no powers of approval or rejection of projects, normally subordinate to Gosstroi (the State Construction Committee) or to individual ministries, design organizations played a systematic, if subsidiary, role in general investment planning. After 1971 they became involved in the elaboration of sectoral and territorial 'development and location schemes'. They have, in the case of large and important projects, also played a role in the preliminary stage of 'examination of the technico-economic feasibility of the envisaged project' (TEO). Once a client had a clear idea of what he wanted, he would present the design organization with an 'assignment for design work', and this formed the basis for initial requests by clients for funds (Dyker 1983, pp. 51–2). The first stage proper in the compilation of the 'design and financial documentation' of a project was, up to 1969, the 'design assignment', which included 'basic technical decisions aimed at securing the most efficient utilization of labour, material and financial resources, in the operation of the envisaged project and its actual construction' (Podshivalenko 1965, p. 135). By a decree of that year the name was changed to 'technical design'. A further decree of 1981 again changed the terminology, this time to the unbelievably clumsy 'design with aggregated cost of construction'. These word games were of no great importance, except in possibly confusing the student, but they did reflect a desire to make the design a more cost-conscious document (of this more on pp. 143–9), and also a more integrated document.

Traditionally, the principal success indicator used in this sector of investment planning has been 'volume of design work' – a variant of the standard gross-output success indicator, usually measured in value terms. In the 1959–65 period cost reduction figured as a major indicator in design work, as it did in industry. The 1965 planning reform made little impact on design. Profit was introduced as a success indicator without serious hitches, but the problem of finding an alternative measure of output, parallel to the introduction of the sales indicator in industry and elsewhere, proved intractable. Under the old regime tranches of volume of design work had been calculated as a simple percentage of the total work to be done, and organizations often received payment for work that was in a quite unusable state. The new idea was to base planning on 'completed stages of design work'. In practice, the degree of arbitrariness in the definition of completed stages remained such that the improvement on the old system was quite marginal (Kudashov 1983, p. 9). We see a similar pattern in relation to the financing of design work. Traditionally done through advances, this was supposed to go fully over onto a credit basis by 1980, and the 1979 planning decree predicated that in the majority of cases credit should be for complete designs, rather than stages (note that this affected financial flows, but not necessarily success indicators and bonus entitlements as such). That decree also announced the general transition of design organizations on to *khozraschet*, to be completed by 1980. That this was to be a fairly limited form of *khozraschet* was underlined by the fact that design organizations still did not have to pay the capital charge. Design organizations were supposed to share to the extent of 5 per cent in the special on-time completion/quality bonuses introduced for the construction industry in 1979 (see p. 141). As with success indicators as such, then, attempted financial reform of the design sector during the Brezhnev era did little more than tinker. The impact of attempts to get away from the crude volume of design work approach was in any case limited by the continued prevalence of piece-work as a method of payment of lower-level design workers (Dyker 1983, pp. 53–4, 57–8).

**The construction industry**

The organizational structure of the Soviet building sector has always been complex in the extreme – traditionally organized in a hierarchy of ministries, *glavki* and trusts, and divided up administratively on the basis of a rather odd mixture of sectoral, functional, and territorial specialization. There were three main 'bricks and mortar' ministries. The Ministry for Heavy Industrial Construction (Mintyazhstroi) basically covered the coal and metallurgy industries, but for historico-locational reasons did in fact do most of the basic construction work in the Ukraine and south-west Siberia. The Ministry of Industrial Construction (Minpromstroi) had a similar duality of specification, involving chemicals, oil-processing and petro-chemicals on the one hand and on the other the oil-rich regions of the Volga-Urals. The Ministry of Construction (Minstroi) concentrated on engineering, light industry, the food industry etc., and also had its 'own' territories. The subordinate organizations of these ministries were all territorially specialized. But the installation of high-technology equipment, especially imported, was the preserve of the Ministry for Installation and Special Construction Work (Minmontazhspetsstroi). This was (in theory) a crack organization, highly centralized, possessing a nation-wide network of technologically specialized *glavki* and trusts (Dyker 1983, pp. 72, 204–5), with a degree of regional specialization only at the lowest level.

A decree of 1979 laid down that the construction industry should transfer on to the association system, with the clumsily christened 'production-construction and installation association' (PCIA) as the basic unit, replacing the trust. However, this measure was never properly implemented. By 1982, the year of Brezhnev's death, PCIAs were doing just 10 per cent of total contractual construction work (Podshivalenko 1983, pp. 91, 93). A decree issued by his short-lived successor, Andropov, reaffirmed the trust as the basic operational unit ('Uluchshat' planirovanie. . .' 1984). An increasingly high percentage of total construction work (nearly 90 per cent by the Brezhnev era) has been carried out by regular 'contractual basis' organizations, subordinate either to specialist construction intermediate organs or to clients. The rest has been done on an 'in-house' basis by units, often small and *ad hoc*, invariably subordinate to client organizations.

As with design organizations, the traditional principal success indicator in the building industry has been a variant of gross output. 'Gross volume of work' is defined as the total value of work done, including unfinished work, plus the value of bought-in materials. During the period 1959–65 cost reduction had the status of major success indicator in construction, like other industries. As in design, the 1965 planning reform brought the immediate introduction of profit as a success indicator, and the beginning of a series of attempts to find an alternative measure of work completed. Pilot schemes in the late 1960s experimented with various kinds of value-added-based indicators, but in 1970 it was total marketed output (*ob"em realizuemoi produktsii*) which was nominated as the official successor to gross volume of work, though the alternative indicators survived at the purely experimental level. Two problems quickly became evident with this modifed sales indicator. First, like straight sales, it is still a gross indicator. Second, it can run into the problem of arbitrarily defined stages in the same way that design indicators can. In the middle to late 1970s more than three-quarters of total construction work was being planned on the basis of conventional stages, usually defined in terms of type of construction work, rather than integral stage of project as such.

But the Kosygin/Brezhnev reform in construction did try to create a direct incentive for timely completion by establishing operationalization (*vvod v deistvie*) as a third key success indicator. This change was backed up by an attempt in 1966 to strengthen the procedures of the State Operationalization Commission, so that it would only pass as completed new capacities capable of actually starting production. In the experimental Belorussian system, first set up in the mid-1970s in a couple of that republic's construction ministries, operationalization became the key indicator. Significantly, that experiment also sought to measure output exclusively on a completed project basis.

In construction, as in design and industry proper, changes in success indicators were to be accompanied by changes aimed at increasing sensitivity to financial parameters. Not only would operationalization of new capacity become crucial to bonus payments, it would also become the basis of payment for work done. By 1978, 60 per cent of total accounts for construction work were being settled on the basis of completed project. (Under the Belorussian system, all accounts were settled on this basis.) But serious problems arose in connection with the finance of work in progress. It was clear that the modified planning arrangements could not work properly on the basis of the old system of advances from clients, since advances were in practice indistinguishable from intermediate payments. On the other hand, exclusive use of the completed project indicator as a basis for settling accounts demands some method of calculating putative output and profit by the quarter, if only so that bonuses can be worked out and credit flows regulated. This may help to explain why, in 1979, 85 per cent of total unfinished construction was still being financed from clients' advances.

Minor innovation in the management of the construction sector was not restricted to the sphere of success indicators. There was also a trend to the extension of the *khozraschet* principle upwards and downwards from the level of the trust. The Belorussian Ministry of Industrial Construction was itself put on *khozraschet*, using the same indicators as its subordinate organizations, while the *khozraschet* brigade, commonly called the Zlobin brigade after the man who originated it, was widely introduced.

Similar to the link arrangement in agriculture, the Zlobin

brigade system gave the work-team a specific task, extending over three months or more, (with luck) the requisite supplies etc, and left it to get on with the job, subject to an upper limit on total wages and bonus payments. Contemporary reports claimed that the system improved the quality of work, shortened lead-times by up to 20 per cent, and raised productivity 20–25 per cent. But its success was limited by persistent supply problems – building workers are of course dependent on the outside world in a much more continuous way than agricultural field workers – and by the resistance of managers who found it too complex, and who were reluctant to give up their traditional prerogative to switch work-teams around, as priorities and the supply situation evolved. These problems help to explain why the system was introduced more successfully in residential than in industrial construction. It is, of course, much easier to break down the former than the latter into convenient 'building-blocks'.

None of this, then, was terribly satisfactory, and it is not surprising that the 1979 planning decree took another bite at the problem of how to plan construction. The basic principle was to be universalization of the Belorussian system, which had shown clear, if modest, results in reducing lead-times and volumes of unfinished construction. This boiled down to the following main elements:

1 Full transition to accounts by finished project or stage by 1981.
2 'Self-financing' to become a key financial principle.
3 Further extension of the Zlobin system.
4 Key success indicators to be: operationalization, marketable output (*tovarnaya produktsiya*), profit and labour productivity, measured in terms of NNO or similar indicator.

These proposals still left a number of key points unresolved. Apropos of 2, it was clear that unfinished construction would now be financed from own resources or from bank credit. It was quite unclear whether the principle of self-financing was to extend into the sphere of fixed capital on the model of the Ministry of Instrument-Making. In relation to 4, experience with the Belorussian experiment had shown that clashes could occur between the demands of the operationalization and marketable output indicators, inasmuch as the latter implies saleability, but not necessarily sale, thus once again representing only a very marginal modification of the gross volume of work indicator. A 1980 ruling stipulated that output could only be counted as marketable once the capacities involved were actually in operation (Podshivalenko and Evstigneev 1980, p. 49). This would effectively have turned the marketable output indicator into an alternative (quantitative) expression of the operationalization indicator. But at the end of the Brezhnev era the problem remained unsolved, with marketable output being, in practice, counted on the basis of State Operationalization Commission certificates as issued, before actual confirmation. This could mean a divergence of up to one year's work between reported marketable output and operationalization (Podshivalenko 1983, p. 91).

A Gosstroi decree of early 1980 defined the concept of normed conventional-net output (*normativnaya uslovno-chistaya produktsiya*) as basically the normed wage bill, plus the sectoral average rate of planned accumulation taken as a percentage of the normed wage bill – clearly an alternative to NNO which could be used with planned loss-making enterprises. (As many as 25 per cent of construction organizations were loss-makers in 1983 – Podshivalenko 1983, p. 92.) It was this variant which was largely used in attempts to refine the measurement of labour productivity in construction, though without great success. The trouble with normed conventional-net output is that because it ultimately depends in both parts on the normed wages fund, it creates an incentive to overbid for normed wages fund in order to make it easy to turn out a given volume of marketable output with less than normed wage expenditure, thus recording higher normed than actual net output. As we saw, NNO creates an incentive to execute a given volume of work with less than normed labour inputs, but the fact that the other element in the formula – normed profit – is completely independent serves as a constraint on overbidding for normed wages fund. For with given prices a higher normed wage bill should, *ceteris paribus*, mean a lower normed level of profit, leaving NNO coefficients unchanged, but incentive funds, production development funds etc. reduced in size. Even if normed levels of profit are not adjusted, the value of any 'fat' on the normed wages fund will only get through to the NNO coefficients on a reduced basis. The absence of safeguards against overbidding of this kind with the normed conventional-net output indicator meant that it could produce substantially exaggerated reported figures for labour productivity growth. In addition, contemporary sources pointed out that normed conventional-net output did not actually introduce a positive incentive to economy on materials, though it obviated the incentive under the traditional system to use materials amply. Thus on general productivity grounds the experimental indicator obtained very low marks indeed (Kudashov 1983, pp. 8–11). The whole saga of normed conventional-net output does, indeed, stand as a monument to the heights of ineffectual fussiness which the reform efforts of the late Brezhnev period could reach.

It is not at all clear that there was ever any systematic implementation of the 1979 measures. As the Brezhnev era drew to a close, construction specialists were still speaking of the 'cult of the gross' as a central problem in the industry. Success indicators apart, the basic system of remuneration in building remained heavily output-oriented, with about 85 per cent of workers on piece-rate systems of one kind or another. A special decree of 1979 did establish specific bonus coefficients relating to on-time completion and quality, but incentive-fund arrangements remained generally emphatically quantity-based (Dyker 1983, pp. 81–3). The investment decree of 1984 returned to the fray, but without coming up with any substantial, clear-cut proposals for the reorganization of construction ('Uluchshat' planirovanie. . .' 1984).

## The Investment Bank and the Construction Committee

It is a striking fact, against the background of the burden of short-term planning which made it impossible for Gosplan to pay proper attention to the medium and long term, that no specialist investment planning bodies existed during the Stalin period. Gosstroi USSR (State Committee of the USSR Council of Ministers for Construction Affairs) was created on 9 May 1950. Stroibank (Investment or Construction bank) was created on 7 April 1959, taking over the competences of a number of specialized banks, including the Agricultural and Industrial banks. Thus the final stages of extensive growth were marked by attempts at concentration in the field of investment planning and finance (Dyker 1983, pp. 48–50, 69–71, 96–8).

Within the structure of the Gosstroi system, organs of *ekspertiza* (design monitoring organizations) were empowered to reject proposals outright on general efficiency grounds. But this did not happen very often, and when it did happen the determined ministerial administrator was often more than a match for his colleague in *ekspertiza*. When, for example, Glavgosekspertiza (Main State *Ekspertiza*) threw out the design for a building materials factory in the late 1970s on the grounds that two existing factories of the same type had shown disappointing results, the ministry simply changed tack and submitted designs for two similar factories in different areas. The lowest level of *ekspertiza* organ was, in fact, actually subordinate to the ministry rather than to Gosstroi, so that very little could be expected of it on the strategic decision-making dimension. On the more detailed level *ekspertiza* organs were charged with seeing that standard designs and financial norms were observed, and that costs were kept down and proper measures taken to raise effectiveness. Designs were sometimes thrown out at this stage on grounds of technical obsolescence, and *ekspertiza* often managed to get estimates down a little. But here again the effectiveness of the monitoring organs was fairly low. It is clear that *ekspertiza* had neither the resources nor the clout to make any substantial difference to the overall level of investment effectiveness.

The picture is similar in relation to another member of the Gosstroi family, the State Operationalization Commission. As noted earlier, the Comission had, prior to 1966, so very formal a remit that it had little chance to be effective. Subsequently a consistent effort was made to give more strength to its elbow, but without a great deal of success. Complaints about its ineffectuality were still common in the Brezhnev era, and one *cause célèbre* reported in *Pravda* in 1980 concerned the signing of an operationalization certificate for a factory that did not exist. Such ludicrous extremes reflected a number of powerful factors tending to neutralize the *raison d'être* of the Commission. First, although individual commissions were ultimately responsible to Gosstroi, they tended to be dominated in practice by local and departmental interests, certainly in relation to run-of-the-mill projects. Second, the traditional orientation of the whole system towards short-term output maximization meant that there was always pressure to pass a project, so that it could start producing something. Last, formal operationalization meant a reduction in officially reported unfinished construction, that was, of course, pure virtue.

Gosstroi USSR itself has always been much concerned with legislation, promulgating building regulations, revising norms etc., and has continually tended to get behind with this work. That may provide the key to an understanding of the comparative ineffectuality of the whole Gosstroi system in relation to investment effectiveness. As with Gosplan, the burden of routine work seems to have made the maintenance of any kind of longer-term perspective impossible.

Stroibank shared with *ekspertiza* the right to veto dubious projects, and this right was exercised systematically. In addition, the bank had the power to withhold finance to projects not furnished with the requisite design and financial documentation. Cost-paring work by Stroibank produced economies of over 20 per cent in some cases during the 1970s, though on average economies achieved came to just about 1 per cent of total estimated value during that decade. The bank was frequently criticized for concerning itself rather less with the quality aspects of design work. Construction organizations were obliged to submit to Stroibank annual intra-project title lists (*vnutripostroechnyi titul'nyi spisok*), which permitted monitoring of costs and gestation periods, and formed the basis for planning the amount of short-term credit needed to finance unfinished construction. It was not uncommon for projects to be excluded from intra-project title lists because of inadequate financial cover. As with designs, the impression is that Stroibank was a more effective monitor of construction work in relation to costs than quality factors, without ever looking anything like strong enough to reverse the upward trends in investment costs which strengthened throughout the Brezhnev period. Overall, Stroibank seems to have been a somewhat more muscular inspection organization than Gosstroi, though it has been suggested that this may reflect bias in the sources (Green 1984).

In 1982, the year of Brezhnev's death, it was decided to create a 'Unified Investment Planning System', ESPKS, based on an integrated information base containing design characteristics and parameters of all projects. The system was designed to help Gosplan itself, Gosstroi, and Stroibank to shift the emphasis in their work away from *ex-post* criticism to *ex-ante* planning and continuous monitoring (Bulgakov 1983). This represented at once an admission of the essential marginality of the existing structure of investment planning and inspection bodies, and a monument – one of the last – to the dream of 'perfect computation'.

## 'THE MORE COSTLY, THE BETTER'

There is a very special paradox attached to the development of planning instruments in the design and construction sectors. Because of the unique character of many investment projects it was in practice very difficult to value design and construction work except in terms of the actual costs involved. Thus crude output maximization could easily turn into crude cost maximization. But because of the scale and lead-times of projects, it proved equally difficult to evolve any kind of operational sales-type indicator parallel to that introduced in industry in the 1960s. Thus the area of the Soviet economy which most badly needed to get altogether away from the cult of the gross was the one which remained most at its mercy, just at the time when trends to capital productivity were such as to place a very high premium indeed on improved cost-effectiveness in the investment sphere. Against the background of our assessment of Gosstroi and Stroibank, we can perceive a special lacuna in this crucial area of the Soviet economic system. Can we, indeed, really talk about Soviet investment *planning* at all? Recalling the points made about ministerial overbidding for investment resources in Chapter 1, we can now start to build up a more complete picture of the kinds of perennial problems that have affected the Soviet investment scene.

Let us begin by going back to *raspylenie sredstv* – excessive investment spread. However substantial the element of pure overbidding, design and construction organizations have undoubtedly made an independent contribution to this problem. Delays in the delivery of technical documentation have presented chronic difficulties. Hold-ups in deliveries affected 1,293 projects, with a total estimated value of 58 billion roubles (nearly half the value of annual investment) in 1979. It has been quite common for projects scheduled for operationalization during the given year to be without working drawings, and design organizations were blamed for 20 per cent of cases of failure to meet planned completion dates in the 1970s. The tradition of centralization left a powerful imprint on the design sector, leaving it at once the victim and the instrument of 'petty tutelage'. In the late 1960s only 20–35 per cent of the working time of design organizations was taken up by work on the actual designs, though the figure does seem to have improved to 40–60 per cent by the mid to late 1970s. The rest of the time went on the process of getting approval for designs from various organs. Now of course the existence of the success-indicator problem did make some degree of scrutiny over design organizations imperative – the command principle always tends to beget centralization. But top-heavy 'multi-level' checking by other subordinate organizations, each with its own axe to grind, was always likely to have a greater impact in terms of increasing design work-loads than on the quality of designs.

Perhaps even more overwhelming has been the tradition of an extraordinary degree of detail in the designs themselves. Of course, under the given planning system, building organizations could not be trusted to sort out the more economic details of designs, but by the Brezhnev era most of them were well enough equipped with engineers to permit some devolution of purely technical decision-taking; yet the design for the Lipetsk metallurgical factory, for example, filled 91 volumes and 70,000 pages, and that of the Baranovichi automatic production line factory 220 volumes. Sheer clumsiness in the way forms had to be filled in compounded both kinds of petty tutelage. In addition, design organizations were obliged to drop work on a given project when its planned time ran out, and go on to the next project. If we put all this bureaucratic maladroitness together with the success-indicator-induced incentive to maximize the volume of design documentation, we have most of the elements for an understanding of the causes of chronic lateness in the delivery of documentation.

Yet there were other factors, less specifically internal to the design organizations themselves. The structure of the design sector has always been excessively complex, and it was the rule, rather than the exception, for design work on big projects to be shared among a large number of organizations, commonly as many as 50 to 70. Despite the multitude of different organizations, rational specialization has often been lacking. For instance, no large-scale specialized organizations serving construction in internal trade and catering were developed during the Brezhnev era, despite the purported shift in priority towards the consumer. From the point of view of scale and specialization, then, it was difficult for design organizations to fulfil their 'production' potential. Could not even a conservative leadership have effected a substantial improvement here? In practice no, because so many design organizations were departmental, and atomization in design was to a considerable extent a function of the powerful tendencies to organizational autarky which we pin-pointed in Chapter 1 as a major obstacle to the intensification of the Soviet economy. 'Dwarf design organizations, duplicating the work of existing units, continue to sprout in our town. . . . It would appear that this happens because of some deep-seated tendency to departmentalism. So the organization's small, well at least it's mine!' (Kirillov 1975).

Table 6.2  Cost escalations on selected projects, early 1970s (million roubles)

|  | Estimated costs | |
| --- | --- | --- |
|  | Envisaged for 1973 in the five-year plan | Confirmed by the annual plan for 1973 |
| Ust'-Ilim hydro-electric station | 690.3 | 1,025.0 |
| Oil pipeline Ust'-Balyk to Kurgan to Ufa to Al'metevsk | 520.0 | 649.9 |
| Oil pipeline Kuibyshev to Tikhoretskaya | 143.5 | 267.0 |
| Abakan rolling-stock factory | 293.0 | 500.9 |
| Tuvaasbest combine | 43.2 | 91.9 |
| Rybina printing equipment factory | 25.5 | 44.2 |
| Kostroma cylinder and piston factory | 52.9 | 236.4 |

Source: Isaev 1973, p. 33.

Backwardness in design techniques was a further factor slowing down work tempos. This was no doubt partly conditioned by quantitative success indicators, but was exacerbated by the politically conditioned reluctance of the Soviet government to permit wide distribution of photocopying equipment. Lastly, design organizations did a great deal of work on projects that had not been finally approved – between 1962 and 1966 design work on above-limit projects valued at 12 billion roubles was left unused (the annual value of total investment was at that time around 50 billion roubles). This was clearly related to ministerial overbidding for investment resources: 'for many clients the design has become simply a document on the basis of which resources for construction can be obtained' (Kudryadtsev et al. 1968, p. 51). As well as further increasing the burden of work on the design sector, that kind of bureaucratic politics also bred deep contempt for the whole investment planning process, delivery dates included, amongst design workers content to plod on and earn their bonuses for val (Dyker 1983, pp. 59–63).

We saw in Chapter 1 that delays in the investment cycle make it difficult to keep a close rein on capital costs. Table 6.2 illustrates just how serious the problem of cost-hikes on big projects was during the early 1970s. Over the Brezhnev period as a whole, the average degree of escalation was 30–40 per cent (Dyker 1983, p. 63;

Kuz'mich, 1983, p. 55). Note that these figures cover only cost-hikes that were eventually absorbed into the official estimates; some escalations occurring at the construction site level may never have been so absorbed. The notoriously inflationary trend of Soviet machinery prices, particularly with regard to special pieces of equipment not covered in the standard price lists, was certainly a factor in cost-hikes, both directly and as a basis on which design organizations could cover up other forms of escalation. A survey covering the period 1971–5 blamed design errors and increases in machinery prices, taken together, for almost a quarter of capital cost escalations (Dyker 1983, pp. 63–4). Given that the success-indicator regime presented design organizations with few inducements to cost sensitivity, this is perhaps not a surprising figure. In fact, however, cost-hike elements apparently directly related to the work of design organizations may on closer examination turn out once again to have been rather a reflection of economy-wide tendencies.

'To get construction started at any cost, and that means having to prove that the given project is economically highly attractive – that is in many cases the unspoken behest to the design worker' (Perepechin and Apraksina 1980). Ministries often put extreme pressure on design organizations to understate estimated capital costs, just so that a given project could be squeezed into the below-limit category. When Promstroiproekt (a general industrial design organization), for example, estimated the cost of the production block of Sibgipromez (a specialist ferrous metallurgy design organization) in Kemerevo at 5.2 million roubles, the Ministry of Ferrous Metallurgy simply cut this to 2.5 million roubles – the then limit – on confirmation. In the end the project cost 5.8 million roubles (Shavlyuk 1979). This helps us to understand how intermediate planning bodies were able to pursue their organizational-autarkical aims with such persistence. It is hardly fair, however, to place the 'blame' on the shoulders of the design workers.

What about straightforward mistakes in design? There can be no doubt that the quantitatively oriented planning regime tended to create a blasé attitude to errors amongst design workers. The fact that the estimated cost of the phenol-acetone and nitric acid divisions of the Saratov chemical combine rose by 10.5 million roubles is clearly not unconnected with the 1,700 changes and corrections that had to be made to the design (Vovchenko 1965,

p. 25). Again, however, we have to be very careful about imputing blame. Kudashov, for instance, portrays 'corrections' in designs presented by construction organizations as basically a ploy by the latter to fuel their own quest for *val*.

> Here also, 'the dearer the better'. In any case, the last word . . . in the end always lies with the builder. And sometimes when it comes to the last word the designer may lose his voice altogether: construction organizations have created a powerful barrier on the road to reductions in estimates consisting of estimate-contractual and technical services whose role in the agreement of designs comes down in practical terms to a search for anything that will make construction more expensive.
>
> (Kudashov 1983, p. 89).

We can confirm that the construction stage has been an independent source of inflationary pressure by looking at figures on material expenditures and wage costs. A survey of 1,587 construction organizations undertaken in 1960 by Stroibank revealed excessive utilization of basic materials, in relation to norms, averaging 20 per cent. Evidence from the 1970s suggests no substantial improvement in the position. In the Brezhnev period workers were sometimes paid anything up to quadruple time for doing illegal overtime on their official day off, and *shabashniki* – 'lump' workers – were making 2–4 times the 'normal' wage in western Siberia (Dyker 1983, pp. 85–6). Unit wage costs in relation to output in eastern Siberia rose 10–20 per cent in a number of key construction organizations during 1975–82 (Bezdelev 1983). Given that there must have been some capital-deepening in the organizations concerned over that period, and in the absence of any major adjustment of the general level of construction wage rates, a very considerable element of pure inflation must have been present here.

Under the traditional system, wages fund planning, if we can call it that, was based on a particularly crude application of the ratchet principle, with the annual fund being based on the previous year's actual wage expenditure, even if that had been above plan ('Zarabotnaya plata. . .' 1968). From 1983 the wages fund was supposed to be planned on the basis of norms relating to planned volumes of work. The trouble with that idea is that different types of work vary in labour-intensity and therefore require different wage–output norms. As long as construction output indicators remained essentially crude and unreformed, the scope for fiddling the planned wages fund by fiddling the 'assortment' of planned construction work remained unlimited (Bezdelev 1983). At a more specific level, the system of tariffs which was supposed to keep piece-rate earnings more or less in line with a putative normal wage for each grade of worker did not work properly. In 1979 the 'tariff' accounted for only 50–60 per cent of total earnings. This was apparently closely related to fiddling on the estimated wage costs of auxiliary work (Komarov 1979). Lastly, bonus funds and regional supplement moneys were often abused (Dyker 1983, p. 85).

What were the roots of this building-site inflation? Obviously, the success-indicator system did not encourage economizing attitudes. More specifically, storming patterns induced by the tyranny of short-term output plans impelled managers to take a cavalier attitude to costs. As we saw earlier, an average of nearly 50 per cent of housing completions was concentrated in the last quarter of the year over the period 1953–73. But in the last quarter labour productivity has normally fallen to just 65–70 per cent of its normal level (Dyker 1983, pp. 94–5). This has reflected the taking on of large numbers of additional workers, often of low calibre, but presumably at very good effective wage rates. Of course the intensity of storming patterns is conditioned as much by the milieu in which construction organizations have operated as by their own planning regime, and much the same could be said of many of the other operational problems which manifest themselves at the actual construction stage. It is to that milieu that we now turn.

## THE CONSTRUCTION INDUSTRY AND THE PATTERN OF THE TRADITIONAL SOVIET PLANNING SYSTEM

We have seen that supply uncertainty has been an endemic characteristic of the over-centralized Soviet planning system. But supply uncertainty has affected construction so acutely that it merits specific treatment in the present context. To put the problem into general perspective: according to the Deputy Minister of Minstroi USSR the 1979 plan for deliveries to the ministry was

*Table 6.3* Percentage fulfilment of plans for construction of enterprises producing non-metallic building materials

|  | 1976 | 1977 | 1978 |
|---|---|---|---|
| Ministry of Heavy Industrial Construction | 22.8 | 46.2 | 73.9 |
| Ministry of Industrial Construction | 92.0 | 83.0 | 99.2 |
| Ministry of Construction | 84.2 | 69.3 | 67.8 |
| Ministry of Transport Construction | 57.2 | 89.6 | 84.2 |

*Source:* Lifatov 1980, p. 21.

150 million roubles short of requirements. Taking into account the fact that not all planned deliveries arrive, the total gap was 200 million roubles, representing 4 per cent of the requirements of the annual plan. We must add considerably to this to take account of poor quality and misdirected deliveries, so that the overall picture of supply uncertainty in this particular case is very stark indeed.

Turning to more specific supplies, it has been remarked that building enterprises, despite the old proverb 'Do not cut off the branch you are sitting on', seem to have been particularly bad at building factories for the building materials industry. The point is graphically underlined by the figures in Table 6.3. In consequence, non-metal construction materials have often been in outright deficit. Some areas have been served better than others, and the network of establishments run by the Ministry for Building Materials itself has always been territorially extremely unevenly distributed. The ministry has had virtually nothing in north-western Siberia, the north-east, and some north-western provinces of the RSFSR. Nevertheless there were 35,000 construction materials establishments in the Soviet Union in the late 1970s, and one might be tempted to cite excessively small scale as a cause of supply difficulties. The direction of causation did, in fact, tend to be in the oppositive direction, with organizations building up their own 'dwarf-workshops' as a hedge against supply uncertainty. The officially reported number of building materials associations and independent enterprises in 1979 was just 3,864.

The situation with regard to steel deliveries and the supply of construction equipment has been similarly unsatisfactory. Even paint brushes have been a major problem. Lastly, poor coordination of the delivery schedules of equipment for installation has often caused both delays in completion and accumulations of uninstalled equipment. Most obviously, supply uncertainty of these various types could only exacerbate the problem of excessive lead-times, generally lowering the quality of work, especially finishing work, and thus fortifying a tendency already present for success-indicator reasons. But evidence from the late Brezhnev era showed that it also intensified the cost problem. Poor quality and specification in supplies of gravel and sand resulted in a rate of above-normal utilization of cement reaching 20 per cent. Additional labour expenditures on fitting of up to 70 per cent were required in construction administration No. 28, a subdivision of the Mosstroi-6 trust, in order to excise defects in ceiling slabs. Excessively early deliveries of equipment have an obvious cost in terms of the implicit rate of interest, but in the absence of adequate storage facilities the costs could be much greater. In some cases veritable scrap-heaps of valuable equipment have accumulated on sites (Dyker 1983, pp. 88–91).

Organizations endeavouring to safeguard their supplies through building up an autarkical position would naturally be concerned to acquire direct control over the purveyance of building services, and there can be no doubt that the production potential of the Soviet construction industry has been stunted by organizational fragmentation, just as has that of design organizations. The Institute of Construction Economics has estimated that the optimal size for primary building organizations corresponds to an annual value of work greater than 1.5 million roubles, and on this basis over 60 per cent of such organizations were of suboptimal size in 1960 during the *sovnarkhoz* period. The situation had, however, been worse under the old ministerial system, and it rapidly deteriorated when that system was reinstated in 1965. Material from the early 1980s suggests that the labour productivity lead of large, integrated construction associations over specialized (frequently departmental), may be of the order of 100 per cent (Dyker 1983, p. 92). All this helps us to understand the paradox of a top-priority activity like investment apparently moving forward on something of a shoe-string at the level of the actual building site. It is because bureaucrats have perceived the necessity of overbidding in the scramble for investment votes that supply to the building site has been such a problem. It is in turn because construction capacity has been seen as something too important to leave to the construction ministries that it has been prevented from developing on a concerted national pattern. Much the same thing can be said about the design sector.

If we place these factors side by side with the pressures of gross-output-based success indicators, we can hardly be surprised at the persistence of quality problems in Soviet construction, and in particular of perennial underachievement in relation to technology. The technology of construction management remained backward, with basic elements like critical path analysis not fully assimilated, and even the level of basic bricks-and-mortar technology left a lot to be desired – prefabricated blocks, for example, were still not in general use at the end of the Brezhnev period (Dyker 1983, pp. 86–7). But it is the quality and technological level of the finished investment project that really matters in this connection, and in turning our attention to that variable we implicitly pose a wider question: long lead-times and cost-hikes apart, just how suboptimal has the ultimate return to the Soviet economy from its investment effort been?

## INVESTMENT PLANNING AND INVESTMENT PAY-OFFS – THE PRE-*PERESTROIKA* RECORD

A *Pravda* editorial from 1974 noted that seven blast furnaces commissioned in 1973, plus the converter plants of the Karaganda, western Siberian and Chelyabinsk steelworks, did not have automatic control systems, and censured designers for this. A report from 1978 blamed conservatism on the part of design organizations in relation to new materials for excess capacity in new, advanced construction materials factories (Dyker 1983, p. 57). This is rather unfair, since regulations prevailing at the time in some cases forbade designers to use light construction materials, once again confirming that we are talking about a whole complex of planning problems rather than just the sins of particular organizations. Specific defects in commissioned projects could often be laid more directly at the door of building organizations. Because finishing work produced less gross output than earlier stages, it tended to be systematically neglected. Reports from the 1970s demonstrated that the reforms of the 1960s had done nothing to alleviate the problem. Thus in Azerbaidzhan 'completed' schools were left without running water or window glass, with unpainted walls and unfinished classrooms. New houses in Lithuania lacked proper insulation, and the removal of a light switch could leave a hole right through to the next house. Gas pipeline builders in the Komi autonomous republic, located in north European Russia, neglected construction of compressor stations in favour of maximizing the length of actual pipe laid, as the easiest way to fulfil output targets (in this case unofficial output targets set at the ministerial level). Pipeline capacity in the absence of compression is only 30–35 per cent what it should be (Dyker 1983, p. 84).

Yet there is an aspect to the question of pay-offs that is more fundamental than anything thrown up by these quaint success-indicator anecdotes. We saw in the first section of this chapter that formal Soviet investment appraisal criteria cannot provide the planners with a unique array of desirable investment starts, even if they are used consistently. We observed in earlier chapters that to the extent that ministries and enterprises etc. have had control over project choice they have tended to go for projects that would safeguard their own supply position, rather than those that would come out on top on the Present Value or any other general criterion. Just how often have the Russians put the wrong factory in the wrong place? We cannot hope to answer this question conclusively, but the attempt is worthwhile because it helps us to see how micro-economic issues tie in with some of the great developmental issues we broached earlier on.

There is an official list of Soviet 'principles of location of productive forces'. It runs as follows:

1 Location of enterprises as near as possible to raw material sources and centres of consumption.
2 Even distribution of economic activity throughout the country.
3 Rational division of labour between economic regions, and complex development of the economy of each region.
4 Raising of the economic and cultural level of all backward national areas to that of the most advanced.
5 Elimination of the distinction between town and country.
6 Strengthening of the defence capacity of the country.
7 International division of labour within the socialist bloc.

If we allow for a certain awkwardness of presentation, there is little here that would raise the eyebrows of a left-of-centre spatial planner in the west. Locational decisions should be made with due account taken of optimal transport patterns and regional natural advantages. At the same time matters of social justice and ethnic peace should quite properly be taken into consideration. Principles

2 and 5 go rather beyond that, but they were in fact quietly dropped by Soviet writers on location during the Brezhnev period (Dyker 1983, pp. 114–17). We would not, then, expect anything very abnormal in the way of spatial decisions to come out of the observance of the official locational principles. Once again, if we want to get to the nub of the matter, we have to look at the organizational picture.

As we saw earlier, there have traditionally been two stages in the process of feasibility study in the Soviet Union. The 'development and location scheme', worked out for sectors and regions, would aim to present an overall picture of likely directions of medium- and long-term development. Within this context, feasibility studies proper (TEOs) would then be elaborated for major individual projected investment starts. In practice this system has been extremely weak.

> The quality of schemes still does not meet contemporary requirements. In many of them the 'point of departure' is not properly assessed, and the latest achievements of science and technology and other factors are not taken into consideration. . . . Multiple variants in terms of location and output levels, taking intersectoral links into account, are rare.
>
> (Shiryaev 1977, p. 29)

The problem of inadequate TEOs was one of the main themes of the colloquium on design work held in Moscow in May 1974, and new regulations greatly increasing the stress on feasibility studies swiftly followed the recommendations of that colloquium. These new regulations proved, however, to be ineffectual, and the 1981 design decree returned to the problem. This time the approach was to abolish the TEO as such, and integrate its content back into an upgraded system of schemes (Dyker 1983, pp. 51–2, 67). That represented a commendable recognition of the interdependence of investment decisions, indeed an embodiment of locational principle 3, but the 1984 investment decree re-established the separate TEO. What was it that made feasibility studies such a difficult area?

First, they were entrusted to design organizations or ministries. The latter, as we shall elaborate, were very far from placing top priority on locational niceties. Ministerial penchants may also have been guilty in a less direct way. To the extent that it was departmentalism that created the 'atomization without specialization' pattern which has characterized the general structure of the

design organization system: (a) an appropriate specialized organization might simply not exist in the case of a given project, and
this would affect fundamental decisions more than it would the
detailed working out of drawings etc.; (b) a very large number of
organizations might be working on the same project, which would
make it extremely difficult for any one of them to cope adequately
with general strategic questions, and indeed might leave it unclear
who was responsible in this area. 'Thematic plans are confirmed
late and often changed. Ministries chop and change the allocation
of design projects, which makes stability in plans difficult'
(Fedorenko and Yandovskii 1976, p. 37). Equally important has
been the tendency for early-stage work to be undervalued in terms
of estimates of the total cost of a design, thus making it 'less
advantageous'.

> In some sectors of industry, and also with some large-scale
> construction projects, limits [i.e. on maximum expenditures] for
> the compilation of technico-economic feasibility studies for
> development and location are for unknown reasons very much
> on the low side, which is often one of the reasons why design
> work and construction of projects is carried on without adequate
> economic foundation.
>
> (Khikmatov 1969, p. 86)

Paralleling this, there has been no special financial provision for
clients to pay for the elaboration of feasibility studies (Mironov
1983).

The big problem with the 1981 provisions was, of course, that
they actually increased the role of the ministries in this whole area
by increasing the status of the sectoral development and location
scheme. The ministries, however, remained more interested in
fiddling estimates, to get projects in as below-limit and to cover up
cost-hikes, than in proper examination of locational issues
(Kuz'mich 1983). Inevitably, perhaps, the 1984 resuscitation of the
TEOs was left to the ministries to organize. Ministries, indeed,
seem to have had so much effective power over the investment
process, and so many good departmental reasons for doing 'bad'
things, that we may wonder, as Khrushchev wondered as early as
1957, whether the whole system of administered investment in the
Soviet Union has not been rather disastrous from the point of view

of effectiveness. In Chapter 1 we argued, on an essentially macroeconomic basis, that ministerial overbidding for investment resources and organizational autarky have to be seen as integral elements of the strategy of using fixed capital investment as a key instrument of resource mobilization. Thus the functional defensibility of the former very much depends, in the first instance, on our assessment of the latter and of its relevance to a particular period of Soviet economic development. Now we must expand on the mesoeconomic and microeconomic levels, and try to assess the impact of organizational patterns on regional development, and on individual projects.

Apart from inducing an 'abnormal' degree of labour-intensity, the main problem with the tendency to organizational autarky is that it distorts locational patterns, and may result in grossly excessive transport hauls.

> The ministries see the Irtysh steppe as just a site for enterprises. Having built the factories, they usually start to supply them from afar with 'their own' raw materials, though these are produced in adequate quantities in Pavlodar [local big town] – but by other ministries.
>
> (Poltoranin and Sevest'yanov 1977)

Transport organizations, still heavily oriented to gross-output-type success indicators, have had no incentive to minimize hauls, and in any case transport capacity is one of the things that ministries have tended to 'collect'. An inspection in 1976 of nine provinces in the RSFSR, for example, revealed that over the previous two years departmental lorry parks had grown by a total of 470,000, while those of specialist transport organizations had grown by only 62,000 despite the fact that costs in the former were 1.2 to 2.3 times what they were in the latter (Sergienkov 1976). Under the *sovnarkhoz* system the tendency to excessive toing and froing was halted, but localistic penchants produced, by contrast, a powerful tendency to 'duplicating capacities'. In central Asia, for example, each of the four republics, to which the *sovnarkhozy* had been made co-extensive, built their own cable and general metal goods factories in the early *sovnarkhoz* period. (Subsequently a single central Asian *sovnarkhoz* was created, precisely to counteract these tendencies) (Dyker 1983, p. 40). Thus, under the regional economic councils less fuel was wasted on cross-hauls but more potential economies of scale were passed over.

We should note, however, that intermediate-level organizational autarky does lead to sacrifice of economies of scale under the ministerial system as well. Because ministries have had to operate mainly within the framework of the existing pattern of enterprises, because their effective independence has been largely restricted to real or bogus reconstruction of existing plants, they have not been in a position to fully 'rationalize' their autarkical preferences. Engineering Ministry X might well prefer to supply all its Moscow main-activity factories with components from a single components factory under its jurisdiction, and located in Moscow itself. Unless, however, it has been lucky enough to inherit such a plant, it will have had to look further afield for capacities 'suitable' for ancillary production lines. The outlying regions of the Soviet Union have always had their frameworks of small engineering plants, often originally built up with local needs (especially maintenance needs) in mind. Notoriously, the ministries have tended to distort these local complexes away from their original purpose, and to press them into service as components shops for national production complexes. This pattern can be seen very clearly in, for example, the case of the engineering industry in Tadzhikistan, the most peripheral of the central Asian republics (Dyker 1983, pp. 150–7). The conclusion is inescapable that it is the peculiar half-way house of traditional Soviet investment planning – neither properly centralized nor properly decentralized – that has made organizational autarky such a wasteful phenomenon. We are talking here about the way things are and always have been rather than any movement towards change. Nevertheless there is striking confirmation here of the general principle that comes through time and time again in our discussion of successive attempts at systemic reform in the Soviet economy – namely, that attempts to mix specific bits of centralization and decentralization against the background of a generally high degree of centralization (which is what ultimately conditions organizational autarky) are bad news.

So much for internal economies of scale. When we come to consider external economies of scale, economies which accrue as the build-up of agglomerations reduces transport costs and makes for a secular upward trend in labour productivity among regional labour forces, the case is little different. The ministerial penchant for long cross-hauls has certainly prejudiced the interests of complex development, and ministries have been markedly unwilling to push investment into labour-surplus rural areas and small towns where it might be presumed that productivity prospects would be long-term rather than medium-term. In the case of central Asia, where, with birth rates still very high, rural labour surpluses have remained much more significant than in other parts of the Soviet Union, they were accused of taking the attitude that 'Uzbekistan [is] ... reducible to a single point – Tashkent' (Zakirov 1965, p. 67). The Gas and Oil Ministries were likewise pilloried for failing to develop infrastructure and build up a stable local labour force in western Siberia (Dyker 1983, pp. 157–74). But at the level of regional development the authorities have in many cases been able to mobilize a sufficient counterweight to departmentalist tendencies. The record in Siberia is patchy, with the integrated development of the Urals–Kuzbass combine contrasting with a west Siberian experience which has shown Gosplan in a rather weak and helpless light. In eastern Siberia giant hydroelectric stations completed in the 1960s and 1970s permitted the development of an integrated power-intensive industrial complex, though departmentalism was partly to blame for substantial excess capacity in early years (Dyker 1983, pp. 119–33). In central Asia one can draw a sharp contrast between the messiness of location patterns at the plant-by-plant level, especially in engineering, and the considerable successes recorded at the level of the region as a whole. Starting from a situation c. 1930 characterized by an almost complete absence of industry but the existence of a fairly developed cotton cash-crop agriculture, the Soviet authorities demonstrated the strength of their *sui generis* capital-ample approach with substantial and sustained capital transfers into the region, invested mainly in agriculture, irrigation, education and agriculture-related light industry. Industrial labour productivity in central Asia as a whole remained well below the national average, while the combination of high rates of natural increase and sustained mechanization in agriculture has produced a growing problem of open rural unemployment, especially among the young. But from the standpoint of 1980, Moscow must gain fairly high marks in the central Asian case for maintaining a balance of specialization and regional self-sufficiency, at least at the intersector level, sometimes in the face of some opposition from departmental and local interests. As the ecological cost of that specialization (see Chapter 5) became subsequently increasingly apparent, so the overall balance sheet of Soviet central Asian development came, it must be said, to look increasingly negative.

The power of centralized command has been demonstrated not only in the positive form of providing impetus for complex development in pioneer areas. However much we may suspect that the central Soviet authorities themselves may have indulged in particular kinds of 'investment good fetishism', they were in the pre-*perestroika* period fairly successful in preventing local political establishments from doing the same. There were exceptions, and the giant Nurek hydro-electric station, built to a capacity of 2.7 million kilowatts in mountain-bound Tadzhikistan with no clear idea at the time of who was going to use the electricity, is an outstanding one (Dyker 1983, pp. 140–50). But that scheme had been pushed through during the *sovnarkhoz* period, when the regionalization of industrial administration undoubtedly increased the political leverage of local political cadres. What we can say with confidence is that state investment in the Soviet Union has not in the past been systematically distorted by local pressures for prestige projects, job-creation etc.

Finally in this section, we must say a word about production externalities. Predictably, ministries and enterprises have a bad record on pollution, and the Caspian Sea and Lake Baikal had already been seriously damaged by industrial excesses by the 1970s. Because a proper transfer price for land has never been charged in the Soviet Union, a whole category of costs which are mainly internalized in western market economies are externalized in the Soviet Union. For instance, the construction of a mid-Yenisei hydro-electric station at Abalakovo, eastern Siberia, controversial but heavily promoted by the Energy Ministry in the late 1970s, would have submerged large volumes of high-quality timber and a considerable amount of valuable agricultural land (including market garden areas) at virtually no cost to the Ministry. Some progress was made during the Brezhnev period towards closer central control in relation to this problem (the mid-Yenisei project was in fact scrapped a couple of years after Brezhnev's death), but the continued failure of the Soviet authorities to introduce a generalized framework of rental payments, for land or exhaustible resources never mind other less concrete gifts of nature, remained a major obstacle to the development of any kind of system of automatic penalizing of polluters. Of course with the big industrial ministries dominating the premium sites in the cities, the immediate effect of the introduction of systematic rents would have been to make a terrible

*Table 6.4* Soviet incremental capital–output ratios (ICORs), 1966–83

| Years | ICORs | Years | ICORs |
|-------|-------|-------|-------|
| 1966–70 | 3.5 | 1979 | 13.3 |
| 1971–5 | 5.2 | 1980 | 7.4 |
| 1976 | 5.0 | 1981 | 8.8 |
| 1977 | 6.5 | 1982 | 7.2 |
| 1978 | 6.2 | 1983 | 7.3 |

*Sources:* Various editions of the *Economic Survey of Europe* (Economic Commission for Europe).

mess of balance sheets. Ministerial vested interest may, then, have been a major independent factor, conspiring with generally conservative attitudes to hold up developments in this area.

There was, perhaps, some excuse for the ecological complacency of the Brezhnev period. Environmental problems certainly existed, but they were still essentially localized, having little general impact on production trends. The Aral Sea was shrinking, but the effect of this on the ecology of the region had not reached calamitous proportions. Chernobyl' was still in the future, though here, as elsewhere, the sins of omission of the 1970s were storing up trouble on a massive scale for a future generation of leaders.

But let us now try to make a general assessment of the Soviet investment record to 1983. In looking more closely at project choice we have largely confirmed the picture that emerged from a consideration of the problems of costs and excessive lead-times. External economies of scale and political toughness apart, the microeconomics of Soviet investment planning have been as bad as the macroeconomics. This does not provide an explanation for the downward trend in Soviet capital productivity, except to the extent that we can argue that these various problems have actually been getting worse. There is certainly evidence that the average lead-time actually lengthened in the 1970s (Dyker 1983, p. 36), but the dramatic trend illustrated in Table 6.4 can hardly be explained in this way. Rather that trend reflects the resource availability factors discussed earlier, especially in relation to energy supplies, and the intensification of the general planning problem as the economy became bigger and more complex. There is, however, clearly some sense in which the Soviet Union was able to 'afford' specific weaknesses in investment planning in the period of extensive development. Equally clearly, it can no longer do so. That, in a nutshell, is the special problem facing the post-Brezhnev Soviet leadership in this crucial area.

## GORBACHEV'S RECONSTRUCTION OF THE INVESTMENT PLANNING SYSTEM

In 1986 the pattern of organization of the construction industry was simplified. The old system which had mixed sectoral and territorial principles of specialization on the basis of a two-level union-republican structure was replaced by one based primarily on the territorial principle. Thus the Ministry of Heavy Industrial Construction was replaced by Minyugstroi (the Ministry of Construction for the South), the Ministry of Industrial Construction by Minuralsibstroi (the Ministry of Construction for the Urals and Siberia), and the Ministry of Construction by Minsevzapstroi (the Ministry of Construction for the North and West). To these was added the newly created Ministry of Construction for the East (Minvostokstroi). The old Ministries of Transport Construction and Construction for the Oil and Gas Ministries survived, though their structures were also territorialized to some extent. The Ministry of Installation and Special Construction was transferred onto a union-republican basis, so that each republic had its own Minmontazhspetsstroi. Finally, independent ministries of construction were created for each union republic.

The old system of intermediate administration based on *glavki* was replaced by a network of territorial and functionally specialized associations. At the same time, the authorities tried to counter the fragmentation that has been so characteristic of the executive end of the investment–construction cycle by creating a network of integrated design–construction associations. By the beginning of 1988 there more than fifty of these. More generally they sought, from 1985 onwards, to increase the size of the average building trust in order to achieve a better approximation to the optimal scale of operations and to provide a sounder basis for transition to full self-financing. At sub-trust level, the collective contract, as developed in agriculture, was programmed to provide the basis for a more effective incentive system at the level of the building site (Balakin 1988). As part of the transition from the traditional system of passive banking based on the monopoly of

Gosbank and Stroibank to a more active, pluralistic system,
Stroibank was abolished in July 1987. The bulk of its business was
taken over by a new bank, the Bank for Industrial Construction
(Promstroibank).

These measures had, in the event, little impact on patterns of
investment activity. The organizational hierarchy of the construction industry remained fragmented and overcomplex:

> What they did essentially was to create construction committees
> in cities and provinces. Under this dispensation the urgent
> business of the day can only be addressed through the
> preparation of appropriate decrees and decisions, the determina-
> tion of staffing levels, salaries and privileges, and also through
> designation of individuals for specific jobs (as a rule, with even
> higher salaries, because these committees have the status of all-
> union ministries). But whenever it comes to any fundamental
> transformation of production structures, all the enthusiasm of
> these executives and specialists just disappears, and everything
> remains as before.
>
> (Kaplan 1989, p. 10)

As of 1989 only 40 per cent of the annual volume of construction
work in the country was under the jurisdiction of Gosstroi (Ivanov
1989, p. 11). The scale of operations of the average building trust
remained at least 25 per cent too small. Even where optimal scale
was reached, anomalies in the pricing system ensured that many
construction organizations continued to make losses, making a
transition to full self-financing impossible (Balakin 1988, p. 62). As
if to emphasize the degree of indecision on the crucial pricing
dimension, the capital charge for construction organizations was
abolished in 1986 and then reinstated in 1988 (Timofeev 1989,
p. 79). Success-indicator changes introduced in 1986 abolished the
marketable output indicator, but put nothing in its place, thus
effectively putting construction organizations back on gross output.
The pattern with the system of settling accounts between
contractor and client was the same: 'It changed at some point in
the 1960s, was subsequently many times "perfected", and in 1986
we arrived, in practical terms, back at the position of 20–30 years
ago' (Ogon' 1989, p. 13). Again, the old quality coefficients for
construction were abolished in 1986 without anything being put in
their place (Merkin 1989, p. 17). The introduction in 1987 of the
principle of negotiated prices between client and contractor was a

significant step forward, but its impact was dissipated by the
inability of the authorities to give the client real power to bargain
over things like lead-times, technology, etc. (Volosatov 1990,
pp. 50–1). Meanwhile, the degree of 'petty tutelage' over building
enterprises seems to have diminished not one whit. As of 1989
those enterprises were still receiving a total of 6,888 indicators from
higher authorities, involving completion of 160 quarterly forms and
a further 258 forms of varying frequency (Betrozgov 1989, p. 72).
While design organizations had been a major target of the
Leningrad system, a more brutal form of the Shchekino system
aimed at producing sharp cuts in staffing levels (Dyker 1987a,
p. 65), they stood accused in 1989 of continuing to 'churn out
obsolescent design documentation, based on the heaviest possible
building elements and the most expensive materials' (Merkin 1989,
p. 15). Design offices remained largely uncomputerized (Bulgakov
1989, p. 29). In 1988, 40 per cent of all designs were sent back by
*ekspertiza* to the client ministries for correction (Bulgakov 1989,
p. 14). Around the same time the development of integrated
design–construction associations had still not really taken off
outside the residential building sphere, and this was proving a
serious obstacle to the development of the turnkey project
approach to investment plan implementation ('O perestroike
upravleniya. . .' 1989, p. 36). In housing construction itself the
work of design–construction associations was, we are told, being
severely hampered by their subordination to local soviets, casting
further doubt on the whole conceptual basis of the 1986
'decentralization' (Mikhel' 1989, p. 30). Held back by inadequate
legislation and conservative-minded staff, the 'new' investment
bank has tended to continue the tradition of Stroibank in its
relations with clients – interfering on details and ignoring the big
issues of medium- and long-term profitability (Zaichenko and
Sharov 1989; Tsypkin 1989). Under the old dispensation the latter
had, of course, been strictly the preserve of the planners.

Perhaps even more telling was the failure of the 1986 measures
to have any impact on the key interstitial weaknesses of the Soviet
investment planning system. In particular, the essential nature of
'planning' documents seemed to have changed not one whit:

Unreal title 'lines' [properly title lists] can be used as the basis
for obtaining perfectly real building materials, and using them,

at least to some extent, on already started projects for which
these materials have been allocated in inadequate quantities . . . against norms for economizing on use of materials and
planned levels of utilization of production capacity in the
building and building materials industries of 100 per cent and [!]
more.

(Kolosov 1989, p. 89)

Again, on the crucial issue of TEOs:

When some of our economists base their arguments on the
market as it exists in capitalist countries, they fail to take
account of the fact that that market is based on a comprehensive
and wide-ranging informational network, and a complex of
highly specialized engineering firms, covering the whole gamut
of production technology, and keeping right up to date on all
technological innovations, on automation, and on economic
trends. This makes it possible for industrial firms to avoid fatal
errors in choosing where to invest their capital. . . . It is vital
that Gosplan USSR, together with the State Committee for
Science and Technology and the environmental services, should
work out and have approved at governmental level a fundamentally new methodology for the elaboration of TEOs and TERs
[technico-economic calculations]. That elaboration should be
done by *consultant engineering firms* [emphasis added].

(Yakovlev 1989, pp. 41, 43)

In September 1989 the Soviet government promulgated yet another
set of measures on the planning and management of capital
investment. The main elements in this new legislation were as
follows:

1 From 1990 success indicators, calculation of profit, and settling
  of accounts should be based on 'finished construction output'
  (*gotovaya stroitel'naya produktsiya*). For projects with a lead-time of
  more than one year, finished construction output might be
  reckoned in terms of operational complexes within the project as
  a whole, and for those with lead-times of more than two years in
  terms of completed buildings or installations.
2 Work in progress should be financed by construction organizations' own resources and/or bank credit. Bank credit should be
  advanced on the basis of estimated cost of construction. The
  interest on those credits should be counted as part of total

estimates. Bank credit for construction should be financed on the basis of the funds which clients would otherwise have had to pay in advances, with the banks paying an annual rate of interest of 0.5 per cent for the use of these funds.

3 The turnkey approach to project planning should be generally introduced for residential and infrastructural investment, and also brought in selectively in the production investment sphere. There should be special bonuses for on-time or ahead-of-time completion of turnkey projects. Gossnab and Gosplan have been instructed to work out a special system for supplying materials to turnkey projects.

4 Above-norm volumes of unfinished construction should be penalized at the rate of 6 per cent annually. Failure to complete projects on time would incur the same penalty in cases where the finance came from enterprise funds. In the case of centralized investments, the penalty for missing completion dates was set at 0.5 per cent per month.

5 For design organizations, full payment of completion bonuses might only be made if the project reached full-capacity production levels within the normed period.

6 The capital charge should be waived for production projects completed ahead of time for the period up to their planned operationalization date, and the funds thus made available shared among the various organizations involved.

('O nekotorykh. . .' 1989)

This is a terribly disappointing package. It is not devoid of good elements, but even those are mostly derivative of the more positive reform attempts of the 1970s. Taken as a whole, the measures are hopelessly fussy and centralist, even for projects financed from enterprise profits, and simply do not address the basic issue of how the market mechanism can be brought into this most difficult of areas. Indeed the whole style of the package reeks of Brezhnevite *sovershenstvovanie* (perfecting) – strikingly, that word still appears again and again in the contemporary literature on investment and construction problems – i.e. it simply ignores the issue of what *radical reform* can mean in the given context. Thus the whole tenor of system rebuilding in the investment sphere seems to be fundamentally out of step with systemic trends in the economy as a whole. Why so? To lay the basis for a preliminary attempt at explanation, let us now turn to a consideration of investment policy under Gorbachev.

## INVESTMENT POLICY 1985–90: ACCELERATION VERSUS RECONSTRUCTION

*Table 6.5* Investment trends, 1986–9 (annual rates of growth)

|  | 1986 | 1987 | 1988 | 1989 | 1986–89 |
|---|---|---|---|---|---|
| Gross investment | 8.3 | 5.7 | 6.2 | 0.6 | 5.2 |
| Operationalizations | 5.9 | 6.8 | −1.3 | −2.0 | 2.4 |
| Volume of unfinished construction | 9.7 | 10.5 | 13.0 | 13.9 | 11.8 |

*Source: Narkhoz* 1988, *Plan Fulfilment Report* for 1989.

Table 6.5 presents the basic aggregate data on investment over the first four years of Gorbachev's first five-year plan. The general picture is clear enough. The degree of overstretch on the investment front has increased sharply, and by 1989 the whole construction sector seemed in danger of seizing up altogether. The watershed year was 1988, and this is confirmed by the statistics on new starts. In 1986 a total of 3,700 new projects were initiated, worth an estimated total of 48.5 billion roubles. In the following year those figures were cut to 3,200 new projects and 38.5 billion roubles; this helps to explain why the operationalizations record was rather better in that year. But in 1988 the total number of new starts rocketed to 4,500, with total estimated value increasing by more than 50 per cent ('O perestroike upravleniya. . .' 1989, pp. 30–1). Only some two-thirds of planned completions were actually implemented. The Soviet economy was clearly quite unable to cope with this, and indeed nothing had been done to resolve the situation by the beginning of 1990. There is some disagreement about its impact on lead-times. One authoritative source states that average construction times fell from 9.5 years in 1985 to 7.7 years in 1988 ('O perestroike upravleniya. . .' 1989, p. 29). Another, equally reliable source states that there has been no significant improvement over the period in question (Zholudev and Kolotilkin 1990, p. 32). In an age of anticipated fundamental structural change, and deepening controversy over the meaning of Soviet growth statistics, we should not place too much weight on incremental capital–output ratios. For what it is worth, however,

ICORs have, on the most optimistic estimates, remained in double figures throughout the Gorbachev era.

Was the whole thing planned? Certainly the aggregate growth targets embodied in the 1986–90 five-year plan were ambitious, with the annual rate of increase of national income programmed at 4.1 per cent, backed up by a proposed rate of increase of fixed investment of 4.3 per cent coupled with a substantial reduction in lead-times (Dyker 1987a, p. 83). In the event, over the first four years of the quinquennium there was a shortfall of 38 billion roubles on national income and an overshoot of 6 billion roubles on investment (Denisov 1989, p. 48). Was it simply the result of a failure to introduce meaningful reform into the investment and construction sector? To a degree, the answer must be yes. But we will dig deeper into the roots of Gorbachev's economic ills if we pursue the proposition that the overall strategy of the five-year plan itself may have created serious obstacles to the effective reform of the sector.

In the early days of Gorbachev's reform drive the term *uskorenie* (acceleration) was as current a slogan as *perestroika* (restructuring). To the extent that Gorbachev – still a relative novice in the art of national economic policy-making – was seeking the obverse of *zastoi* (the stagnation of the Brezhnev era), that was perhaps understandable. But it reflected a regrettable failure to break with the Soviet tradition of mechanistic growthmanship, precisely the tradition which had brought the Soviet economy to the crisis it faced in the mid-1980s. In Gorbachev's defence it must be said that this line of combining restructuring with acceleration bore the imprimatur of no less a figure than Abel Aganbegyan, doyen of Soviet economic reformers and the dominant voice in the economic counsels of the Soviet government from 1985 to 1989. Before long Gorbachev, under the more discerning and cautious influence of Leonid Abalkin and Nikolai Petrakov, would recognize that there could be no meaningful acceleration until after restructuring was completed. The 1986–90 five-year plan, however, was founded on the premise that the two could go together, and indeed that the technical restructuring of the production profile of the Soviet economy could be implemented independently of any radical restructuring of the planning system.

The restructuring priorities of the five-year plan were heavily concentrated on machine building, as the key to the re-equipment of the rest of Soviet industry and the linchpin of technical progress.

Aggregate machine-building output was planned to grow by 7.4 per cent, as compared to an average of 6 per cent actually achieved 1981–5, and the annual rate of renewal of active capital stock in machine building itself was to be raised to 10–12 per cent. High-technology engineering sectors were programmed to increase output 1.3 to 1.6 times as fast as the average for the whole sector.

Our final assessment of how successful the 1986–90 machine-building programme was in its own right will be left until Chapter 7. For the present, let us simply note that the implications for the construction industry of a plan which sought an increase in aggregate growth rates, combined with a shift in resources towards technology-intensive branches, could hardly be anything else but ominous. As we saw, Soviet construction plans have always tended to be taut, building materials supply always a bottleneck. But under the strain of *uskorenie* policies, the situation by the late 1980s was such that metal and cement requirements were 14–18 per cent undersupplied, even assuming that all delivery plans were met (Merkin 1989, p. 15). The shortfall for bricks and timber was, respectively, 25 per cent and 40 per cent (Zholudev and Kolotilkin 1990, p. 30). Over the same period some 40 per cent of construction labour stand-downs were caused by breakdowns in supplies of materials (Mikhel' 1989, p. 29). Ironically, in an age of machine-building priorities, a survey of behind-schedule invest-ment projects found that some 20 per cent of planned machinery deliveries had not arrived. At the same time, stocks of uninstalled equipment increased by 16.5 per cent from 1988 to 1989 (Zholudev and Kolotilkin 1990, pp. 30, 34).

This pattern of intensifying supply uncertainty had two major secondary effects. First, by frustrating attempts to cut lead-times, it effectively stymied efforts to improve X-efficiency in construction and design. It was precisely because of the impossibility of monitoring revenue and profitability over gestation periods approaching 10 years that the Soviet authorities gave up on the search for a meaningful sales indicator for construction in 1986 ('O perestroike upravleniya. . .' 1989, p. 35). It was again to a great extent because of this that by 1989 some 100 billion roubles' worth of design documentation relating to unfinished construction had accumulated, making a nonsense of attempts to make the design management and incentives structure more sensitive to up-to-dateness (Bulgakov 1989, p. 16). Perhaps even more important, the degree of imbalance between supply and demand meant that such cautious moves in the direction of marketization as were implemented in the late 1980s tended simply to create opportunities for monopoly profits, rather than improving the allocation of resources.

It is completely natural that in conditions of monopoly and general deficit, monopolists orient themselves to short-term profit, resorting to every trick in the trade – using any excuse to jack up prices, getting rid of the cheap end of the product range etc. Under these conditions enterprises and organizations do not need technical progress.

(Solov'ev, 1989, p. 65)

This underlying situation has indeed been one of the principal factors which has prevented the system of negotiated prices developing into a proper market for construction goods and services ('Posle vystuplenii. . .' 1989, p. 37).

In 1988, 40 per cent of total state investment was financed from enterprise-retained profits. By 1989 the figure had risen to 49 per cent. Why, it may be asked, has such a sustained movement in the direction of self-financing not produced some movement in the direction of a more cost-conscious investment set-up? The paradox is, of course, only an apparent one. We left the new decentralized investment arrangements in the mid-80s, struggling in a general environment still dominated by central planning. By the late 1980s the general environment had changed a good deal in the direction of the market principle, but the specifically investment/construction environment had changed very little. It is significant that for the crucial year of 1988 a breakdown of those very poor aggregate operationalization figures shows that while 68 per cent of planned centralized investment completions were actually commissioned, only 65 per cent of the corresponding magnitude for decentralized investment was passed as completed. The 31 per cent shortfall reported for supply of equipment to decentralized investment projects (Zholudev and Kolotilkin 1990, p. 30) may seem like explanation enough for that pattern. Equally important, however, is the fact that re-equipment (upgrading) investment, now wholly financed from enterprise retentions, on the whole continued to fail to upgrade, but rather to leave the technological level of plants much the same as before (Zholudev and Kolotilkin 1990, p. 36). The general pace of reform was clearly still not rapid enough to break the habits of defensive investment which enterprise directors had built up through decades of over-centralization and supply uncertainty, habits intrinsically inimical to considerations of cost-efficiency.

## AN INTERIM CONCLUSION

The evolution of the investment scene seems, then, to provide further evidence for a number of our basic propositions. The reform process is only as strong as its weakest link, and meaningful reform is simply incompatible with formal growth targeting. But we must end the chapter by disturbing the neatness of this conclusion. For while it may be possible for the Soviet authorities to abandon aggregate growthmanship, how are they to restructure the production capacity of the Soviet economy without some notion of sectoral priorities, and some budgetary means of implementing these priorities, even against the background of some kind of market system? This brings us back to a whole range of problems which go far beyond the field of investment and construction as such, a range of problems which we first adumbrated at the end of Chapter 4. It is now time to pull the threads together and address these, the issues on which the future of the Soviet economy will surely turn.

# Chapter 7

# *Perestroika* in crisis

I am amazed: what kind of lives have we lived?
What have we constructed, what raised up?
And why, for what reason?
On the building site there is – NOTHING!

(By the Soviet poet K. Yershkov; translated by the author, who
heard Ershkov recite this and other verses at Poet's Corner in the
Arbat, Moscow in May 1990.)

## PROFILE OF A POLICY FAILURE

By the middle of 1990, after five years of Gorbachev's leadership,
the Soviet economy was in deep crisis. Output was falling – for the
first time since the beginning of the first five-year plan. (National
income dropped 2 per cent over the first six months of that year,
industrial output by 0.7 per cent – *Plan Fulfilment Report* for the first
half of 1990.) Perhaps part of the story is more accurate reporting,
as Soviet statisticians grapple more successfully with the problem
of concealed inflation in production indices. But there cannot be
the slightest doubt that the overall economic situation in the Soviet
Union at mid-1990 could be described – most optimistically – as
stagnation.

Yet the aggregate view gives the least disturbing perspective on
the contemporary Soviet economic position. At the level of
individual product groups we see output of key inputs like fertilizer
and cement falling sharply, while that of consumer items like
textile materials and clothes and refrigerators marks time or shows

*Table 7.1* Soviet growth rates, 1986–91

|  | NMP<br>(official Soviet) | GDP<br>(western estimates) |
|---|---|---|
| 1986 | 4.1 | 2.4 |
| 1987 | 2.3 | 1.5 |
| 1988 | 4.4 | 1.5 |
| 1989 | 2.4 | – |
| 1990 | 4.0 | −4.0 |
| 1986–90 | 1.8 | 0.3 |
| 1991 (estimates) | 5.0 | −5.0 |

*Source:* Official Soviet statistics; Economist Intelligence Unit.

small decreases. It is reported that output of electric irons is growing rapidly, yet it is impossible to obtain an iron in Soviet shops; that production of soap powder has increased although Soviet housewives are unable to acquire a packet for love or money. Is it that people are hoarding irons?

> You may ask: what is the population ironing? You cannot help suspecting that ironing is now replacing washing. In point of fact, why wash, when there is nothing to wash with, if you can steam your washing from below with an iron with an iron-adaptor (forgive the technical term), and put it back on your poor body, exhausted with the chase round the shops.
>
> (Petrenko and Borin 1990)

But the most disturbing situation is with respect to food supplies. The official statistics admit that the output of meat, fish, vegetable oil, salt, and tinned fruit and vegetables has fallen. But the food crisis visible in every *gastronom*, on every pavement, is infinitely worse than the bare statistics indicate. Queues seem to stretch as far as the eye can see, and where there is no queue there is nothing on the shelves. Restaurants, even those patronized mainly by foreigners, frequently run out of supplies, and most Soviet cities have now introduced local regulations which forbid the selling of foodstuffs to anyone who cannot prove local residence. Another Arbat poet suggested in May 1990 that if the Central Committee of the Communist Party of the Soviet Union did not hurry up and do something to feed the people, the people would eat the Central Committee.

Is there a hint from the official production series of any real

*Table 7.2*  Structure of capital investment by sector of industry
(percentage of total investment for the whole economy)

|  | 1976–80 | 1981–5 | 1986–7 |
|---|---|---|---|
| Production of the means of production | 30.7 | 31.4 | 32.4 |
| Production of the means of consumption | 4.3 | 4.3 | 4.1 |
| By industrial complex: | | | |
| Fuel and energy | 10.5 | 12.9 | 14.4 |
| Metallurgy | 4.0 | 3.6 | 3.5 |
| Machine building | 8.5 | 8.7 | 9.0 |
| Chemicals and timber | 5.2 | 4.1 | 3.6 |
| Building materials | 5.5 | 4.9 | 4.7 |

*Source:* Loginov 1989, p. 24.

restructuring? Certainly some of the drop in aggregate output may
be attributable to a new consciousness of the importance of
ecological considerations, and to the process of conversion of
military production capacities. Certainly, output of the main
electronics lines, both industrial and consumer, is growing rapidly.
But the Soviet economy remains utterly backward in every aspect
of microelectronic technology, and this manifests itself most starkly
on the dimension of telecommunications, still a nightmare for
anyone in the USSR – Soviet or foreign – trying to do business.
There may be some inklings of intensification in one or two sectors
of the economy, but the overall productivity picture reveals a
sluggishness which is little different from that which prevailed in
the late Brezhnev period. On the most optimistic calculation, total
productivity in the Soviet economy continues to decline, as it did
during the 1970s and early 1980s. Table 7.1 reveals some
differences in Soviet and western assessments of Gorbachev's
growth record, particularly in relation to year 1988, but the
general trend is clear enough. At the beginning, the pure 'new
broom' effect, as discipline was tightened and vodka production
cut, combined with some positive short-term impact from the
*uskorenie* policy to produce a measurable kick in aggregate economic
performance. But a high price was to be exacted for this brief
period of success. By 1988 the novelty of the new disciplinarianism
was beginning to wear off, and illicit distillation was developing
into a serious social problem. More fundamentally, as Table 7.2
shows, the early years of the Gorbachev era produced absolutely no
restructuring of the Soviet capital stock whatsoever. The share of

fuel and energy in total investment continued to grow and grow, that of chemicals fell sharply, while that of machine building, supposedly the linchpin of the 1986–90 five-year plan, grew almost imperceptibly. It goes without saying that the share of the consumer goods industries also fell.

It would be unfair to blame this pattern wholly on the *uskorenie* policy. After all, the Soviet fuel industry does face unique technical problems, and secularly rising unit capital costs in oil and gas extraction are inevitable. But as we saw at the end of Chapter 4, there is a powerful argument to the effect that fundamental misconceptions of Soviet energy planning were not sloughed off in the middle to late 1980s as they should have been, and it seems clear that the renewed obsession with quantitative growth during that period was one of the main factors lying behind the failure to do so. In any case, by 1989 the level of output of oil was again falling in absolute terms (it had been one of Gorbachev's early triumphs to reverse the downward trend which had initially appeared in 1985), while the rate of growth of gas output was also falling sharply.

Still, the *uskorenie* policy had been abandoned by 1989, perhaps even earlier. With Abalkin succeeding Aganbegyan as senior economic advisor, the fantasy of reconstructing and accelerating all at the same time was finally laid to rest. The 'Abalkin plan', published at the end of 1989 (Abalkin 1989c), was cautious on time-tabling, relegating comprehensive *perestroika* to the medium term. On this scenario a fully-fledged market-based system, including stock markets and commodity exchanges and a partially convertible rouble, would not be in place until 1993. Where Abalkin's formulations reflected a genuinely new radicalism was in terms of the whole strategy of economic reform. Echoing calls from the Supreme Soviet, the newly invigorated Soviet parliament, he laid primary stress on system-building, and on the passage of a mass of basic legislation, including laws on property, on taxation, on monopoly policy, and on social security. Following on from that, he called for the setting up of a new network of 'regulatory organs' – auditing services, tax inspection organs, restrictive practice and monopoly commissions – and for crash training programmes to produce the people to staff these new organs.

But Abalkin's studied and cautious radicalism found little echo at the level of operational planning. The state orders system, originally introduced to provide a basis for gradual transition to a free market in industrial supplies, continued to function in practice as an instrument for the maintenance of central planning.

> Unfortunately, the new temporary guidelines for the placing of state orders for 1989 and 1990 give no real grounds for optimism. Maintenance of the command principle in the area of material–technical supply will ensure that enterprises remain largely oriented to gross output, even if there is a substantial reduction of the share of state orders [in total production].
>
> (Radaev 1989, p. 51)

In the event, no such reduction took place, and by mid-1990 state orders were still pre-empting some 85 per cent of total industrial output, including that of exporting firms supposedly enjoying a new freedom to sell to whom they wished under the foreign trade reforms.

The essential contradictions still plaguing the *perestroika* programme were brought into full relief at the end of 1989 when Prime Minister Ryzhkov presented the first draft of a new five-year plan. Only a few weeks after the unveiling of the Abalkin plan, Gorbachev's principal agent of economic policy implementation presented a document which emphasized the continued importance of directive planning and rejected radical options on property relations and monetary reform. In the course of the debate on the draft in the Congress of People's Deputies, radical economist Gavriil Popov, soon to be elected chairman of the Moscow Soviet, accused the government of 'continuing to want to tell hens how many eggs to lay'.

The appointment in January 1990 of Nikolai Petrakov as (yet another) special economic advisor to Gorbachev seemed to signal the start of a new impetus towards accelerated systemic reform. But the publication of key system-building documents was repeatedly postponed through the spring and early summer of 1990. When measures were finally announced, they amounted to little more than a long-overdue reform of food prices. The Soviet public was outraged at the proposed price increases, and the measures quickly withdrawn. (See following section for detailed discussion.) But with the convocation of a democratically elected Supreme Soviet of the Russian Federation, the biggest of the Soviet republics, holding slightly more than half the total population of the Soviet Union, the whole political backdrop to the reform controversy changed radically. The newly elected president of the

Russian Federation, Boris Yeltsin, was the catalyst who provided a political platform for a new and sharper form of economic radicalism. That new radicalism is particularly identified with the name of Stanislav Shatalin.

In August 1990 a group headed by Shatalin produced a 500-day plan for the decisive restructuring of the Soviet economy. The plan was based on the principles of massive privatization, liberalization of prices, budgetary and monetary reform, and the introduction of a western-style social security system, plus selective rationing, to protect the victims of restructuring ('O programme perekhoda. . .' 1990). We leave our assessment of the programme as an economic policy document in its own right to a later stage. Its immediate impact was to signal, effectively, the end of an era, to pronouce Gorbachev's *perestroika* programme mortally ill, if not already dead.

## ANATOMY OF A POLICY FAILURE

It seems that virtually the entire Soviet economics profession, ranging from radicals like Shatalin and Gavriil Popov to 'conservatives' (i.e. gradualists) like Ruben Yevstigneev of the Institute for the Economics of the World Socialist System, and indeed Abalkin himself, agree that *perestroika* has suffered a complete loss of impetus, that there is currently a total lack of direction in Soviet economic policy-making which threatens to turn crisis into catastrophe. Is it a simple matter of 'too little, too late'? Is it just that Gorbachev, for all his extraordinary ability to learn from mistakes and false starts, has not been able to adjust his apparatus-bred ideas quickly enough to cope with a situation that would not stand still? Have Gorbachev's policies been undermined by systematic obstruction on the part of disgruntled Communist Party conservatives? Is it rather the egalitarian conservatism of the Soviet masses, or alternatively the national tensions released by Gorbachev's political liberalization that have knocked the *perestroika* programme off its critical path? Or have, indeed, essentially technical economic problems presented the major obstacles to sustained, practical radicalism? It can hardly be in dispute that political factors have been of crucial importance in the pattern of events that unfolded over the period 1989–90. It is, nevertheless, useful to begin by looking at the more narrowly economic

*Table 7.3* Soviet budget deficits, actual and projected (billion roubles)

|                       | 1984 | 1985 | 1986 | 1987 | 1988 | 1989 | 1990 |
|-----------------------|------|------|------|------|------|------|------|
| Official Soviet figures | –    | 18.0 | 47.9 | 57.1 | 90.1 | 92   | 60   |
| CIA figures           | 11.0 | 17.0 | 49.8 | 64.4 | 68.8 | –    | –    |

*Source:* CIA 1988b; *Narkhoz* 1989, p. 624; budgetary and plan fulfilment documents.

dimension. To what extent were the failures of *perestroika* predetermined by the failures of Brezhnevism?

The traditional analysis of the weaknesses of Soviet-style central planning places primary emphasis on the microeconomic dimension. The insensitivity of the system to quality, to technology, to cost-effectiveness, to what the customer really wants – these are the classic shortcomings of the system dedicated to extensive development, the shortcomings which have produced surpluses of things that no one wants, shortages of the most essential commodities, both consumer and industrial, and a structural rigor mortis which has defied the best attempts of Moscow planners to breathe into the body the life of industrial adjustment.

But there was something more insidious, more deep-seated, in the legacy which Stalinist development tactics left to would-be reformers of the Soviet system. A policy which self-consciously ignores the logic of the market mechanism, and insists on placing investments in accordance with the pecking order of plan priorities rather than that of profitability; which is prepared to countenance the most serious financial irregularities as long as the plan is fulfilled; which imposes organizational forms like the *kolkhoz* for essentially ideological reasons, and against every consideration of X-efficiency in the countryside; and which pursues perfectly laudable social goals, such as the availability of cheap food and public transport for the people, in an essentially open-ended way which makes effective fiscal control impossible: such a policy cannot but produce a pattern of systematic loss-making in the economy and blank cheques in the social sphere. And that pattern must eventually come through in the form of severe pressure on the national budget. Thus generalized soft budget constraints beget hard budget deficits; microeconomic weaknesses build up into macro-economic imbalance. The figures in Table 7.3, though, hardly provide cast-iron proof that the budget deficit was a millstone bequeathed to the reformer Gorbachev by the do-nothing conservative Brezhnev. The fact is that the deficit inherited by Gorbachev from Brezhnev's crony, Chernenko, was a modest 11 billion roubles – less than 2 per cent of national income – if we can accept the CIA estimate in the absence of an official Soviet figure. Nor did the deficit grow rapidly during Gorbachev's first, incomplete year of office. But in 1986, just as the *perestroika* programme was getting into full swing, the budget deficit almost trebled.

This dramatic escalation did, indeed, have something to do with Gorbachev's naïve and ill-considered anti-alcohol drive. Yet the 6.2 billion rouble drop in turnover tax revenue between 1985 and 1986 (*Narkhoz* 1988 p. 624) goes only a little way to explain an increase of around 30 billion roubles in the deficit. By 1988 turnover tax revenue had more than recovered its 1985 level, while the deficit continued to rise. No doubt deductions from the profits of the Soviet drink industry back to the state budget also fell in 1986, but this would not have made a dramatic difference to the overall fiscal position. More significant was the collapse in oil prices from an average of US$35 per barrel in 1983 to one of US$10–12 (subsequently recovering to around US$15) in 1985–6. This cost the Soviet budget some 20 billion roubles annually (Yur'ev, 1989). Thus, the great bulk of the 1986 increase in the deficit can indeed be explained in terms of windfall losses and policy elements which were peripheral to central *perestroika* priorities, leaving the hard-core deficit as inherited from the previous regime.

Why, then, did the budget deficit continue to increase rapidly in 1987 and 1988, as both turnover tax and oil prices recovered slightly? The simplest explanation is that the hard-core deficit grew. In this case there is substantial evidence to suggest that the simplest explanation is the correct one. Let us focus on meat and milk subsidies, one of the biggest elements on the budgetary expenditure side, one which vies with defence itself as a burden on the Soviet economy. In a key speech delivered at the end of 1987, Gorbachev railed at the wastefulness of these subsidies, and pledged to reduce them as a priority objective (Gorbachev 1987). At that time meat and milk subsidies were accounting for some 10 per cent of national income. Yet by 1989 total agricultural subsidies, of which the great bulk go to the meat and dairy sector, had risen to 90.2 billion roubles – almost exactly the level of the budget deficit, and 12–14 per cent of national income. The official forecast was that they won't rise to 98.5 billion roubles in 1990 (Pavlov 1989). Soviet economists estimate that procurement price increases which came into force on 1 January 1990 could increase that latter figure to 160 billion roubles (Borozdin 1989, p. 25).

Why has Gorbachev totally failed to implement such a crucial element in his programme? For part of the explanation, we need merely turn back to the concluding sections of Chapter 5. Organizational reform in agriculture has flattered to deceive, and the critical breakthrough in terms of establishing a proper farmer class in the Soviet Union has still not been made. In increasing a range of procurement prices in early 1990 Gorbachev seemed merely to be repeating the mistakes of the Brezhnev period in presupposing that in agriculture better procurement prices automatically equal better incentives. But in May 1990 the Soviet President did press a significant new initiative on the issue of food subsidies. He proposed that bread prices should rise by 50 per cent from mid-1990, that meat prices should rise by 130 per cent from the beginning of 1991, and that fish prices should go up 150 per cent and milk prices double on 1 January 1991. These may sound like radical proposals to western ears, yet in truth they were limited enough in their scope. They maintained the principle of central price-fixing, thus essentially side-stepping one of the central issues of radical reform (of this more in a moment). And while 130 per cent sounds a lot, it must be set in the context of a free-market price for meat (15–20 roubles per kilo) which is 7–10 times the price of meat in state shops. There was nothing here, then, to shake the foundations of the edifice of central planning, and no real promise of a total removal of disequilibria in the foodstuffs market. Nevertheless the initiative met with a uniformly hostile reception, amongst the Soviet population and conservative and radical politicians alike. In June the Supreme Soviet voted to postpone the increase in the price of bread, and at the same time sent the Soviet government off to reconsider its whole strategy of economic reform.

Our provisional verdict must be, then, that, yes, the Soviet budget has grown in the Gorbachev period from the seeds sown under previous regimes. Gorbachev can certainly be faulted for failing to reverse the trend, for failing to attack the essential problem of soft budget constraints. But by 1990 Gorbachev had to share the blame with Soviet public opinion, and with a range of liberated oppositionists, from arch-conservative Yegor Ligachev to maverick radical Boris Yeltsin. How ironic, when we remember that Gorbachev, the archetypal Communist Party apparatus man, had unleashed the forces of *glasnost'* and democratization in the period 1987–9 because he perceived that without freedom of information and expression, economic reform would be a non-starter.

But we are getting ahead of the story here. Before expanding on this central theme of interaction between economic, political, and social dimensions, let us pause to spell out exactly what massive budget deficit and deep-seated macroeconomic imbalance mean for the process of economic reform.

## THE PRICE OF BUDGET DEFICIT

The budget deficit is to a great extent the result of the inability of central planning to allocate resources efficiently. A rising budget deficit can be taken as a rough proxy for the increasing urgency of systemic reform. Yet under conditions of Soviet socialism, the budget deficit stands as perhaps the biggest single technical economic obstacle to effective *perestroika.*

Budget deficits are common enough in western market economies, albeit not on the relative scale of the Soviet deficit. (At late 1990, it must be said, the Bush administration in Washington was threatening to set a new standard.) Thus at its height, Ronald Reagan's deficit of the early 1980s represented some 4 per cent of US national income. 'Normal' budget deficits can be absorbed quite easily by the money markets which exist in all the developed economies. (On this criterion Reagan's deficit was, certainly, an abnormal one.) In the UK, for instance, the government can issue short-term Treasury Bills to cover temporary deficits. In the past the definition of socialism as understood in the Soviet Union has excluded the existence of a money market. This means that there are only two possible ways of financing budget deficits. The first is by borrowing abroad, a tactic followed by a number of east European countries in the late 1970s with disastrous results. It is not clear the the USSR is in a position to borrow abroad on the scale necessary to have a significant impact on the budget deficit. (Of this more when we come to look at the balance of payments issue *per se.*) What is clear is that the Soviet government has up to now excluded this option. That leaves only one way of bridging the gap – the emission of new currency. Thus a budget deficit of 90 billion roubles more or less adds that amount to the money supply – in 1989 it was plain to every Soviet citizen that the extraordinary increase in the number of brand-new rouble bills in circulation boded no good.

It was at the end of 1988 that the *perestroika* programme first started to address the essential problem of prices. The legislation permitting the formation of cooperatives had already created one small area of decontrolled price formation in the Soviet economy. Attempts to free-up the system of state orders in the autumn of that year gave directors of state enterprises new rights in the area of price fixing. It soon became apparent that the degree of aggregate excess demand, reinforced by the monopoly power enjoyed by many Soviet enterprises unrestrained by foreign competition, was such that price liberalization meant in many cases a licence to charge any price you liked. This, indeed, was one of the reasons why attitudes to the cooperatives soon began to turn hostile, and why restrictions on the coops were introduced at the beginning of 1989. By that time the rate of open inflation had escalated to some 10 per cent. Further restrictive measures taken in the course of 1989 may have reduced the open inflation rate to around 5 per cent. The hesitant wave of liberalization of late 1989/early 1990 raised it again to 15–20 per cent.

However, as Nikolai Shmelev puts it, 'we do not really know which is in reality dearer – gold or bricks' (Shmelev 1989b, p. 274). One of the great intellectual breakthroughs within the Soviet economic establishment in the period 1988–9 was the increasing acceptance of a series of key propositions; that all-encompassing central price-fixing is not only impossible, but actually undesirable; that a market economy operating with wrong prices is worse than useless; that a market economy can only produce an efficient allocation of resources on the basis of efficiency prices; and that only the market can generate such prices. The terrible truth that became evident in 1989 was that in conditions of extreme macro-economic imbalance any attempt to allow the market to generate its own prices would almost certainly lead to rapid hyper-inflation.

Let us pause for a moment to probe more deeply into the nature of Soviet repressed inflation. It is clear that much of the cumulative Soviet budget deficit represents money paid out in the wage bills of unprofitable enterprises and farms benefiting from soft budget constraints; money which simply has no counterpart in the volume

*Table 7.4* Total savings deposits (billion roubles)

| 1970 | 1980 | 1985 | 1986 | 1987 | 1988 | 1989 |
|------|------|------|------|------|------|------|
| 46.6 | 156.5 | 220.8 | 242.8 | 266.9 | 296.7 | 337.7 |

*Source: Narkhoz* 1988 p. 96; *Plan Fulfilment Report* for 1989.

of marketable goods and services produced by those same enterprises and farms. Where does that 'unspendable' money go? Some of it goes to finance the ever-growing turnover of the second economy (Grossman 1989). Some of it goes under the mattress – to the extent of something between 70 billion roubles and 200 billion roubles (Hanson 1989, p. 1). Much of it goes into savings bank deposits. The figures in Table 7.4 show the extraordinarily rapid and sustained growth of total savings deposits from 1970 onwards. From 1985 the figure has grown annually by an increment which increased from just over 20 billion roubles in 1986 to over 40 billion roubles in 1989. No doubt some of these savings are genuinely voluntary. It is equally clear, however, that the bulk of them simply represent the forced savings imposed by the repressed inflationary gap.

By 1990, then, the Soviet government faced a serious problem of policy blockage. In the absence of any commitment to rapid removal of the budget deficit, it was not clear that the best designed *perestroika* programme in the world could progress beyond the drawing-board stage. No wonder, then, that there was a sense of loss of focus and impetus. But the blockage was not an absolute one. As Poland showed in 1990, it is possible to get rid of huge budget deficits quite rapidly (Charemza 1990). Is the Soviet economy a suitable case for such 'shock therapy'? Before seeking to answer that question we must look in turn at the Soviet authorities' other main economic policy headaches.

**THE PRICE OF EXTERNAL DEFICIT**

Historically, the Soviet Union has a strong balance of payments record. Weak in the export of manufactures, she has been strong in that of energy materials, with oil and gas exports making up some 70 per cent of total exports over recent decades. Imports of grain and machinery have sometimes put a strain on the hard-currency balance of trade, but gold exports, usually worth US$2–4 billion

*Table 7.5* The Soviet hard-currency external balance (US$ billion)

|  | 1983 | 1984 | 1985 | 1986 | 1987 | 1988 | 1989 | 1990 |
|---|---|---|---|---|---|---|---|---|
| Balance of trade | 1.3 | 2.2 | −0.8 | −3.9 | 0.4 | −2.7 | −6.5 | −4.9 |
| Balance of payments, current account | 1.5 | 3.0 | 1.0 | −1.0 | 1.5 | −1.5 | −4.5 | −3.0 |

*Source:* Economist Intelligence Unit.

per annum in recent years, ensured that the hard-currency current account remained in healthy surplus, taking one year with another, up to the mid-1980s. In 1986, under the strain of the collapse in oil prices, a large balance of trade deficit and a small current account deficit appeared. An export drive in the following year succeeded, however, in clearing both deficits. From 1988, however, a new trend sets in. Hard-currency trade deficits start to grow rapidly, and in 1989, for the first time, the Soviet Union runs a current account deficit on a massive scale. These trends are paralleled by a rapid increase in the volume of the Soviet external debt. The reader will note that it is not possible to explain debt trends purely in terms of apparent current account trends. Moscow appears to have borrowed much more than she strictly needed, for example, to cover the 1986 deficit. In 1987 the hard-currency current account is in healthy surplus, yet gross and apparent net debt rise again. It seems likely, then, that an element in Soviet borrowing in the second half of the 1980s has gone into off-shore funds, or simply to increase reserves. Nevertheless the fact is that Soviet debt service (interest plus amortization) had reached 5.3 billion roubles by 1989, an alarming 32 per cent of total exports to the west. The debt service figure was expected to rise to 6.2 billion roubles in 1990 (Pavlov 1989). These figures reflect the fact that the overwhelming bulk of of Soviet external liabilities are of a fixed-interest character. To February 1990 the USSR had managed to attract just 1.5 billion roubles of international equity capital under the rubric of the 1987 joint venture legislation (Kheifets 1990). By early 1990 the Soviet Union was running into serious payments difficulties as she tried to repay credits taken out for the purchase of grain in 1989. In May 1990 a number of Japanese steel companies suspended shipments to the Soviet Union as the pile of unpaid bills mounted. It is no wonder that the Soviet Union is in danger of

*Table 7.6* Soviet hard-currency external debt (US$ billion)

|                                      | 1975 | 1980 | 1985 | 1986 | 1987 | 1988 | 1989 |
|--------------------------------------|------|------|------|------|------|------|------|
| Gross debt                           | 10.6 | 17.6 | 27.0 | 36.0 | 36.5 | 38.0 | 46.3 |
| Net debt(BIS reporting<br>banks only) | 7.6  | 9.0  | 13.9 | 21.2 | 22.5 | 23.5 | 29.2 |

*Source:* Bank for International Settlements; Economist Intelligence Unit;
*Ekonomika i Zhizn'*, no. 12, 1990, p. 6.

losing its triple-A credit rating on the international financial
markets.

Why the dramatic loss of control of the balance of payments
from 1988 onwards? We cannot blame oil price trends – as we saw,
the Soviet Union coped remarkably well with the Third Oil Shock.
What about the foreign trade reforms of 1986 and 1987, as detailed
in Chapter 4? It certainly looks from the figures as if those reforms
had a much more decisive impact on hard-currency imports than
on hard-currency exports, with the former growing 68 per cent
from 1987 to 1989, and the latter just 15 per cent (official Soviet
statistics). Did this represent a new, decentralized modernization
drive on the part of Soviet enterprises eager to exploit their new
prerogatives in relation to importing? In fact, Soviet machinery
imports for hard currency (valued in constant prices) actually fell
slightly as a proportion of total imports from 1987 to 1988 and may
have fallen more sharply from 1988 to 1989, though they almost
certainly grew marginally in terms of current prices (*Vneshnie
Ekonomicheskie Svyazi SSSR* 1989, p. 18; *Ekonomika i Zhizn'*, no. 15,
1990, p. 4). The increased import demand of the late 1980s, the
bulk of it financed on credit, may, then, simply have reflected the
impact of excess aggregate demand, which would take us straight
back to the budget deficit. The failure of exports for hard currency
to take off is surely primarily a result of the continued pre-emption
of the great bulk of the output of all Soviet enterprises by state
orders, which is in turn a result of the failure to introduce decisive
marketization. (Significantly, joint ventures themselves generated a
total of just 128 million roubles of exports in 1989, as against 431
million roubles of imports – Kheifets 1990, p. 3). On our earlier
reasoning, this can in turn be blamed on the budget deficit. There
is no obvious way in which these hypotheses could be rigorously
tested, but it seems highly plausible to suggest that the factors

lying behind the sharp deterioration in the Soviet Union's external balance in 1988 and 1989 are the same factors that have been of determining importance in relation to domestic macroeconomic balance. Note, however, that removal of the budget deficit would not automatically remove this pressure on the balance of payments, just as it would not automatically remove domestic inflationary pressure, since it would not automatically neutralize the accumulated frustrated purchasing power engendered by earlier budgetary deficits.

## THE PRICE OF DEMOCRATIZATION

It is hard to dispute Gorbachev's conclusion that economic reform would not be possible without political reform. What is less clear is whether economic reform is possible *with* political reform. The Soviet President seems to have expected, in common with many western commentators, that democratization would produce a natural majority of cautious liberals – in economic and political terms – who would back *perestroika*, while at the same time recognizing that politics is the art of the possible. If so, he has been sorely disappointed.

Three dominant political themes, distinct but intertwining, developed in the late 1980s: nationalism, political pluralism, and popular attitudes to the market mechanism. All of them represented either results or responses to the initiatives of *perestroika*. None can claim precedence in terms of importance, but the nationalism issue was, perhaps, the first to break in purely temporal terms. So let us begin by addressing it.

As Gorbachev developed the self-financing model during 1987 he went increasingly beyond the basic, enterprise-specific, Sumy model. The new idea was to extend the principle on a territorial basis. Union republics in particular would be permitted, indeed encouraged, to set themselves up as *khozraschet* units, trading with the rest of the union on a market-oriented, profit-and-loss basis, and (presumably) organizing the intrarepublican economy on the same basis. There was an echo here of Khrushchev's *sovnarkhoz* reform of 1957 – no good omen – and it must be said that there are few models from standard economic theory for the setting up of such territorially based corporations. But in the context of the Soviet Union's unique ethnic and territorial profile, it made a good deal of pragmatic sense. Gorbachev clearly perceived that *glasnost'* was bound to produce a resurgence of the various nationalisms of the 50 per cent of the Soviet population that is not Russian, these having simply been repressed under previous regimes. He also perceived that the vastness of the Soviet Union demanded a special approach to regional economic decision-taking, whatever the economic system.

The laboratory was the Baltic region. The three Baltic republics – Estonia, Latvia, and Lithuania – had originally been annexed to the Russian Empire in the eighteenth century and had won their independence after the Russian Revolution. They were forcibly incorporated into the Soviet Union in 1940, after the signing of the Soviet–Nazi Pact of 1939 which effectively partitioned Eastern Europe between Germany and the Soviet Union. The populations of the three republics suffered much from the characteristic Stalinist visitations of death, imprisonment, and deportation, and were never reconciled to Soviet rule. But their geographical advantages, combined with a cultural heritage (non-Slav languages, Lutheran or Roman Catholic religion) which kept them looking west even in periods of Soviet isolationism, and kept them working hard even when the economic system gave them few reasons for doing so, ensured that by the 1960s the Baltic was the most prosperous and developed region of the Soviet Union.

Even before Gorbachev came to power, Estonia, Latvia, and Lithuania, together with the Belorussian republic which lies south of Lithuania, were being used as a forcing ground for more market-oriented economic experiments. As Gorbachev sought to radicalize his *perestroika* programme, it was logical enough for him to seek for allies in these Soviet fragments of the Nordic world, and the Baltic populations responded, enthusiastically embracing the role of storm-troopers of radical economic reform. It looked as if Gorbachev had done a deal.

In early 1988, though, it all started to go wrong. In February of that year a murderous dispute broke out between two of the major nationalities of Soviet Transcaucasia – the Christian, Indo-European Armenians and the Muslim, Turkic Azerbaidzhanis. The dispute arose over a small territory – Nagorno-Karabakh – which is an enclave within Azerbaidzhan, but largely inhabited by Armenians. The Armenians demanded the incorporation of the territory into the Armenian republic. The Azerbaidzhanis rejected this, and within a few days an appalling pogrom was launched against local Armenians in the Azerbaidzhani city of Sumgait which left at least thirty-four people dead. In the succeeding escalation of the conflict Soviet troops were deployed, and a number of Azerbaidzhanis and Armenians killed by those troops. This deployment did not prevent the development of full-scale civil war between the two nations, a civil war which continues to smoulder to the present day. What it did succeed in doing was alienating both Armenians and Azerbaidzhanis to the extent that both groups began to demand independence from the Soviet Union. In the Azerbaidzhani case these developments were closely intertwined with the emergence of Muslim fundamentalism. (The Azerbaidzhanis are Shiah Muslims, like the Iranians, and like their fellow-Azerbaidzhanis who live on the other side of the Soviet–Iranian border from Soviet Azerbaidzhan.)

The really important characteristic of this tragic tale of ethnic sectarianism is that it had absolutely no economic dimension whatsoever. We may see in it a certain expression of the general sense of frustration that all Soviet citizens feel at the inability of the economic system to satisfy basic human needs. Beyond that, the Nagorno-Karabakh dispute represented an atavism having as much to do with economic reform issues as the Serbian–Albanian dispute in Yugoslavia.

The first bitter lesson Gorbachev had to learn in the realm of nationalities policy, then, is that liberalization may, in Soviet conditions, produce reversion to the tribalism of the past rather than any impetus towards the *perestroika* of the future. The second lesson, perhaps even more bitter, came in 1989, as he began to lose his grip on the situation in the Baltic. There the idea of republican *khozraschet* had caught the national imagination to such an extent that increasingly radical local leaders began to articulate developments of the idea which went far beyond Moscow's original blueprint. Total local control over all the assets within the republic, an independent joint ventures regime, separate national currencies and, finally, a separate citizenship law which would impose severe residence restrictions on people not of the titular nationality – was this simply not a programme for total national independence? By early 1990 it had become clear that it was exactly that, as first Lithuania, then Latvia and Estonia, issued formal declarations of independence. Up to that point Gorbachev had continued to seek some form of compromise which would have kept his models for a Soviet market economy within the Soviet Union. But Lithuania's declaration of independence was too much, and Gorbachev imposed an economic blockade on Lithuania. By mid-1990, with the blockade lifted, it looked as if some kind of new compromise might finally be reached, though there is general, resigned, agreement amongst Moscow intellectuals that the Baltic republics will ultimately go their own way. In the meantime the prevailing situation, in what had been one of the most promising regions from the point of view of thoroughgoing *perestroika*, simply makes the Soviet authorities' critical path to a market economy that much more difficult to negotiate.

The nationalism theme intertwines tightly with the theme of political pluralism. Well before the official ending of the one-party system at the beginning of 1990, nationally based parties like Sajudis in Lithuania and Rukh in the Ukraine had emerged as standard-bearers of democratization. But the new pluralism transcended the purely ethnic/regional dimension. After the first partially democratic elections to the USSR Supreme Soviet in 1989, the Inter-Regional Group of Deputies quickly emerged as a radical political alliance, uniting individuals as contrasting as Andrei Sakharov and Boris Yeltsin. A closely related and overlapping development within the Communist Party itself saw the articulation of a Democratic Platform (*Demokraticheskaya Platforma*), bringing together many people of democratic and progressive, though not necessarily militantly radical, inclination. At the Communist Party Congress held in July 1990 sections of the Democratic Platform formally split from the Communist Party, with Boris Yeltsin, President of the Russian Republic, the most notable of the individual apostates. Meanwhile, conservative communists have been permitted to form a new conservative platform through the medium of the reborn Russian Communist Party (separate from, but still operating within the framework of the Soviet Communist Party), which held its first Congress in mid-1990.

Outside the ranks of the Supreme Soviet and the Communist Party, 1990 witnessed a flowering of new political groupings of a liberal slant – Democrats, Social Democrats, Constitutional Democrats, and a new Confederation of Labour. Their newspapers were freely on sale on the street corners of Moscow, helping to meet the apparently insatiable appetite of Muscovites for information. The sellers of these newspapers were occasionally man-handled by the police (*Ekspress-Khronika*, 17 April 1990), but the pluralization of the media seemed already irreversible.

Not all the new non-communist political movements, however, were of liberal complexion. One of the most powerful, though also one of the loosest, new groupings to emerge was *Pamyat'*. Dating back in its origins to the mid-1980s, *Pamyat'* initially simply represented a trend of mainly Russian thinking concerned about the damage and neglect suffered by buildings, including church buildings, under Soviet rule. Indeed there are still elements within *Pamyat'* which cling to that essentially cultural and idealist platform ('Chto my znaem. . .' 1990). But the dominant element within the movement has taken on a markedly conservative-Russian-nationalist, anti-semitic complexion – in short has tended towards fascism.

Gorbachev has frequently laid the blame for the slow pace of *perestroika* on obstruction by conservative Party bureaucrats. There is some truth in this allegation. At the same time it must be emphasized that election after election in the Soviet Union during 1989 and 1990 has demonstrated that Party conservatives – even the more articulate and forceful ones – enjoy little support among the populace. The failure of leading conservative Yegor Ligachev to win election to the post of Deputy General Secretary at the July Congress of the CPSU underlined the ultimate weakness of the conservatives even within the Party itself. Perhaps because they realized that a conservative platform has no appeal to the masses, many delegates of conservative inclination at the Congress must have voted against Ligachev.

So much for the good news. The bad news for the cause of *perestroika* is that the radicals may enjoy hardly more mass support outside the 'revolutionary' cities of Moscow and Leningrad than the Party conservatives. Indeed the proceedings of the first Congress of People's Deputies of the Russian Republic, which was convened in May 1990, confirmed that the dominant political ethos in Russia itself now, as in the non-Russian republics, is one of nationalism. It is not necessarily the nationalism of *Pamyat'* – Boris Yeltsin, for instance, or Gavriil Popov, are both very far indeed from a *Pamyat'* platform. Yet both those leaders have supported the assertion of Russian sovereignty within the Soviet Union, and of the proposition that the Soviet authorities have no right to legislate on specifically Russian matters. These notions threaten to undermine the whole legal and political basis on which the Soviet government seeks to implement its policies.

Popular attitudes, however, have an impact on the process of restructuring which goes far beyond the realm of politics *per se*. It is easy to assume, especially on the basis of Polish, Hungarian, and East German experience, that *perestroika* means a welcome restoration for the masses of not only the market mechanism in a very general sense, but also of the traditional sticks and carrots of the market economy – high wages for those who work hard, low wages, even the threat of job loss, for those who do not. There are, indeed, many individuals in the smaller east European states who would favour the Thatcherite, rather than the West German/ Swedish model of the 'social market economy'. The Soviet Union, however, is very different from eastern Europe. Nowhere is this more apparent than on the dimension of popular attitudes to the market mechanism.

In January 1990 the Moscow Centre for the Study of Public Opinion, a prestigious organization whose director, Tatyana Zaslavskaya, had started the whole *perestroika* process in 1982 with her *Novosibsirsk Report*, carried out a survey on attitudes to private property in the Soviet Union (Lyalyushkin *et al.* 1990). The survey produced a somewhat confused picture, mainly because most Soviet citizens are vague about the distinction between private (*chastnyi*) and personal (*lichnyi*) property. Nevertheless the overall pattern of attitudes was well contoured. There was a clear, two-thirds majority in favour of leasehold, joint ventures, and worker-owned enterprises. On joint-stock companies of the KamAZ type (see Chapter 4, p. 97), opinion was fairly evenly divided. But only 36 per cent of the respondents were in favour of wholly foreign-owned firms, only 30 per cent in favour of cooperatives as presently existing, and only 27 per cent in favour of enterprises owned by individual Soviet citizens. Just 23 per cent thought that individual private ownership of large-scale industrial plants was acceptable, and there was a small majority against permitting the hiring of labour by private entrepreneurs. Just 32 per cent of the sample said that they would take advantage of any legalization of private entrepreneurship, with lack of money, lack of the requisite technical knowledge, and lack of confidence that the government might not change its mind being the main factors conditioning the negative responses of the other 68 per cent. There was wide regional variation in the responses, with Latvia producing a clear majority in favour of private property and Russia much more doubtful. The Centre's conclusions were threefold. First, too much liberalization in relation to private property could well induce a backlash against private entrepreneurship. For that reason it would be better to concentrate on collective forms of property in the short run. Second, any programme for the *de-étatization* of property in the Soviet Union must be backed up with a comprehensive state poverty programme in order to avoid undesirable social side-effects. Third, interregional variations in attitudes are so great that no single model of marketization/privatization for the whole of the Soviet Union is practicable.

There is little comfort for Gorbachev in these conclusions. Social programmes are uncontroversial, but will place an additional burden on a beleaguered budget. Variations in attitudes between different Soviet nations present no analytical problems, but would seem to lend support to the Yeltsin/Popov line on the proper legislative balance between all-union and republican legislatures rather than Gorbachev's. Finally, the validity of the conclusion on collective forms of property as a vehicle for private entrepreneurship is thrown into doubt by the extreme unpopularity of the existing cooperatives, which are, after all, a form of collective property.

## WHAT IS TO BE DONE?

It is clear that in the presence of so many economic and political complications, the inherent tendency must be for the *perestroika* process to lose momentum and for the Soviet system to default to a more traditionally Soviet economic model. But just to present the problem in that form reveals a ray of hope. In truth, there is no traditional Soviet economic model to default to! So if the only way is forward, how is the Soviet leadership to pick its way between the precipices and swamps created by sixty years of economic and political stasis?

It emerged from our analysis in the early part of this chapter that no significant further progress with restructuring can be made until the budget deficit is removed or radically reduced. Current plans to cut the deficit are simply not far-reaching enough to make more than a marginal impact on the blockage. What options are open to a Soviet government seeking to emulate the Polish government of Tadeusz Mazowiecki in cutting the budget deficit to zero or near zero within a year or so?

There are ways in which the Soviet government could, in the short run, make some positive impact on budget revenue. A more sophisticated alcohol policy would leave the alcohol industry to increase output in response to demand, but subject to high rates of tax, so as to ensure that there was no 'vodka-gap' for the bootleggers to fill. That would be good for the exchequer and good (or at least better) for the health of the Soviet people, though it would no more remove the budget deficit than the anti-alcohol policy that created it in the first place. Again, the progressive tax on cooperative wages introduced in early 1990, though flawed in its formulation, does represent a perfectly sensible principle for correcting the 'natural' distribution of income, thus helping to reconcile ordinary Russians to the nature of market incentives, while at the same time doing something for budget revenues. The same can be said for the law on profits tax passed in July 1990, which introduced the progressive taxation principle for all domestic enterprises (but not, it appears, for joint ventures). On the other hand, policies of 'milking the rich' have made but a minor impact on the income of the state even in countries where there are plenty of rich to be milked. In the Soviet Union, for the time being at least, the number of people properly qualifying for some kind of super-tax remains absolutely tiny. In total, then, there is scope for short-term 'incremental' improvement in the budget revenue position, but it must be measured in tens rather than hundreds of billions of roubles. Of course in the long run, as the principles of the market economy take hold and real economic growth begins again, budget revenues could be expected to rise substantially and painlessly. But that would be a result, not a cause, of effective restructuring.

Turning to more radical options – what about privatization? Large-scale privatization of Soviet industry is, with due respect to the authors of the 500-day programme, surely a medium- rather than short-term prospect since it presupposes a certain amount of initial 'socialist asset-stripping' in order to bring enterprises somewhere near to profitability, and would require the setting up of some kind of stock-market unless the government were prepared simply to give enterprises to the workers (which would of course help neither the budget nor the cause of restructuring). A Soviet stock-market is, in turn, inconceivable as long as the Soviet Union lacks a currency able to act as an effective store of value and means of exchange. But with so much money in savings accounts, surely the authorities could find some way of tapping it? Selling off state-owned housing is one possibility, though the poor quality of the bulk of Soviet housing might be a significant obstacle to such a policy. (Alternatively, the notional rents of today could be replaced by something more like economic rents. That might, of course, upset people as much as swingeing food price increases.) But one area where privatization could certainly make an immediate and substantial impact on budget revenue is in relation to land. Whether on the basis of leasehold or freehold, land for agriculture or development, provided it is outside badly polluted areas, is a prime resource for which demand could be expected to match supply in the event of a sell-off. Because land is a tangible asset, the problem of the weakness of the rouble is irrelevant. But the agriculture issue is a huge issue, which encompasses expenditure as well as revenue sides of the budget. So we leave it for the present, to return to it at the conclusion of our discussion of the budgetary issue.

At the level of short-term, emergency action, then – privatization of land apart – it seems that we must concentrate on the expenditure side of the budget. Within that dimension, perhaps the most obvious area for economies is in the field of defence expenditure. President Gorbachev gave to the Supreme Soviet in May 1989 the first official 'true' figure for total defence expenditure. The figure he gave – a projected figure for 1989 – was 77.3 billion roubles (Gorbachev 1989b). This represents some 11–13 per cent of Soviet National Income (depending on exactly how the latter is calculated), which is remarkably close to the estimates of the CIA (1988a), which seems to afford enormous scope for cuts in an age of galloping disengagement at the east–west military level. Yet according to the CIA Soviet defence expenditure actually grew 3 per cent in 1989 by comparison with 1988 (CIA 1989), and Gorbachev himself, in another 1989 speech, implied precisely such a trend (Gorbachev 1989a). The apparent paradox is not so difficult to fathom. Military expenditures in any given year are a function of procurement and manning decisions taken years earlier, and in a system like the Soviet, with its weakness for long lead-times, that might be many years earlier. Military production facilities are not usually directly convertible to civilian-good production except on a fairly marginal scale, even in the cases where the organizations concerned are already manufacturing a lot of consumer goods (Grishchenko 1989). Of course, they could simply be closed down but that would only create a whole new range of problems, including budgetary problems (of this more on p. 200). In addition, new elements in the situation like the large-scale repatriation of Soviet troops from eastern Europe are likely to impose new and massive costs on the Soviet budget. In a word, military restructuring, far from offering the Soviet government a 'free shot', is not much less problematic than industrial restructuring.

In his May 1989 speech Gorbachev said that military spending would be cut by 10 billion roubles over the period 1990–1. This formulation seemed to reflect a sharp awareness of the structural difficulties constraining defence expenditure cuts, leaving open as it did the option of only beginning to cut in 1991. Even if all the 10 billion roubles proposed for cuts were concentrated in that year we would, of course, still be talking about a reduction of only some 13 per cent on the present 1990 defence budget. In an authoritative article from early 1990, Soviet defence economist I. Yudin suggested that by 1992–3 annual Soviet military expenditure would be down to around 50 billion roubles. (Yudin 1990). He bases this on the assumption of partial professionalization of the Soviet Army (a measure that has since been promulgated), and of a radical reorganization of military administration. Even so, he is positing a reduction in the military burden on the budget of less than 30 billion roubles – and even that only in two to three years' time. The conclusion is inescapable, then, that the demilitarization of the Soviet economy, though of great potential importance, is a medium-term, rather than a short-term option. As such, it cannot play a central role in attacking the short-term budget problem.

While there is no disputing that the defence burden on the Soviet economy is a heavy one, it is placed firmly in perspective when we look at the biggest single item in the Soviet budget – 'allocations to the economy', which came to 242.8 billion roubles in 1988, 52.8 per cent of total budgetary expenditure and 7 per cent more than in 1987, and some three times as much as defence spending (*Narkhoz* 1988, pp. 624–5).

What exactly are 'allocations to the economy'? About one-half of the total is accounted for by non-returnable investment grants. In the light of the total failure of the Gorbachev government to bring any order whatsoever into the chaotic capital investment sector, as documented in Chapter 6, it is perhaps not surprising that the trend in this item is still upwards. The other main item under allocations to the economy is subsidies, including food subsidies. Again, as we saw earlier in this chapter, the Soviet government has signally failed to stop continued escalation in the level of food subsidies.

But while this is a sorry tale, it does, surely, point the way to a possible solution. Why not a 'short, sharp shock' treatment for centralized investment? With half of total investment now financed from retained profits, the upgrading requirements of existing enterprises are surely adequately taken care of. And with new investment projects in the Soviet Union taking anything up to ten years to complete, would it matter one whit if centralized investment were simply closed down completely for a couple of years, especially if the prize were a launching-pad for a genuinely radical reform which would, *inter alia*, shorten lead-times dramatically?

The answer, in terms of short-term output trends, is almost certainly: no, it would not. The problem is that some medium- and long-term issues cannot simply be put on ice. Let us cast our minds back to the energy proposals of Professor Aksenov described at the end of Chapter 4. In the long run, these proposals would, on Aksenov's reasoning, generate vast investment economies. But a new energy strategy requires *different* energy investments right now. A total centralized investment freeze would simply block off the option of a new investment strategy. Again, the appalling state of the Soviet transport network, one of the reasons why 30 per cent of food production never reaches the consumer, is a problem which must be attacked *now*, though the fruits of a new road and rail programme would not be reaped for many years.

Big though the energy problem is, however, it is not the biggest of the Soviet Union's long-term economic headaches. One of the bitter-sweet fruits of *glasnost'* has been a new awareness, at all levels, of the terrible extent of environmental damage bequeathed to the Soviet Union by a quantity-obsessed development strategy. Perhaps the best known and most dramatic instance of this damage is presented by the Chernobyl' case. Following on an explosion at the Chernobyl' (Ukraine) nuclear power-station in 1986, a vast area of the western Soviet Union suffered serious radiation pollution. At a meeting of the 'Moscow Tribune' club, held in the Moscow House of Academic Ecologists on 14 April 1990, distinguished biologist A. G. Nazarov reported on a new scientific

study which had been done of the effects of Chernobyl' on the basis
of recently declassified information and field trips to affected areas
(*Ekspress-Khronika*, 17 April 1990, p. 2). Nazarov cited the following
data: 100,000 square kilometres are polluted by radiation for the
next 150 years, including 30 per cent of the territory of the
Ukraine, 75 per cent of that of Belorussia, and parts of Bryansk,
Tula and Kaluga provinces in the Russian republic. Four million
people live in the affected areas, of which 200,000 require urgent
resettlement and 1.5 million gradual resettlement. It is estimated
that the total cost of such a resettlement would be 180 billion
roubles – some 75 per cent of the total value of budgetary
allocations to the economy in 1988. Other assessments suggest a
somewhat less dramatic scenario, but no one disputes that a
massive *state* investment effort is required to implement a proper
post-Chernobyl' clean-up.

While Chernobyl' is perhaps the only one of the Soviet Union's
ecologicial disasters to have achieved world-wide notoriety, it is not
unique. The case of the Aral Sea discussed in Chapter 5 is only the
most dramatic instance of the rape of the Soviet Union's
waterways. Even the springs of the North Caucasus, long famous
for their curative powers, are now threatened with pollution. In
old-established industrial areas like the eastern Ukraine, rates of
cancer among the population are abnormally high. In the present
context it is not important how much worse the Soviet ecological
problem might be than that in comparable countries. What
matters is simply the size of the problem in absolute terms.

Faced with environmental problems on this scale, in addition to
vast infrastructural investment requirements, it is clear that the
Soviet government cannot simply freeze centralized investment
expenditure. There are few prospects for the privatization of the
Aral Sea. The urgency of the ecological issue does, indeed,
strengthen the argument for cutting off financial support to
traditional, obsolescent industries, though even there the hazard of
socially unacceptable unemployment levels would counsel a
gradual approach (see pp. 200–1 for further discussion). The fact
is, however, that on environmental and infrastructural grounds
alone, it is simply not realistic to envisage swingeing reductions in
the volume of public sector investment in the Soviet Union.

That leaves us with subsidies, and in particular with agricultural
subsidies. However tricky an issue this is from the political point of
view, the food complex does offer the Soviet government the one

possibility of making a major dent in the budget deficit more or less overnight – the one genuine 'free shot'. Meat and bread are ridiculously cheap in the Soviet Union, many state and collective farms ridiculously inefficient. But in the face of stubborn public hostility to food price increases, how is the free shot to be taken?

This is perhaps the one area of policy-making currently exercising the Soviet government for which a market-led approach could well simplify rather than complicate matters. The paradox of public attitudes to food prices is that for the majority of the Soviet population living outside the big cities, meat at two roubles a kilo is a pure fiction. For meat is not available to them in state shops at *any* price. In Moscow it is only available if you are prepared to queue for hours and hours. The mistake President Gorbachev made in May 1990 was to alter radically, by government fiat, a parameter that had come to have great symbolic importance for the Soviet people, but which, because of institutional blockages, had no impact on the real problem – namely, agricultural supply. An alternative approach would eschew any such arbitrary dispositions, and simply seek to improve supplies to the existing collective farm markets at which peasants have traditionally sold their private plot surpluses (in 1988 these accounted for 5 per cent of total food retail turnover, 2.2 per cent in terms of constant prices) (*Narkhoz* 1988, p. 102). This would take the pressure off the state retail sector, reduce the length of queues, place the onus on the peasants themselves to get their produce to market in one piece, and ultimately bring collective farm market prices down. Meat, for example, would continue to be available at two roubles a kilo for those who could get it, and would become much more widely available at a price – say in the region of 5–10 roubles a kilo – accessible to most Soviet citizens and without the precondition of queueing. The free market would gradually take over the leading role in the provision of foodstuffs on an unsubsidized basis. (This would, of course, require substantial new investment in extended collective farm markets, small individual retail outlets etc.) (Schaffer 1990). It appears that the agricultural strategy of the 500–day plan may, indeed, follow this line of reasoning.

There is, perhaps, an element of sleight-of-hand here, a trick to neutralize the peculiar kind of money illusion, or rather price illusion, which afflicts a large part of the Soviet population. The reality, however, is that such a policy would focus on improving supplies, leaving prices to look after themselves. It would, of course, be successful in such a focus only if it explicitly addressed the whole issue of conditions of agricultural supply, only if it sought to back up a free market in produce with a free structure at the production level. This brings us nicely back to the whole issue of privatization of agriculture. A leasehold/freehold system in agriculture is the first, though not the only, condition for radical improvement in food supplies. Privatization of land will add to budget revenues, just as privatization of food retailing will help to cut budget expenditures. All of this could be implemented within a single year, and the budget deficit brought to near-zero.

A radical privatization policy on agriculture would provide one more bonus. As we noted at the beginning of this chapter, the Soviet deficit on hard-currency balance of trade was US$6.5 billion in 1989. For the same year total grain imports were worth something more than US$6 billion. It would be unrealistic to imagine that agricultural privatization could by itself remove the Soviet trade deficit. Indeed grain production is the one area of agriculture where medium-sized family farms are unlikely to provide comprehensive answers to efficiency problems. But if we view the transformation of the big, grain-growing collective and state farms into genuine cooperatives as a dimension of privatization, the agricultural card could become almost as big an ace in relation to external balance as in relation to internal, budgetary balance, permitting the Soviet authorities to re-establish a degree of external equilibrium without having to wait for the macro-economic effects of renewed budgetary soundness to percolate through to the external sector.

What other short-term options might contribute to a re-establishment of external financial balance? As we saw earlier, the debate on military conversion has produced fairly cautious evaluations of the potential for switching military production capacities to specific civilian lines, for 'beating swords to ploughshares'. But those evaluations have in turn engendered a new approach to conversion. If conversion of production lines *per se* is difficult, why not keep the production lines as they are and seek conversion in terms of markets? This is the origin of the idea, now widely canvassed in the Soviet Union, that military and space production potential could be switched from the domestic to the hard-currency export market. Now there can be no doubt that Soviet ballistics and space station technology is on a par with the best in the world. But a fascinating proposal put forward by the head of one of the USSR's leading space design institutes places the whole idea in a revolutionary new perspective (Tarasov 1990). The proposal is for the construction of a 100-ton experimental factory in outer space, for the production of unique semiconductors, medicines, and types of optical glass. It is estimated that the project would cost 1.2 billion roubles, and would generate gross earnings of 3–8 billion roubles. The projected lead-time is three years, so that with a 1991 start, the experimental factory would come on-stream in 1994. Reference back to Chapter 6 suggests, however, that, under current Soviet conditions those three years could well turn into ten.

In practice, then, the Soviet military-industrial complex is likely to turn into a major exporter only in the medium term. It turns out, upon examination to provide but a special case of a general proposition. The medium- to long-term future of the Soviet hard-currency balance of trade will, short of a dramatic and permanent rise in the price of oil which even the Persian Gulf crisis of 1990 hardly seems to promise, depend on the ability of the USSR to develop its capacity to export manufactures on a large scale. Such a development will be a consequence, not a condition, of effective *perestroika*. In mapping out a programme for the removal of the budget deficit as the first of those conditions we have, along the way, already made proposals for far-reaching systemic reform, particularly in relation to agriculture. What other initial conditions would have to be met for *perestroika* to really take off?

Much of the foregoing discussion has focused on the inherent inefficiency of the feudal-bureaucratic form of state administration of the economy which has dominated in the Soviet Union in the past. Central planning, it has been demonstrated, is incorrigibly wasteful, and is by its very nature unable to cope with the tasks of intensive development. The quicker the whole edifice inherited from Stalin can be dismantled and the more the Soviet economy can be privatized, the better.

But these propositions, indisputable in themselves, raise as many questions as they answer. If central planning is to go, what form of central economic policy-making is to take its place? The 'regulated market' currently favoured by the Soviet leadership is, perhaps, something of an empty economic box – the experience of indicative planning, east and west, gives little ground for optimism on the prospects for developing a system of 'generalized market research' as the basis for a new kind of Soviet *concertation*, even if we assume away the ethnic-centrifugal forces which seem to grow daily stronger in the USSR. But indicative planning or no indicative planning, the Soviet authorities, or the Russian/ Estonian/Ukrainian etc. authorities, will be left with the problem of how to run the parts of the economy left in the state sector when all possible privatizations have been implemented. We have already seen how the current infrastructural and environmental priorities of the government make the maintenance of a high rate of centralized investment inevitable. We can add that the very depth of the Soviet industrial restructuring problem excludes the option of simply putting every enterprise on full self-financing, and then closing down or selling off any which become insolvent. A large part of the Soviet capital stock requires total renewal, and simple arithmetic tells us that that will take at least ten years even with the maintenance of a high investment ratio. Much of the rest requires redeployment – the kind of reorganization which is implemented in western countries through receivership and stock-markets. The Soviet government has already pin-pointed the need to develop institutions such as receivership (Abalkin 1989c). The 1990 basic legislation on the setting up of joint-stock companies discussed in Chapter 4 provides a legal framework for share issues. The 500-day plan aims to set up a stock exchange within 100–120 days. But a fully-fledged Soviet stock-market is, as we saw earlier, inconceivable until *after* the initial phase of restructuring is complete – that is, until financial and monetary equilibrium and partial rouble convertibility are established, and the minimum of industrial reorganization sufficient to ensure that potential investors would feel confident that they were investing in *something* implemented. (One wonders, in any case, whether even the London Stock Exchange could handle industrial reorganization on the scale required by the Soviet Union.) A 'shock-therapy' approach to these industrial restructuring problems would simply destroy a large part of the Soviet economy and create massive unemployment. Such an approach might hold out the prospect of an industrial phoenix in the the next century, but if in the meantime it passes through stages which generate intolerable social and political tensions it is very likely to bring the whole strategy of reconstruction crashing down long before any such benefits can be reaped.

If a large part of the Soviet economy is bound to remain within the state sector, then, how is the government to ensure that waste and inefficiency in that sector does not simply cancel out any gains made in the new private sector and that the old feudal-bureaucratic regime will be replaced by cost-effective stewardship of public funds – in short, by a modern public sector on the western model? More specifically, how will hard budget constraints be imposed on enterprises which cannot reasonably be expected to make a profit in the short term? How will the Soviet government ensure that the massive environmental projects that lie ahead will not turn into financial and ecological disaster, on the model of Brezhnev's non-Black Earth Programme? What role, within such projects, will be played by subcontracting, including subcontracting to foreign firms? If that role is large, how will the tendering process be handled? How will the Soviet government finance desperately needed new road programmes? Wholly through the central budget? By a combination of central and local funding? Should they consider the possibility of charging tolls? If so, should they leave the administration and maintenance of toll roads to the private sector, on the French model?

There is as little experience of addressing these problems in the Soviet Union as of running a large, wholly private sector. There is, of course, a long track-record of public enterprise in the west, though it yields as many negative lessons as positive, as many failures as successes. One thing is clear: you cannot run a public sector without civil servants, a breed unknown in the Soviet Union. And this is just one dimension of a general problem of education, training, and attitudes which may be as critical for the future of *perestroika* as any more technical issue.

Perhaps Leonid Abalkin was speaking half in jest when he said in a *Der Spiegel* interview in 1989 that there were fewer than twenty people in the Soviet Union who understood finance and marketing (Abalkin 1989b). But he returned to the theme of education for *perestroika* in the 'Abalkin plan' of November 1989 (Abalkin, 1989c). Coming back to the industrial restructuring theme, it is clear that institutions like receivership cannot be effectively created in the Soviet Union until there are people trained specifically to man the institution. The quest for a cost-effective economy may take economics as its compass, but it will require a good deal of prosaic accountancy before the map is complete. Significantly, the plans to turn the KamAZ lorry plant into a joint-stock company have highlighted the crucial importance of sophisticated auditing services to provide valuations of elements of capital stock. At present, only foreign firms can provide those services (Korotkov and Ul'yanov 1990). And while education will be crucial in building up the required kinds of human capital at the elite level, it will be equally important in modifying the mind-set of the Soviet population at large. We have seen more than once how popular attitudes and popular prejudices can neutralize even quite modest attempts at reform. Until Soviet schools, universities, and media can cajole (some socialists would say brainwash) the people into accepting that high demand must mean high prices, that incentives to produce what the people need must mean high incomes for those who deliver the goods, and that there are no jobs for life, then the cause of fundamental restructuring will remain a beleaguered one.

Possibly the greatest immediate obstacle preventing critical acceleration in the restructuring programme, though, is the problem of relations between the Soviet nations. Or rather it is the problem of the single Soviet market. It does, in truth, matter little from the economic point of view, and from the point of view of systemic restructuring, if the Soviet Union ceases to exist in the form we have known in the past. As has been amply demonstrated by post-war experience in western Europe, the enormous benefits that accrue from large, integrated markets are not conditional on the existence of single state administrations, single armies, or single sovereignty. Whether their maximal exploitation is dependent on the existence of a single currency remains a hotly debated point, but to date the European Community has managed pretty well without even that. Now as we have seen throughout this book, spatial integration has always been the weakest point of the Soviet economy. In the absence of a market, with the pressures and weaknesses of an over-centralized system, the tendency to autarky of one kind or another was always very powerful. Hesitant attempts at reform of the Khrushchev variety tended to make things worse rather than better.

It is one of the most striking characteristics of the degeneration of *perestroika* that occurred during 1989/90 that this tendency has returned with a vengeance. By mid-1990, as we saw earlier, it was impossible to shop in food stores in many Soviet cities without proof of local residence. Following on Gorbachev's spring 1990 economic blockade of Lithuania in response to the latter's unilateral declaration of independence, the Moscow Soviet, under its radical economist mayor Gavriil Popov, entered into direct negotiations with the Lithuanian government on the possibility of swopping fuel for food supplies. Early 1990 also saw the government of Uzbekistan, the biggest of the central Asian, republics, cutting deliveries to other republics. August of that year brought a new twist to the autarky theme. It was reported that the Supreme Soviet of the Russian Federation, fresh from a consideration of the 500-day plan, had passed a law forbidding the sale of Russian natural resources through joint ventures etc. 'without the permission of the appropriate (i.e. Russian Federation) authorities'. Clearly an essentially political gesture intended mainly for the attention of President Gorbachev, the report was nevertheless deeply disturbing in that it showed an insensitivity to international business confidence factors which bodes ill for Soviet/Russian involvement in the international division of labour. The combination of marketizing radicalism and xenophobic populism is a bizarre one to western eyes, and it can hardly be a functional one. But it is that combination which currently dominates the Parliament of the Russian Federation.

It is perhaps not surprising that local leaderships take autarkic measures in the face of critical immediate food shortages. To the extent, however, that they identify regional self-sufficiency with 'true' independence, they are certainly sorely mistaken. But perhaps here again it is the system rather than the people that should take the blame. In a prescient article published in 1989, Estonian economist M. Bronshtein argued that a half-way house on the principle of the market economy, and on the principle of market relations between regions, could well produce the worst of all possible worlds, with regional authorities seeking to subvert residual central directive powers by retreating into regional autarky (Bronshtein 1989). Consideration of the painful history of Yugoslavia in this connection (see Dyker 1990) fully supports Bronshtein's thesis. Here again, we find powerful confirmation of a general thesis that has pervaded this chapter. Meaningful *perestroika* has to be deeply radical from the word go, and that means that the Soviet government will have to show great courage, not only in the strictly economic field but also in the political, if the present deadlock is to be broken. An imaginative approach to the problem of reconstituting the Soviet Union, possibly as a commonwealth of independent states, is absolutely vital if the nations of the Soviet Union are to discover, perhaps for the first time, where their real common economic interests lie. The model should probably be the Treaty of Rome, and the Soviet government might do well to abandon its plans for a new Treaty of Union in favour of a looser configuration under the rubric of a 'Treaty of the Third Rome'.

## CONCLUSION: CAN THE SOVIET UNION DO IT ALONE?

It was a frequently expressed view in economist circles in Moscow in mid-1990 that effective *perestroika* was impossible without large-scale economic aid from the west. Indeed Deputy Prime Minister Abalkin said as much to a visiting European Commission delegation in May of that year. The Community, or at least some of its members, seemed inclined to respond affirmatively. From the point of view of reduction of international tension this is, no doubt, very positive. But amidst all the talk of Marshall Plans and the like for the Soviet Union, it is perhaps worth reiterating some of the basic points that have emerged from the foregoing analysis, namely:

1  The Soviet crisis is a systemic crisis. While the goal is the total restructuring of the production profile of the economy, the instrument is, and can only be, the total restructuring of the economic system.
2  There is absolutely no evidence that the Soviet Union is a capital deficit region. On the contrary, the economic history of the country since 1930 is the history of investment ratios consistently in the region of 25–30 per cent of national income, comparable to high-investment western economies like the West German and the Japanese. The problem in the Soviet Union has been the escalating inefficiency with which the investment funds so effectively mobilized have been used. That brings us straight back to the systemic variable.
3  It follows from 2 that there is no macroeconomic reason why the Soviet Union should run persistent balance of payments deficits. Given the exporting strength of the Soviet Union in Ricardo goods like oil, gas, and timber, there is equally no micro-economic reason. (Note the total contrast with the smaller east European countries on this point.)
4  Policy response on the part of the west to current Soviet international payments problems should, therefore, proceed from the premise that these are essentially liquidity problems. That in turn would suggest that action to facilitate increased Soviet

involvement in the international financial community, and in particular membership of the IMF with the 'overdraft' facilities that this brings with it, may be more apposite than any programme of long-term aid, on the basis of either grants or loans on special terms.

5 Against the background of a dramatic fall in the level of international tension, it is absolutely right and proper that western-imposed restrictions on east-west trade, including the COCOM list of goods deemed strategic which may not be exported to the Soviet Union, should be dismantled. This will aid technology transfer. But that technology transfer will, of course, be ultimately effective only if the domestic Soviet economic system is capable of assimilating it.

6 Everything should be done to encourage the free flow of private capital to the Soviet Union. This is the most effective vehicle for technology transfer, and it has the great advantage of not imposing an automatically recurrent burden on the balance of payments. Once again, however, it must be stressed that the main obstacles to a flowering of foreign investment are of a domestic systemic nature.

That *perestroika* must mean an abandonment of Stalinist national autarky and the Soviet Union joining the world economic system as a full member, is indubitable. But the internationalization of *perestroika* is essentially a stage-two assignment. The first job, a job still hardly begun, is to fashion a Soviet economic system which can respond to market pressures on a world scale, on a national scale, and on a local scale. That task can only be accomplished by the leaders and peoples of the Soviet Union.

# Postscript

By April 1991 the situation had changed little from mid–1990. Output continued to fall and macro-economic imbalance to grow. Against a background of escalating discontent amongst the non-Russian nationalities and some heavyhandedness in Moscow's policy, particularly in the Baltic, the 'war of laws' between Gorbachev and Yeltsin continued unabated, with no sign of any effective Gorbachev–Yeltsin coalition emerging. A wave of strikes centring on the coal industry, which developed in March and April, generated increasingly politicized demands, culminating in widespread calls for Gorbachev's resignation. Against this political background, there is simply no basis on which the tough and radical policy initiatives required by the Soviet Union (or its successor states) can be implemented.

## The budget deficit

The budget deficit was officially reported at 58.1 billion roubles for 1990, representing a 33.9 billion reduction on the 1989 deficit. There are indications that this may represent something of an understatement of the true deficit. Even as it stands, however, and in the continued absence of a Soviet money market to provide a fiscal cushion, it adds very substantially to the repressed inflationary gap, as was evinced by growing shortages and lengthening queues towards the end of 1990. The early signs are that the budgetary position may worsen again dramatically in 1991 and 1992, as non-Russian republics tend increasingly to withhold payments to the central budget. According to new finance minister, Vladimir Orlov, the deficit had reached 31.1 billion roubles for the first quarter of 1991 alone.

## The monetary overhang

New prime minister Valentin Pavlov, who took over when Nikolai Ryzhkov suffered a heart attack in December 1990, came to the hot seat with the dubious credentials of a man who, as finance minister, had presided over the final loss of control over the Soviet money supply. His first major initiative, launched in January 1991, gave little cause for optimism on the policy-making future. Fifty and one-hundred-rouble bills were withdrawn from circulation, with the proviso that holders of such bills would be given other bills on a one-to-one basis up to a maximum of 1,000 roubles. Thus the measure involved an element of confiscation. It was purportedly aimed partly at flushing out dirty mafia money. But while the growth in commercial gangsterism was one of the most dramatic features of 1990, it is clear that by the beginning of 1991 the mafias were operating mainly in hard currency. The other aim of Pavlov's 'currency reform' was to reduce the excess money supply, and thus reduce repressed inflationary pressure. But with the on-going budget deficit continuing to add to the overhang, Pavlov's measure, intensely irritating though it was to the Soviet population, seemed but a drop in the macro-economic ocean.

## The problem of prices

On 2 April 1991 a series of sharp increases in state retail prices was announced. Beef went up by 250 per cent, flour by 200 per cent, bread by 100–300 per cent, depending on type, men's suits by 130 per cent and school exercise books by 400 per cent. The measures bore a striking similarity to the abortive measures announced by Ryzhkov in mid-1990. The underlying situation had changed somewhat in the meantime in that the Soviet population had had time to become used to the idea of big price increases, while a process of 'rolling' upwards adjustment in prices was already under way during the winter of 1990–1. So the price increases are likely to stick this time. Nevertheless the initiative displays all the underlying weaknesses of the original Ryzhkov price initiative. It is an exercise in *central planning*, continuing and consolidating the tradition whereby the government in Moscow determines not just the general profile but also the details of the price system. In promising to pay out 164 billion roubles in compensatory income adjustments, the Soviet government has made sure that the measures will have at best a marginal impact on the size of the budget deficit. And while the price increases may cut the length of some queues, and stop small boys playing football with bread rolls, to use Gorbachev's favourite example, they will do nothing to attack the crucial underlying problem of incentives to agriculture, since under the existing agricultural set-up there is no direct way the new prices can act as signals to agricultural producers. With the Soviet government continuing to vacillate over agricultural privatization the chances of a market-led solution to the food supply problem are currently very slim.

## The problem of external balance

In light of the $4.9 billion deficit on hard-currency balance of trade reported for 1990 the Soviet balance of payments looks increasingly precarious, and the prospects for 1991 and 1992 are not good. With Soviet oil output falling fast (by 6 per cent in 1990), and world oil prices likely to remain weak through 1992, there is little chance of any substantial increase in Soviet export earnings. At the same time the burden of interest payments on foreign debt is growing all the time, while repayments schedules are due to bulge in 1991. Over the period 1991–2, then, the Soviet Union will be looking to borrow heavily abroad – and will have some difficulty in finding willing lenders. While the western powers, and in particular the EC, are clearly anxious to facilitate continued reform in the Soviet Union, and are already making substantial gestures in terms of technology transfer and educational and training programmes, there are no prospects for large-scale public-sector capital transfers to the Soviet Union. Amidst deepening political uncertainty in the country itself, the prospects for private capital inflow appear equally dim.

## A chink of light

Amidst all the bad news, there are some encouraging signs. However poor its public profile, the cooperative movement continues to develop, and is now accounting for some 7–10 per cent of Soviet national income. Late 1990 and early 1991 witnessed a wave of legislation, at union and republican (notably RSFSR) level, covering issues like privatization, taxation, principles of audit and cost accounting, breach of contract, unemployment, and the like. As long as the movement towards a market economy remains stymied, and as long as the war of laws continues, none of this will have any operational impact. But it does mean that one crucial element in the original Abalkin plan of 1989, the creation of a body of basic commercial and financial law, is being quietly implemented. Thus when the next wave of *perestroika* begins to gather strength, at least one precondition that was conspicuously absent in the late 1980s will be firmly in place.

# Glossary

| | |
|---|---|
| *apparatchik* | Communist Party apparatus man |
| *arenda* | leasehold |
| *chastnyi* | private |
| CMEA | Council for Mutual Economic Assistance |
| CRE | coefficient of relative effectiveness |
| *ekspertiza* | design monitoring organization |
| *fondootdacha* | output–capital ratio |
| *gektarshchik* | 'hectarer' |
| *glasnost'* | 'openness' |
| *glavk* | main administration (within ministry |
| Gosagroprom | State Agro-Industrial Committee |
| Gosbank | State Bank |
| Goskomtrud | All-Union State Committee for Labour and Social Problems |
| Gosplan | State Planning Commission |
| Gossnab | State Supply Committee |
| Gosstroi | State Construction Committee |
| *gosudarstvennyi zakaz (goszakaz)* | 'state order' |
| *khozraschet* | 'business accounting' |
| *kolkhoz* | collective farm |
| *kolkhoznik* | collective farmer |
| Komsomol | Young Communist League |
| *kontrol'nye tsifry* | 'control figures' |
| *krai* | province |
| KTU *(koeffitsient trudovogo uchastiya)* | labour coefficient |
| *lichnyi* | personal |
| Minstroi | Ministry of Construction |
| *naryad* | allocation certificate |
| NMP | net material product (Marxian definition of national income which excludes 'unproductive services') |

| | |
|---|---|
| NNO | normed net output |
| *ob"edinenie* | association |
| *oblast'* | province |
| Orgnabor | organized recruitment |
| PBR | payment by results |
| PCIA | production-construction and installation association |
| *perestroika* | reconstruction, restructuring |
| *planirovanie ot dostignutogo urovnya* | 'planning from the achieved level' |
| Politburo | Political Bureau, Communist Party Cabinet |
| *proektnaya organizatsiya* | design organization |
| Promstroibank | Bank for Industrial Construction |
| *propiska* | residence permit |
| RAPO (*raionnoe agropromyshlennoe ob"edinenie* | district agro-industrial association |
| *raspylenie (sredstv)* | excessive investment spread |
| *samookupaemost'* | self-financing |
| Sel'khozkhimiya | chemicals for agriculture organization |
| Sel'khoztekhnika | machinery for agriculture organization |
| *shabashniki* | 'lump' workers |
| *shturmovshchina* | 'storming' |
| *sluzhba truda* | employment offices |
| *snabsbyt* | supply depot |
| *sovershenstvovanie* | 'perfecting' |
| *sovkhoz* | state farm |
| *sovnarkhoz* | Regional Economic Council |
| Stroibank | Investment Bank |
| *tekhnicheskoe perevooruzhenie* | 'technical re-equipment', upgrading |
| *tekuchest'* | excessive labour turnover |
| TEOs (*tekhniko-ekonomicheskie obosnovaniya*) | feasibility studies |
| *titul'nyi spisok* | 'title list' |
| *tolkach* | 'pusher' |
| *tovarnaya produktsiya* | marketable output |
| *trudoustroistvo* | labour placement |
| *upravlenie* | administration |
| *uskorenie* | acceleration |
| *val, valovaya produktsiya* | gross output |
| *vstrechnye plany* | 'counterpart plans' |
| *yarmarki* | wholesale fairs |
| *zagotovka, zakupka* | procurement |
| *zastoi* | stagnation |
| *zayavka* | indent, requisition |
| *zveno* | link |

# References

Abalkin, L. (1977) 'Upravlenie i ego rezervy', *Pravda*, 27 May, p. 3.
—— (1989a) 'Kakim byt' novomu pyatiletnemu planu?', *Kommunist* (6).
—— (1989b) 'Vorwärts wie eine schildekröte', *Der Spiegel* (15).
—— (1989c) 'Radikal'naya ekonomicheskaya reforma: pervoocherednye i dolgovremennye mery', *Ekonomicheskaya Gazeta* (47), 3–5.
Abouchar, A. (1967) 'Rationality in the prewar Soviet cement industry', *Soviet Studies* 19 (2).
Adam, J. (1980) 'The present Soviet incentive system', *Soviet Studies* 32 (3).
'A esli vniknut'' (1968) *Pravda*, 15 November, p. 2.
Agaev, E. (1981) 'Personal'nyi gektar', *Literaturnaya Gazeta*, 18 March, p. 10.
Aganbegyan, A. (1986) 'Perelom i uskorenie', *EKO* (6).
—— (1989) 'O kontseptsii sotsial'no-ekonomicheskogo razvitiya na perspektivu', *Izvestiya Akademii Nauk SSSR, Seriya Ekonomicheskaya* (9).
Aksenov, D. (1989) 'Strategiya "chistoi" energii', *Ekonomicheskaya Gazeta* (16), 5.
Aksenov, K. (1980) 'Dat' prostor novomu', *Pravda*, 20 September, p. 2.
Aliev, N. (1980) 'Proigryvaet. . .peredovik', *Pravda*, 20 September, p. 2.
Amann, R., Cooper, J., and Davis, R. W. (eds) (1977) *The Technological Level of Soviet Industry*, Yale University Press, New Haven and London.
Andriyanov, V. (1971) 'Problemy kadrov dal'nego vostoka; 2. pereselenets', *Komsomol'skaya Pravda*, 24 July, p. 2.
Bakhtaryshev, Sh. (1980) 'Organizatsiya i oplata truda zhivotnovodov', *Ekonomicheskaya Gazeta* (43), 19.
Balakin, V. A. (1988) 'Uglublyat' perestroiku upravleniya i khozyaistvennogo mekhanizma v stroitel'nom komplekse', *Ekonomika Stroitel'stva* (1).
Barsukov, I. V. (1971) 'Effektivnost' podsobnogo promysla', *Sel'skoe Khozyaistvo Belorussii* (7).
Bergson, A. (1964) *The Economics of Soviet Planning*, Yale University Press, New Haven.
—— (1978) *Productivity and the Social System – the USSR and the West*, Harvard University Press, Cambridge, Mass.
Berliner, J. (1966) 'Managerial incentives and decision-making: a comparison of the United States and the Soviet Union', in M. Bornstein

and D. R. Fusfeld (eds), *The Soviet Economy – A Book of Readings*, 2nd edn, Irwin, Homewood, Ill.

Betrozgov, V. T. (1989) 'Problemy razvitiya i povysheniya effektivnosti investitsionnogo kompleksa strany', *Ekonomika Stroitel'stva* (10).

Bezdelev, V. (1983) 'Zarplata i proizvoditel'nost'', *Ekonomicheskaya Gazeta* (42), 18.

Birman, I. (1978) 'From the achieved level', *Soviet Studies* 30 (2).

Bodashevskii, I. (1968) 'Dva predlozheniya', *Ekonomicheskaya Gazeta* (16), 10.

Bogomolov, F. (1982) 'I stala niva shchedree', *Ekonomicheskaya Gazeta* (8), 14.

Boldyrev, A. (1979) 'Planirovanie v otrasli – na novuyu stupen'', *Ekonomicheskaya Gazeta* (48), 7.

Borozdin, Yu. (1989) 'Ekonomicheskaya reforma i tovarno-denezhnye otnosheniya', *Voprosy Ekonomiki* (9).

Bronshtein, D. F. (1970) 'Kompleks kak uchetnaya edinitsa v promyshlennom stroitel'stve i faktor, sposobstvuyushchii sokrashcheniyu ob"ema nezavershennogo stroitel'stva', in *Metody i Praktika Opredeleniya Effektivnosti Kapital'nykh Vlozhenii i Novoi Tekhniki*, issue 17, Nauka, Moscow.

Bronshtein, M. (1986) 'K kontseptsii khozyaistvennogo mekhanizma APK', *Voprosy Ekonomiki* (2).

—— (1989) 'Nuzhen edinyi rynok', *Izvestiya*, 29 June.

Bulgakov, S. N. (1983) 'Nachinaetsya s plana', *Pravda*, 7 September, p. 2.

—— (1989) 'Stroitel'noe proektirovanie – na novyi kachestvennyi uroven'', *Ekonomika Stroitel'stva* (12).

Bullock, A. and Stallybrass, O. (eds) (1977) *The Fontana Dictionary of Modern Thought*, Collins, London.

Bunich, P. (1967) 'Khozyaistvennaya reforma v promyshlennosti: ee osushchestvlenie i nekotorye problemy', *Voprosy Ekonomiki* (10).

Cave, M. (1980) *Computers and Economic Planning: The Soviet Experience*, Cambridge University Press, Cambridge.

Charemza, W. W. (1990) *Poland's Balcerowicz Plan – Results and Prospects*, WEFA, London.

Chenery, H. and Watanabe, T. (1958) 'International comparisons of the structure of production', *Econometrica* 26 (4).

Chernenko, K. (1984) Report of speech to CC CPSU Plenum, *Ekonomicheskaya Gazeta* (44), 3.

Chernyavskii, L. (1976) 'Stroikam – snabzhenie po zakazam', *Ekonomicheskaya Gazeta* (6), 10.

'Chto my znaem o "Pamyati"?' (1990) *Sodeistvie* (independent Lithuanian newspaper) (7).

CIA (1988a) *Revisiting Soviet Economic Performance under Glasnost: Implications for CIA Estimates*, US GPO, Washington.

—— (1988b) *USSR: Sharply Higher Budget Deficits Threaten Perestroyka*, US GPO, Washington.

—— (1989) *Report on Soviet Economic Performance in 1988*, US GPO, Washington.

Clark, H. Gardner (1956) *The Economics of Soviet Steel*, Harvard University Press, London.

Clarke, R. A. and Matko, D. J. I. (1983) *Soviet Economic Facts 1917–81*, Macmillan, London.

Conquest, R. (1968) *The Great Terror*, Macmillan, London.

Conyngham, W. (1982) *The Modernization of Soviet Industrial Management*, Cambridge University Press, Cambridge.

Cooper, J. (1979) *Innovation for Innovation in Soviet Industry*, Centre for Russian and East European Studies discussion paper, University of Birmingham, June.

Dantzig, G. B. (1963) *Linear Programming and Extensions*, Princeton University Press, Princeton, New Jersey.

Demchenko, V. (1965) 'Ne opekat'!', *Ekonomicheskaya Gazeta*, 13 October, p. 6.

Dementsev, V. V. (1975) 'Finansovyi mekhanizm ob"edinenii', *Ekonomicheskaya Gazeta* (25), 8.

Denisov, G. A. (1989) 'Investitsionnaya kontseptsiya', *Ekonomika Stroitel'stva* (10).

'Deputaty-ekonomisty o radikal'noi ekonomicheskoi reforme' (1989) *Voprosy Ekonomiki* (9).

Devons, E. (1950) *Planning in Practice*, Cambridge University Press, Cambridge.

Dorfman, R., Samuelson, P. and Solow, R. (1958) *Linear Programming and Economic Analysis*, McGraw-Hill, New York.

Drogichinskii, N. (1974) 'Ob optovoi torgovli sredstvami proizvodstva', *Voprosy Ekonomiki* (4).

Dyker, D. A. (1976) *The Soviet Economy*, Crosby Lockwood Staples, London.

—— (1981a) 'Planning and the worker', in L. Schapiro and J. Godson (eds) *The Soviet Worker*, Macmillan, London.

—— (1981b) 'Decentralization and the command principle – some lessons from Soviet experience', *Journal of Comparative Economics* 5 (2).

—— (1983) *The Process of Investment in the Soviet Union*, Cambridge University Press, Cambridge.

—— (1984) 'The economy', in D. R. Jones (ed.) *Soviet Armed Forces Review Annual*, vol.7, Academic International Press, Gulf Breeze, Fl.

—— (1987a) 'Industrial planning; forwards or sideways?', in D. A. Dyker (ed.) *The Soviet Union under Gorbachev: Prospects for Reform*, Croom Helm, London.

—— (1987b) 'Agriculture: the permanent crisis', in D. A. Dyker (ed.) *The Soviet Union under Gorbachev: Prospects for Reform*, Croom Helm, London.

—— (1990) *Yugoslavia: Socialism, Development and Debt*, Routledge, London.

Economic Commission for Europe (1977a) *Economic Bulletin for Europe*, 29, United Nations, New York.

—— (1977b) *Economic Survey of Europe in 1976*, Part I, United Nations, New York.

—— (1978) *Economic Survey of Europe in 1977*, United Nations, New York.

—— (1983) *Economic Survey of Europe in 1982*, United Nations, New York.

—— (1984) *Economic Survey of Europe in 1983*, United Nations, New York.

Efimov, A. N. (1957) *Perestroika Upravleniya Promyshlennost'yu i Stroitel'stvom v SSSR*, Gospolizdat, Moscow.

*Ekonomicheskie Problemy Agrarno-Promyshlennoi Integratsii* (1976) Kolos, Moscow.

*Ekspress-Khronika* (1990) (independent news sheet, Moscow) (16).

Ellman, M. (1970) 'The consistency of Soviet plans', in M. Bornstein and D. R. Fusfeld (eds) *The Soviet Economy - A Book of Readings*, 3rd edn, Irwin, Homewood, Ill.

—— (1979) *Socialist Planning*, Cambridge University Press, Cambridge.

Engels, F. (1962) *Anti-Dühring*, 3rd edn, Foreign Languages Publishing House, Moscow.

Erlich, A. (1960) *The Soviet Industrialization Debate*, Harvard University Press, Cambridge, Mass.

Fedorenko, K. G. and Yandovskii, G. V. (1976) 'Kapitalovlozheniya i kontrol' Stroibanka', *Finansy SSSR* (2).

Fedorenko, N. (1968) 'Ob ekonomicheskoi otsenke prirodnykh resursov', *Voprosy Ekonomiki* (3).

Fedotov, V. (1989) 'Silovym priemom', *Ekonomicheskaya Gazeta* (15), 12.

Fel'dman, G. A. (1928) 'K teorii tempov narodnogo dokhoda', *Planovoe khozyaistvo* (11 and 12).

Ferberg, A. (1966) 'O kapital'nykh vlozheniyakh na rekonstruktsiyu deistvuyushchikh predpriyatii', *Voprosy Ekonomiki* (1).

Fil'ev, V. (1983) 'Shchekinskii metod i perspektivy ego dal'neishego razvitiya', *Voprosy Ekonomiki* (2).

Filippov, P. (1983) 'V chem sila gektara', *Ekonomicheskaya Gazeta* (24), 13.

Fridenberg, V. (1957) 'Voprosy kombinirovaniya proizvodstva', *Voprosy Ekonomiki* (9).

Galkin, D. (1976) 'Povysit' effektivnost' rekonstruktsii', *Ekonomicheskaya Gazeta* (1), 7.

Gerschenkron, A. (1966) *Economic Backwardness in Historical Perspective*, Harvard University Press, Cambridge, Mass.

Gillula, J. W. and Bond, D. L. (1977) 'Development of regional input-output analysis in the Soviet Union', in V. G.Treml (ed.) *Studies in Soviet Input-Output Analysis*, Praeger, New York and London.

Gladyshev, A. (1966) 'Obshchestvennye fondy potrebleniya i migratsiya naseleniya', *Planovoe Khozyaistvo* (10).

Glushetskii, A. (1990) 'Vysoki li dokhody u kooperatorov?', *Ekonomika i Zhizn'* (2), 11.

Gofman, K. and Petrakov, N. (1968) 'Tsenoobrazovanie s pozitsii tekhnicheskogo progressa', *Ekonomicheskaya Gazeta* (27), 11.

Golub', E. (1974) 'Bol'shoi konveier', *Pravda*, 13 May, p. 1.

Gorbachev, M. S. (1987) Speech in Murmansk, published in *Ekonomicheskaya Gazeta* (41).

—— (1989a) Speech to the Plenum of the CC CPSU on 25 April 1989, published in *Pravda*, 27 April.

—— (1989b) Speech to the Supreme Soviet on 30 May 1989, published in *Ekonomicheskaya Gazeta* (23).

Gorushkin, V. (1969) 'Za schet fonda razvitiya. . .', *Ekonomicheskaya Gazeta* (15), 6.

Granick, D. (1980) 'The ministry as the maximising unit in Soviet industry', *Journal of Comparative Economics* 4 (3).

Gray, K. R. (1979) 'Soviet agricultural specialisation and efficiency', *Soviet Studies* 31 (4).

Green, D. W. (1984) Review of *The Process of Investment in the Soviet Union* by D. A. Dyker, *Soviet Studies* 36 (2).

Greenslade, R. (1976) 'The real National Product of the USSR 1950–75', in Joint Economic Committee, US Congress, *Soviet Economy in a New Perspective*, US GPO, Washington DC.

Gregory, P. and Stuart, R. (1981) *Soviet Economic Structure and Performance*, 2nd edn, Harper & Row, New York.

Gribov, V. (1976) 'Sovershenstvovanie planirovaniya i finansirovaniya kapital'nykh vlozhenii', *Planovoe Khozyaistvo* (7).

Grishchenko, B. (1989) 'Konversiya: vzglyad iznutri', *Ekonomicheskaya Gazeta* (21).

Grossman, G. (1989) *Sub-Rosa Privatization and Marketization in the USSR*, Berkeley-Duke occasional papers on the second economy in the USSR, no. 17, November, WEFA, Bala Cynwyd.

Gusev, N. (1970) 'Sel'skoe khozyaistvo v zavershayushchem godu pyatiletki', *Ekonomika Sel'skogo Khozyaistva* (3).

—— (1971) 'Sel'skoe khozyaistvo v pervom godu novoi pyatiletki', *Ekonomika Sel'skogo Khozyaistva* (2).

Hanson, P. (1968) *The Consumer Sector in the Soviet Economy*, Northwestern University Press, Evanston, Ill.

—— (1983) 'Success indicators revisited: the July 1979 Soviet decree on planning and management', *Soviet Studies* 35 (1).

—— (1984) 'Brezhnev's economic legacy', in *NATO Colloquium 1984*, NATO Economics and Information Directorates, Brussels.

—— (1989) *Inflation Versus Reform*, Radio Liberty Research, April.

—— and Hill, R. M. (1979) 'Soviet assimilation of western technology: a survey of UK exporters' experience', in Joint Economic Committee, US Congress, *Soviet Economy in a Time of Change*, US GPO, Washington, D.C.

Heal, G. (1973) *The Theory of Economic Planning*, North Holland Publishing House, Amsterdam and Oxford.

Hirschman, A. (1958) *The Strategy of Economic Development*, Yale University Press, New Haven.

Holzman, F. (1957) 'The Soviet Urals-Kuznetsk combine', *Quarterly Journal of Economics* 71 (3).

Hunter, H. (1964) 'Priorities and shortfalls in pre-war Soviet planning' in J. Degras and A. Nove (eds) *Soviet Planning: Essays in Honour of Naum Jasny*, Blackwell, Oxford.

Hutchings, R. (1976) *Soviet Science, Technology, Design*, Oxford University Press, London.

Isaev, V. (1973) 'Puti povysheniya effektivnosti kapital'nykh vlozhenii', *Voprosy Ekonomiki* (8).

Ivanov, A. P. (1989) 'V Mezhotraslevoi nauchno-issledovatel'skoi assotsiatsii ekonomiki stroitel'nogo kompleksa SSSR', *Ekonomika Stroitel'stva* (10).

Ivanov, L. (1968) 'Na tekh li dorogakh ishchem?', *Literaturnaya Gazeta*, 25 September, p. 10.

Ivanov, V. (1979) Statement in *Ekonomicheskaya Gazeta* (21), 9.

Izrailev, V. (1986) 'Postavshchiki otmalchivayutsya', *Ekonomicheskaya Gazeta* (21), 10–11.

Jasny, N. (1972) *Soviet Economists of the Twenties: Names to be Remembered*, Cambridge University Press, Cambridge.

Joint Economic Committee, US Congress (1982) *USSR: Measures of Economic Growth and Development, 1950–1980*, US GPO, Washington, D.C.

Kalmykov, G. and Filipenko, V. (1966) 'Zolotoe dno', *Don* (10).

Kantorovich, L. (1939) *Matematicheskie Metody Organizatsii i Planirovaniya Proizvodstva*, Leningrad University Press, Leningrad.

—— (1960) *Ekonomicheskii Raschet Nailuchshego Ispol'zovaniya Resursov*, Akademiya Nauk SSSR, Moscow.

—— and Vainshtein, A. (1967) 'Ob ischislenii normy effektivnosti na osnove odnoproduktovoi modeli razvitiya narodnogo khozyaistva', *Ekonomika i Matematicheskie Metody* (5).

——, —— (1970) 'Eshche ob ischislenii normy effektivnosti na osnove odnoproduktovoi modeli razvitiya narodnogo khozyaistva', *Ekonomika i Matematicheskie Metody* (3).

Kaplan, L. M. (1989) 'Osnovnye napravleniya perestroiki khozyaistvennogo mekhanizma v investitsionnom komplekse', *Ekonomika Stroitel'stva* (11).

Karcz, J. F. (1968) 'Soviet agriculture: a balance sheet', in V. G.Treml (ed.) *The Development of the Soviet Economy: Plan and Performance*, Praeger, New York.

Kaser, M. (1975) 'The economy: a general assessment', in A. Brown and M. Kaser (eds) *The Soviet Union since the Fall of Khrushchev*, Macmillan, London.

Katsenelinboigen, A. (1978) *Studies in Soviet Economic Planning*, M. E. Sharpe, White Plains, NY.

Keren, M. (1972) 'On the tautness of plans', *Review of Economic Studies* 39 (4).

Khashkin, G. Z. *et al.* (1976) *Osnovnye Fondy Gazovoi Promyshlennosti*, Nedra, Moscow.

Khashutogov, V. (1976) 'Kogda narushaetsya distsiplina postavok', *Ekonomicheskaya Gazeta* (37), 10.

Kheifets, B. (1990) 'Joint Entrepreneurship in the U.S.S.R. and Prospects for Soviet–South Korean Cooperation', typescript, Moscow.

Khikmatov, A. (1969) *Rezervy Povysheniya Effektivnosti Kapital'nykh Vlozhenii*, Tashkent, Uzbekistan.

Kirillov, N. (1975) 'Kazhdoi stroike – ekonomichnyi proekt', *Ekonomicheskaya Gazeta* (47), 9.

Kolesnevov, S. G. (1971) 'Ekonomicheskoe stimulirovanie i oplata truda v sel'skom khozyaistve' in V. F. Mel'nikov (ed.) *Ekonomika Sotsialisticheskogo Sel'skogo Khozyaistva v Sovremennykh Usloviyakh*, Ekonomika, Moscow.

Kolosov, V. P. (1989) 'Organizatsiya upravleniya stroitel'stvom v sisteme mer po sovershenstvovaniyu investitsionnogo protsessa', *Ekonomika Stroitel'stva* (10).

Komarov, I. (1979) 'Zarplata stroitelya', *Ekonomicheskaya Gazeta* (12), 9.

Koppel', F. and Brig, B. (1969) 'Bol'shoi gorod i ministerstva', *Pravda*, 21 May, p. 2.

Kopteva, A. (1983) 'Khozyaeva polya', *Ekonomicheskaya Gazeta* (36), 16.

Kopysov, I. (1968) 'Krest'yanin i zemlya', *Literaturnaya Gazeta* (6), 10.

Kornai, J. (1969) 'Multi-level programming – a first report on the model and on the experimental computations', *European Economic Review* 1 (1).

Korotkov, P. and Ul'yanov, V. (1990) '"KamAZ": put' v aktsionery', *Ekonomika i Zhizn'* (32), 4–5.

Kozlov, N. (1986) 'Tsena platnoi uslugi', *Ekonomicheskaya Gazeta* (25), 19.

Kritsman, L. (1921) *O Edinom Khozyaistvennom Plane*, Gosizdat, Moscow.

Kudashov, E. (1983) 'Most mezhdu starym i novym', *Ekonomika Stroitel'stva* (9).

Kudryadtsev, V. *et al.* (1968) 'Ekonomicheskie etalony i konkursnoe proektirovanie', *Ekonomika Stroitel'stva* (3).

Kuz'mich, Yu. A. (1983) 'Neobkhodimye predplanovye proektnye prorabotki – put' k povysheniyu effektivnosti kapital'nykh vlozhenii', *Ekonomika Stroitel'stva* (9).

Lavelle, M. J. (1974) 'The Soviet "New Method" pricing formulae', *Soviet Studies* 26 (1).

Lenin, V. I. (1966) 'Ob edinom khozyaistvennom plane', in *Izbrannye Proizvedeniya*, vol. 3, Political Literature Publishing House, Moscow, vol. 3.

Leontief, W. (1936) 'Quantitative input/output relations in the economic system of the United States', *Review of Economics and Statistics* 18 (3).

Liberman, E. (1962) 'Plan, pribyl', premii', *Pravda*, 9 September, p. 3.

Liberman, Ya. (1968) 'Ekonomicheskaya reforma i finansovoe planirovanie', *Planovoe Khozyaistvo* (2).

Lifatov, A. P. (1980) 'Uporyadochit' obespechenie stroek nerudnymi materialami', *Ekonomika Stroitel'stva* (4).

Loginov, V. (1989) 'Plany i realnost'', *Voprosy Ekonomiki* (4).

Luk'yanenko, V. and Moskalenko, V. (1985) 'Na shag vperedi', *Pravda*, 30 December, p. 2.

Lupton, T. (1972) 'On the shop floor: output and earnings', in T. Lupton (ed.) *Payments Systems*, Penguin, Harmondsworth.

Lur'e, S. (1973) 'Dogovor na izgotovlenie i realizatsiyu produktsii podsobnykh predpriyatii i promyslov sel'skogo khozyaistva', *Sotsialisticheskoe Zakonodatel'stvo* (1).

Lyalyushkin, S., Prokoshenko, S., and Zubkov, Yu. (1990) 'Chastnaya sobstvennost' v strane perestroiki?', *Kur'er* (independent Latvian newspaper), April.

Lynev, R. (1985) 'Na khozraschete', *Izvestiya*, 8 August, p. 3.

Marx, K. (1968) 'Critique of the Gotha Programme', in K. Marx and F. Engels, *Selected Works*, Lawrence & Wishart, London.

*Materialy po Balansu Narodnogo Khozyaistva SSSR* (1932) Central Administration of National Economic Records, Moscow.

Matthews, M. (1978) *Privilege in the Soviet Union*, George Allen & Unwin, London.

Medvedev, Z. (1986) *Gorbachev*, Blackwell, Oxford.

Merkin, R. M. (1989) 'Napravleniya radikal'noi perestroiki investitsionnoi deyatel'nosti i khozyaistvennogo mekhanizma investitsionnoi sfery', *Ekonomika Stroitel'stva* (10).

*Metodika Opredeleniya Ekonomicheskoi Effektivnosti Kapital'nykh Vlozhenii* (1981) *Ekonomicheskaya Gazeta* (2 and 3).

Mikhel', A. V. (1989) 'Sovershenstvovanie khozyaistvennogo mekhanizma kak osnova rosta proizvoditel'nosti truda', *Ekonomika Stroitel'stva* (12).

Mirgaleev, A. (1977) 'Shchekinskii metod i ego perspektivy', *Voprosy Ekonomiki* (10).

Mironov, V. (1983) 'Komu vesti predproektnye raboty?', *Ekonomicheskaya Gazeta* (39), 19.

Mitrofanov, A. (1969) 'Kompas ekonomicheskoi effektivnosti', *Ekonomicheskaya Gazeta* (39), 13.

Moskalenko, V. (1986) 'Samofinansirovanie kak metod ratsional'nogo khozyaistvovaniya', *Voprosy Ekonomiki* (1).

*Narodnoe Khozyaistvo SSSR (Narkhoz)*, *Finansy i Statistika*, Moscow, various years.

National Board for Prices and Incomes (1968) Report No. 65, *Payment by Results Systems*, Cmnd 3627, HMSO, London.

Nefedov, V. (1986) 'Orientatsiya khozyaistvennogo mekhanizma APK na intensifikatsiyu', *Voprosy Ekonomiki* (3).

Nove, A. (1961) *The Soviet Economy*, George Allen & Unwin, London.

—— (1968) *The Soviet Economy*, 3rd edn, George Allen & Unwin, London.

—— (1969) *An Economic History of the USSR*, Allen Lane, The Penguin Press, Harmondsworth.

'Ob uluchshenii planirovaniya i ekonomicheskogo stimulirovaniya proizvodstva i zagotovok sel'skokhozyaistvennykh produktov' (1980) *Ekonomicheskaya Gazeta* (52), 5–7.

'Ob uluchshenii planirovaniya i usilenii vozdeistviya khozyaistvennogo mekhanizma na povyshenie effektivnosti proizvodstva i kachestva raboty' (1979) *Ekonomicheskaya Gazeta* (32), special supplement.

'O dal'neishem ukreplenii trudovoi distsipliny i sokrashchenii tekuchesti kadrov v narodnom khozyaistve' (1980) *Ekonomicheskaya Gazeta* (3), 4.

Ogon', Ts. G. (1989) 'Sistema khozraschetnykh otnoshenii v stroitel'stve trebuet izmeneniya', *Ekonomika Stroitel'stva* (11).

'O nekotorykh merakh po uluchsheniyu polozheniya del v kapital'nom stroitel'stve' (1989) *Ekonomika Stroitel'stva* (12).

'O perestroike upravleniya investitsiyami i sovershenstvovanii khozyaistvennogo mekhanizma v stroitel'stve' (1989) *Ekonomika Stroitel'stva* (10).

'O programme perekhoda k rynochnoi ekonomike. Programma minimum – "Mandat doveriya na 500 dnei"' (1990) typescript, Moscow.

Pavitt, K. (ed.) (1980) *Technical Innovation and British Economic Performance*, Macmillan, London.

Pavlov, V. (1989) Budget speech, reported in *Ekonomicheskaya Gazeta* (40).

Perepechin, I. and Apraksina, L. (1980) 'Kakov proekt – takov ob"ekt', *Ekonomicheskaya Gazeta* (6), 7.

Pessel', M. (1977) 'Kredit kak faktor intensifikatsii kapital'nogo stroitel'stva', *Planovoe Khozyaistvo* (1), 51.

Petrenko, V. and Borin, Yu. (1990) 'Utyug s izvilinami', *Krokodil* (14), 4.

Petrov, G. (1982) 'Na osnove kollektivnogo podryada', *Ekonomicheskaya Gazeta* (25), 7.

*Plan Fulfilment Reports*, various years.

'Planovye pokazateli kriterii otsenki' (1979) *Ekonomicheskaya Gazeta* (35), 5.

Podshivalenko, P. (ed.) (1965) *Ekonomika Stroitel'stva*, Political Literature Publishing House, Moscow.

—— (1983) 'Organizatsionnye formy stroitel'stva i upravlenie im', *Voprosy Ekonomiki* (7).

—— and Evstigneev, V. D. (1980) 'Puti sovershenstvovaniya stroitel'nogo proizvodstva', *Ekonomika Stroitel'stva* (5).

Poltoranin, M. and Sevest'yanov, V. (1977) 'Na beregakh Irtysha', *Pravda*, 3 July, p. 2.

Popov, P. I. (ed.) (1926) *Balans Narodnogo Khozyaistva Soyuza SSR 1923–24 goda*, Trudy Tsentral'nogo Statisticheskogo Upravleniya, Moscow.

'Poryadok raspredeleniya pribyli' (1979) *Ekonomicheskaya Gazeta* (47), 10.

'Posle vystuplenii "Ekonomiki Stroitel'stva"' (1989) *Ekonomika Stroitel'stva* (11).

Pospielovsky, D. (1970) 'The "link system" in Soviet agriculture', *Soviet Studies* 21 (4).

Pozdnyakov, V. (1968) 'Razmeshchenie i razvitie podsobnoi promyshlennosti v kolkhozakh', *Ekonomika Sel'skogo Khozyaistva* (5).

'Problemy razrabotki novoi metodiki sostavleniya narodnokhozyaistvennykh planov' (1977) *Planovoe Khozyaistvo* (7).

Pronin, A. (1969) 'Razvitie podsobnykh predpriyatii i promyslov v kolkhozakh i sovkhozakh', *Ekonomika Sel'skogo Khozyaistva* (4).

Protsenko, O. D. and Soloveichik, D. I. (1976) *Planirovanie Dolgovremmenykh Khozyaistvennykh Svyazei*, Ekonomika, Moscow.

Rabinovich, I. A. (1976) *Organizatsiya Snabzheniya i Effektivnost' Proizvodstva*, Tekhnika, Kiev.

Radaev, V. (1989) 'Novoe kachestvo ili starye tempy', *Voprosy Ekonomiki* (7).

Revenok, L. and Pichugin, P. (1981) 'Kogda poryadok na zemle', *Ekonomicheskaya Gazeta* (5), 19.

Reznik, S. D. (1980) 'Trudovaya distsiplina', *Ekonomika Stroitel'stva* (3).

Rogin, S. (1979) 'Ispitany', *Pravda*, 9 October, p. 2.

Ronichev, I. (1985) 'Gol ne v te vorota', *Literaturnaya Gazeta* (45), 11.

Roy, D. (1972) 'Quota restriction and goldbricking in a machine shop', in T. Lupton (ed.) *Payment Systems*, Penguin, Harmondsworth.

Ryzhov, M. (1972) 'Posylayut "tolkachei". . . kogda podvodyat partnery', *Pravda*, 25 February, p. 3.

'Samofinansirovanie – put' k razvitiyu initsiativy' (1986) *Ekonomicheskaya Gazeta* (18), 11–14.

Saushkin, Yu. G, Nikol'skii, I. V., and Korovitsyn, V. P. (eds) (1967) *Ekonomicheskaya Geografiya SSSR*, Part I, Moscow University Press, Moscow.

Schaffer, M. (1990) Conversation with.

Schroeder, G. (1968) 'Soviet economic "reforms": a study in contradictions', *Soviet Studies* 20 (1).

—— and Severin, B. (1976) 'Soviet consumption and income in perspective', in Joint Economic Committee, US Congress, *Soviet Economy in a New Perspective*, US GPO, Washington, D.C.

Schwarz, S. (1953) *Labour in the Soviet Union*, Cresset Press, London.

Selyunin, V. (1989) '"...Prodolzhat' tupikovyi put' nel'zya"', *Pamir* (2).

Sergienkov, I. (1976) 'Kak griby posle dozhdya', *Pravda*, 8 May, p.2.

Shatunovskii, I. (1968) Report published in *Pravda*, 19 December, p. 2.

Shavlyuk, V. (1979) 'Pochemu dorozhaet stroika', *Pravda*, 27 June, p. 2.

Shcherbakov, V. and Yasin, Ye. (1989) 'Khozyaistvennyi kompleks strany: algoritm i struktura upravleniya', *Ekonomicheskaya Gazeta* (5), 6–7.

Shiryaev, G. (1977) 'Uluchshenie proektno-smetnogo dela – vazhnaya narodno-khozyaistvennaya zadacha', *Planovoe Khozyaistvo* (1).

Shmelev, N. (1989a) Seminar at the Bundesinstitut für ostwissenschaftliche und internationale Studien, Cologne, Germany, May.

—— (1989b) 'Economics and common sense', in A. Jones and W. Moskoff (eds) *Perestroika and the Economy*, Sharpe, New York and London.

'Sistema material'no-tekhnicheskogo snabzheniya' (1969) *Ekonomicheskaya Gazeta* (40), 5.

Skorodunov, E. (1966) 'O kachestve radiotovarov', *Sovetskaya Torgovlya* (9).

Sokolov, I. (1969) 'Podsobnye promysly: nuzhdy i perspektivy', *Sel'skaya Nov'* (11).

Solomin, V. (1977) 'Kachestvo planirovaniya i organizatsiya kapital'nogo stroitel'stva', *Voprosy Ekonomiki* (1).

Solov'ev, M. V. (1989) 'Vazhneishee uslovie uskoreniya investitsionnogo protsessa', *Ekonomika Stroitel'stva* (10).

'Sotsial'nye garantii' (1989) *Sotsialisticheskaya Industriya*, 18 April.

'S veterkom' (1968) *Pravda*, 2 December, p. 2.

Tarasov, A. (1990) 'Orbital'nyi zavod', *Pravda*, 17 May, p. 3.

Tarnavskii, G. (1973) 'Obespechenie zakonnosti v dogovornykh otnosheniyakh kolkhozov', *Sotsialisticheskoe Zakonodatel'stvo* (7).

Tatarkin, A., Vazhenin, S., and Ovchinnikov, V. (1988) 'Khozyain, a ne podenshchik', *Ekonomicheskaya Gazeta* (40), 8.

Timofeev, V. I. (1989) 'Sovershenstvovanie khozyaistvennogo mekhanizma v stroitel'stve', *Ekonomika Stroitel'stva* (10).

*Tipovaya Metodika Opredeleniya Ekonomicheskoi Effektivnosti Kapital'nykh Vlozhenii* (1969), *Ekonomicheskaya Gazeta* (39).

*Tipovaya Metodika Opredeleniya Ekonomicheskoi Effektivnosti Kapital'nykh Vlozhenii i Novoi Tekhniki v Narodnom Khozyaistve SSSR* (1960) Gosplan SSSR, Akademiya Nauk SSSR, Institut Ekonomiki, Moscow.

Trapeznikov, V. A. (1970) '"Glagoli" upravleniya: znaet – mozhet – khochet – uspevaet', *Literaturnaya Gazeta*, 12 May.

Tsagaraev, S. (1984) 'Eksperiment i vstrechnyi', *Ekonomicheskaya Gazeta* (28), 8.

Tsygankov, Yu. (1976) 'Effektivnost' nepreryvnogo planirovaniya kapital'nogo stroitel'stva', *Voprosy Ekonomiki* (2).

Tsypkin, G. A. (1989) 'Bank: deyatel'nost' i otvetstvennost'', *Ekonomika Stroitel'stva* (8).

Uluchshat' planirovanie, organizatsiyu i upravlenie kapital'nym stroitel'stvom' (1984) *Ekonomika Stroitel'stva* (7).

Ural'tsev, B. (1984) 'Otvetstvennost' vo vsekh zven'yakh', *Ekonomicheskaya Gazeta* (35), 8.

Urbanek, L. (1968) 'Some difficulties in implementing the economic reforms in Czechoslovakia', *Soviet Studies* 19 (4).

Utochkin, I. and Kuznetsov, M. (1970) 'Promysly – otrasl' kolkhoznogo proizvodstva', *Ekonomika Sel'skogo Khozyaistva* (12).

Vaag, L. (1965) 'Effektivnost', interesovannost'', *Ekonomicheskaya Gazeta*, 20 October, pp. 8–9.

Varavka, V. (1975) 'Plan proizvodstva i portfel' zakazov', *Ekonomicheskaya Gazeta* (52), 14.

Vasil'ev, F. (1968) 'S pozitsii khozyaistvennika', *Sel'skaya Nov'* (7), 10.

Vasil'ev, G. (1986) 'Struktura novaya, a metody...', *Ekonomicheskaya Gazeta* (19), 14.

Vlasov, V. G. (1984) 'Prava i otvetstvennost'', *Ekonomicheskaya Gazeta* (4), 7.

*Vneshnie Ekonomicheskie Svyazi SSSR v 1988* (1989) *Finansy i Statistika*, Moscow.

Volosatov, A. V. (1990) 'Dogovornaya tsena. Chto dal'she?', *Ekonomika Stroitel'stva* (1).

Vovchenko, N. (1965) 'Bystree osvaivat' proizvodstvennye moshchnosti', *Ekonomika Stroitel'stva* (10).

'V Tsentral'nom Komitete KPSS i Sovete Ministrov SSSR' (1982) *Ekonomicheskaya Gazeta* (23), special supplement.

'V Tsentral'nom Komitete KPSS i Sovete Ministrov SSSR' (1985) *Ekonomicheskaya Gazeta* (48), 17–18.

'V Tsentral'nom Komitete KPSS i Sovete Ministrov SSSR' (1986) *Ekonomicheskaya Gazeta* (15), 2, 4 and 5.

'V TsK KPSS i Sovete Ministrov SSSR' (1979) *Pravda*, 29 July, pp. 1–2.

'Vypolnenie plana stroitel'stva – vazhneishaya narodno-khozyaistvennaya zadacha' (1972) *Planovoe Khozyaistvo* (5).

Weitzman, M. (1980) 'The "ratchet principle" and performance incentives', *Bell Journal of Economics* 11 (1).

Wilber, C. K. (1969) *The Soviet Model and Underdeveloped Countries*, University of North Carolina Press, Chapel Hill, NC.

Wiles, P. (1981) 'Wage and income policies', in L. Schapiro and J. Godson (eds) *The Soviet Worker*, Macmillan, London.

Yagodin, L. (1968) 'Tovarishch iz raikoma', *Ekonomicheskaya Gazeta* (44), 26.

Yakovlev, A. M (1989) 'Puti korennoi perestroiki upravleniya investitsionnym protsessom v narodnom khozyaistve', *Ekonomika Stroitel'stva* (10).

Yanowitch, M. (1977) *Social and Economic Inequality in the Soviet Union*, Martin Robertson, London.

Yasinskii, G. (1973) 'Prokurorskii nadzor po delam o khishcheniyakh sotsialisticheskogo imushchestva', *Sotsialisticheskoe Zakonodatel'stvo* (10).

Yudin, I. (1990) 'Tsena rytsarskikh dospekhov', *Ekonomika i Zhizn'* (1), 11.

Yur'ev, R. (1989) 'Raskryvaem tainy byudzheta', *Pravitel'stvennyi Vestnik*, (18), 6.

Zaichenko, D. I. and Sharov, A. N. (1989) 'Sostoitsya li povorot v deyatelnosti bankov?', *Ekonomika Stroitel'stva* (1).

Zakharov, Y. and Petrov, N. (1974) 'Ob"edineniya segodnya', *Pravda*, 7 August, p. 2.

Zakirov, Sh. N. (1965) *Voprosy Razvitiya i Razmeshcheniya Promyshlennosti Uzbekistana*, Nauka UzSSR, Tashkent.

Zangurashvili, V. (1976) 'V srok i polnost'yu', *Pravda*, 8 February, p. 3.

'Zarabotnaya plata – po gotovoi produktsii' (1968) *Ekonomicheskaya Gazeta* (27), 20.

Zaslavskaya, T. (1983) *Doklad o Neobkhodimosti Bolee Uglublennogo Izucheniya v SSSR Sotsial'nogo Mekhanizma Razvitiya Ekonomiki*, Radio Liberty, *Materialy Samizdata* (35/83), 26 August, AC No. 5042.

Zholudev, G. A. and Kolotilkin, A. B. (1990) 'Investitsionnaya programma: khod osushchestvleniya i nereshennye problemy', *Ekonomika Stroitel'stva* (1).

# Index

Abalakovo, 159
Abalkin, L. 100, 102, 167, 174–5, 176, 201, 204
accumulation *see* savings, investment
Achki system 111
Aganbegyan, A. 100, 102, 167, 174
Agricultural Bank 141
agriculture 3–4, 12, 20, 30–2, 51–2, 55, 63–4, 66, 103–28, 158–9, 172, 175, 178–9, 182–3, 193, 197–8; animal 4, 118, 121, 122; crop 20, 31–2, 55, 116, 122–3, 158–9, 182–3, 198; investment 4, 32, 105–9, 113, 117, 123; prices 31–2, 104–8, 112, 114–17, 118–19, 122, 126, 179; procurement, procurement targets 20, 105, 107, 109, 115–16, 118, 124; subsidiary industrial activity 51–2, 63–4, 66, 111, 115; subsidiary, private 12, 105, 115, 120–1, 197
Aksenov, D. 101, 195
alcohol abuse, policy 79, 178, 192
allocation certificate *see naryad*
All-Union State Committee for Labour and Social Problems 54
amortization 80–1, 88, 133
Amu-Darya 127–8
Andropov, Yu. 37, 79–83, 92, 113, 120, 137
anti-alcohol campaign *see* alcohol abuse
'Anti-Party Group' 45

Aral Sea 127–8, 160
Arbat 171–2
*arenda see* lease-holding
Armenia 186–7 *see also* Transcaucasia
assignment for design work 135
association 60–1, 66, 74, 80–1, 94, 105–6, 137, 162
auditing 201–2
autarky, national 4, 13, 205
autarky, organizational 18, 45–6, 53, 55, 61–3, 70, 76, 145, 150, 156–7, 202–3
Azerbaidzhan 112, 152, 186–7 *see also* Transcaucasia

Baikal, Lake 159
balanced growth *see* growth, theories and strategies of
balance of payments 3, 13, 182–5, 198–9, 205–6
Baltic republics 124, 126, 186–8 *see also* Estonia, Latvia, Lithuania
bank credit 49, 52, 81, 85, 88, 136, 139, 143, 164–5
banking, reform of 97–8, 161–2
bankruptcy 200
Belorussia 186, 196
Belorussian system 138–9
Bergson, A. 5, 16, 17
bogey 27, 36–7
Bol'shevichka 47–8
bonuses *see* incentives
Bratsk hydro-electric station 15, 16
Brezhnev, L. 38–9, 47–8, 60, 66–73, 80, 83, 86, 89, 92, 103–6, 108,

For Product Safety Concerns and Information please contact our EU
representative GPSR@taylorandfrancis.com Taylor & Francis Verlag GmbH,
Kaufingerstraße 24, 80331 München, Germany

Printed and bound by CPI Group (UK) Ltd, Croydon, CR0 4YY
12/05/2025
01866925-0001